INDIA AND CENTRAL ASIA

INDIA AND CENTRAL ASIA

TWO DECADES OF TRANSITION

EDITED BY
P.L. DASH

UNIVERSITY PRESS

OXFORD
UNIVERSITY PRESS

Oxford University Press is a department of the University of Oxford.
It furthers the University's objective of excellence in research, scholarship, and
education by publishing worldwide. Oxford is a registered trademark of Oxford
University Press in the UK and in certain other countries

Published in India
by Oxford University Press
YMCA Library Building, 1 Jai Singh Road, New Delhi 110 001, India

ISBN-13: 978-0-19-808963-6
ISBN-10: 0-19-808963-5

Typeset in Berling LT STD 10/14.8
by Sai Graphic Design, New Delhi 110 055
Printed in India at G.H. Prints Pvt Ltd, New Delhi 110 020

Contents

Foreword

With the collapse of the Soviet Union in 1991, there emerged five independent and sovereign states in Central Asia viz. Kazakhstan, Kyrgyzstan, Tajikistan, Turkmenistan, and Uzbekistan. The events in and around Afghanistan—Pakistan corridor have given the Central Asian countries a strategic importance. Consequently, Russia, the United States, countries of the European Union, Japan, China, Iran, Turkey, and India have all vied to gain access to the region and establish economic and diplomatic ties with these countries.

Uzbekistan and Kazakhstan are the most populous amongst them and have also remained politically most stable since Independence. Kyrgyzstan has passed through two revolutions and has adopted the parliamentary system of governance which is at variance with its other Central Asian neighbours who have the presidential system. Turkmenistan has flourished due to easy flow of gas money. Tajikistan went through a civil war during the first five years of Independence but stabilized when the warring factions formed an alliance to govern the country.

There is a cultural affinity between India and the Central Asian countries. The ancient Silk Route and the spread of Buddhism had brought India and Central Asia close to each other in the past. However, during the past two decades no tangible headway has been achieved in developing better commercial and cultural ties.

More than a dozen of Indian and foreign scholars have brainstormed on several issues confronting the countries of independent Central Asia and have come out with an array of analyses from the Indian vantage point, which present to the reader different scholarly views on a wide range of issues. This volume is a collection of scholarly essays published under the auspices of the Nehru Centre, Mumbai and would help us understand the depth of Central Asia from the days of yore to the contemporary times, particularly from an Indian angle.

SHARAD PAWAR
Chairman
Nehru Centre

Acknowledgements

This publication is the result of a seminar organized by Nehru Centre on Central Asia, a region of abiding interest to India. A dozen scholars participated in the seminar and I am grateful to them for the scholarship they brought to the seminar. I would particularly like to thank Professor P.L. Dash for editing the volume and also for writing an introduction to it.

I am deeply indebted to Shri Sharad Pawar, Chairman, Nehru Centre, for writing a Foreword to this publication.

My special thanks to Sonia Khare for copyediting the text. Our librarian, Arati Desai and her team deserve congratulations for all their efforts in bringing out this book.

I.M. KADRI
General Secretary
Nehru Centre

Editor's Note

While writing letters from the prison to his daughter, Indira Gandhi, Pandit Jawaharlal Nehru had paid more than adequate attention to developments in Soviet Central Asia. The *Glimpses of World History* contains pages of panegyrics on Central Asia. Nehru's particular emphasis was on how underdevelopment was overcome far too quickly within two decades in backward Central Asia and how socialism had magnified the temptation for others to emulate the socialist model in other countries suffering from poverty, illiteracy, deprivation, and economic backwardness. Central Asia thus remained the symbol of socialist progress in the eyes of Nehru.

Harking back farther into history, one finds inalienable connections: intense cultural interaction in ancient India with Buddhism spreading knowledge and wisdom along the Silk Road and via that region to China, Mongolia, Asiatic Russia, and beyond. With the advent of Islam, cross-cultural affinity further endeared medieval India to Central Asia. And the interactions continued. The synthesis of Islamic culture with those of already existing Hinduism and Buddhism enriched the cultural canvas of Eurasia in an unprecedented manner. No other region of the world had as much cross-cultural affinity as had the three regions of Asia—West, South, and Central Asia. From archaeological excavations in various countries of the region to well-documented records in archives, museums, and libraries, we find enough evidences of these close affinities between the Central and South Asian peoples.

While the great game between the British and Russian empires in the nineteenth century, in Central Asia, is passé, the Soviet disunion in 1991 catapulted Central Asia to world prominence on altogether different grounds. A region politically volatile and economically unstable threw open an array of security problems for the neighbourhood countries. The growing influence of Islamic radicalism from neighbouring Afghanistan in the early years of Central Asia's independence and a civil war in Tajikistan further accentuated this threat. For the first time, the five independent countries of Central Asia—Kyrgyzstan, Kazakhstan, Tajikistan, Turkmenistan, and Uzbekistan—engaged attention of countries from far and near not only because of their independence, but also due to their strategic, geopolitical, and geoeconomic importance in an area largely Islamic.

Independence also threw upon new challenges of statecraft, diplomacy, and security. The concept of traditional security swiftly underwent radical changes. Many non-traditional security issues continue to dominate the agenda of newly independent states too feeble to effectively tackle them. To analyse and study the emerging political, social, and economic scenario became inevitable and research on the very importance of Central Asian countries became an integral part of academic discourse worldwide. The presence of US troops and acquisition of military bases in the region had sharpened geopolitical jockeying, bringing to afield many interested countries of the world to harness this resource-rich region to their own as well as to the advantage of globalization. The energy-rich countries of the region—Kazakhstan and Turkmenistan—played the Caspian game, while Uzbekistan, the most populous country of the region, came out prominently to play its weighty regional role in competition with Kazakhstan.

Yet, the region remained beset with many paradoxes. Kazakhstan, Uzbekistan, and Turkmenistan are resource rich, while Tajikistan and Kyrgyzstan are scant with resources. Uzbekistan and Kazakhstan are populous, while other three countries are sparsely populated, with barely 5 million people each. Two countries—Kyrgyzstan and Tajikistan—are upstream countries, whereas Amu Darya and Syr Darya take their origin, and three other downstream countries depend on the former two for fresh and potable water, leading to a virtual water war among them. Contemporary problems are in plenitude, while solutions are far too few. Such problems include narcotic trafficking, money laundering, splintering effects of the Afghan imbroglio, terrorism, environmental degradation, food security, and so on. By now, two decades of independence have gone by. Yet, all these problems are inadequately addressed. At least an academic discourse in quest of a theoretical perspective to analyse these issues and possibly find out an empirical way out has taken shape.

Modern nation-state building on the ruins of socialism after achievement of independence has also become a matter of intense academic interest. All five countries gained their political independence from the former Soviet Union and all five of them travelled different systemic path to eke out their political future. It is of interest to note that their electoral profile along with predominantly presidential political system vis-à-vis the emerging parliamentary system of governance in Kyrgyzstan has been the subject of various research themes. In a nutshell, the region offers fascinating academic problems for debate and discourse and for sustained discussions on many valid themes of contemporary relevance facing Central Asia.

The Central Asian region in our neighbourhood is in ferment and India's interest in that region is abiding. India has had a long tradition of linkages with Central Asia. Therefore, it is considered befitting to focus on the area, where countries of the region are shaping up their political future amid many obstacles facing them. This volume is the outcome of a two-day seminar on Central Asia organized by the Nehru Centre, Mumbai, and a humble tribute to the first Prime Minister of India, who envisioned that Central Asia provided solutions to many intricate, socio-economic problems. Maybe, in the globalizing context in the years to come, Central Asia will throw a new paradigm of social, political, and economic development.

P.L. Dash
Professor of International Relations and
ICCR India Chair,
University of World Economy and
Diplomacy, Tashkent, Uzbekistan

1

India and the Importance of Central Asia

SANJAY KUMAR PANDEY

Central Asia's importance for India can be judged from three perspectives: historical-cultural, geopolitical, and economic. The historical and cultural contacts between India and Central Asia date back to the very dawn of history. Since the early times, there has been a constant flow of culture and commerce between the two regions. 'Waves upon waves of immigrants came to India from Central Asia, and many of these were scholars, scientists, technicians and artisans.'[1] They contributed to the rich tapestry of Indian life and culture. This was reciprocated by Indian missionaries and merchants who transmitted religions, arts, and merchandize to that region.

The cultural and economic interaction between India and Central Asia became particularly strong during the Greek and Saka rule, when some areas of northern India and Central Asia became part of the same state formation.[2] The pinnacle of India-Central Asia relations was reached under the Kushana Empire, which included territories of Central Asia and a considerable part of north India. The Kushana period witnessed lively and reciprocal cultural exchanges between Central Asia and India. The carriers of cultural influences in India were primarily the Kushana authorities, functionaries, and soldiers, whereas in Central Asia they were Buddhist missionaries and monks.[3]

However, according to Devahuti, Indians did not migrate to Central Asia in order to settle there. There was no paucity of land in their own country, and the inhospitable mountainous terrain and severe climatic conditions in those regions did not attract them. On the other hand, Central Asia provided them with opportunities for profitable trade and for the missionary spread of Buddhism. 'There are stray instances of politically ambitious settlers, but the overall picture of Central Asia is that of predominantly Indianized—not Indian—populations.'[4]

The interaction between India and Central Asia intensified further when the Islamized Central Asian Turks established their control over north India in the early thirteenth century. During the latter half of sixteenth and seventeenth century, the consolidation of Mughal Empire in India gave a boost to India's interaction with Central Asia. The political stability and economic prosperity under the Mughals led to the growth of India's trade with that region and an increase in the number of Indian traders and bankers there. The colonization of India by the British and the annexation of Central Asia to the Tsarist Empire led to the decline of trade between the two regions and consequent decrease in India's ties with that region.[5] It is very important to remember that with the Partition in 1947 and the creation of Pakistan, India was cut off from its historical and natural neighbours: Iran, Afghanistan, and Central Asia. Thus, serious obstacles emerged in India's interaction with these neighbours.[6]

During the Soviet period, there was a lack of direct political relation between India and the Soviet Central Asian Republics (CARs). The socio-cultural relations between Central Asia and India were mediated through Moscow. The Soviet authorities tried to keep Central Asia aloof from the rest of the world. However, because of the very special relationship that New Delhi enjoyed with Moscow, India was among very few countries which had access to these republics. There was considerable goodwill for India among the people and elites of Central Asia, mainly as a result of the past ties and the popularity of Indian culture and Hindi movies. The disintegration of Soviet Union was a setback for India. The USSR was not only the principal supplier of sophisticated arms, at highly discounted prices, and provided financial support by accepting payments in rupees for Soviet goods, but also extended immense political support to the country in the international arena. Its dissolution removed the main anchor of India's foreign policy.

The Soviet dissolution, however, created new possibilities and prospects for Indian foreign policy. It paved the path for India to re-establish the age-old ties with the five independent countries of Central Asia. India was forced to evolve policies to deal with the new political situation in the Central Asian republics. The 1990s was a decade of change and uncertainty: both India and the Central Asian states (CAS) were revising their domestic polices and perspectives, as well as their approaches to international politics, trade, commerce, diplomacy, cultural values, security, and defence-related issues. In view of these changes, the Central Asian states and India set out to reformulate their national and regional interests, keeping in mind the larger goal of peace, stability, and security, covering South, West, and Southeast Asia.[7]

In 1991 and 1992, India established diplomatic relations with Kazakhstan, Kyrgyzstan, Tajikistan, Turkmenistan, and Uzbekistan and worked with these newly independent states to develop a framework for diplomatic, economic, and cultural cooperation. Besides its long historical connections with this region, India sought good relations for several reasons: to prevent Pakistan from developing an anti-India coalition with the Central Asian states in the dispute over Kashmir; to persuade those states not to provide Pakistan assistance in its nuclear programme; to ensure continued contacts with long-standing commercial and military suppliers; and to provide new opportunities to Indian businesses.[8]

Both India and the five newly emerged Central Asian states soon realized their mutual interests and importance. Both knew that the other enjoyed a place of pre-eminence in their consciousness because of the long historic ties, common heritage, and close friendship and cooperation during the Soviet times. The multiethnic and multireligious structure of the Indian as well as the Central Asian societies creates similar concerns and approaches. In view of this, India upgraded its mission in Alma-Ata and Tashkent to open its embassies. On the other hand, Uzbek President, Islam Karimov visited India during August 1991 and President Nazarabayev of Kazakhstan visited India in February 1992. A slew of agreements were signed in the field of science, technology, culture, and especially economic and investment sectors.

Geopolitically, Central Asia has become an arena for competition between three big players—Russia, China, and the United States through its presence in Afghanistan—and three middle-tier players—Turkey, Iran, and Pakistan. In this setting, and especially in view of China and Pakistan's aversion to India's active involvement in the region, it is very difficult for New Delhi to directly exert influence in Central Asia. This feeling of isolation accentuates India's need to develop a new and cohesive strategy. Discussions about this new strategy have been fruitful and intermittent, arguably because the basic question of what India wants from the region has not been answered. Does India want to balance the big players such as China and Russia in Central Asia? Or, does India seek to balance middle players like Pakistan and Iran? According to Mehmet Ozkan, 'India is an outside power, and may influence the key questions in Central Asia in a mostly indirect way.' He believes India needs to evolve a new strategy toward Central Asia, conceiving the region beyond Pakistan and China. New Delhi can develop a policy of building cooperation with the middle-tier players like Turkey and Iran. India's cooperation with Russia and the United States in Central Asia can also be beneficial, but it is unlikely to secure India's foreign policy objectives.[8]

As opposed to the above view that India at best is a marginal player in Central Asia, American analyst Stephen Blank believes that India's rising profile in Central Asia has not received the attention it deserves. India has the means and skill to pursue its own interests resolutely. He emphasizes that Central Asia has long since become a part of South Asia's broader security calculus and vice versa. India's strategy also reflects major trends in Indian foreign policy that have significant implications. Those trends reflect India's growing economic and military power and its policymakers' increased attention to, and interest in becoming a major pan-Asian player, not just the dominant power on the subcontinent. India's policies toward Central Asia, therefore, take into account all the instruments of power: economics, diplomacy, and military.[9]

India's security interest was negatively impacted in the 1990s when the Russian influence in Central Asia weakened with a commensurate rise in the Chinese influence. This situation got partly stabilized with the growing United States presence in the region since 2001. There is a growing convergence between the United States and Indian interests, especially their reluctance to see the region fall under the exclusive influence of any one country. These shared strategic interests include facilitating the reconnection of Central Asian states to the world economy and helping them sell their energy and other products in the global market. But New Delhi and Washington differ in their approach concerning the usefulness of Pakistan and/or Iran to reconnect Central Asia with the outside world.[10]

As a buffer, the usefulness of Central Asia for India is three-fold: to prevent the creation of an 'Islamic belt' allied to Pakistan, to forestall encirclement by either China or the USA, and finally to insulate India from narcotic terrorism that now plagues its northern borders. This security dimension has driven Indian investment in Afghanistan and military cooperation with Tajikistan.[11] According to Anita Inder Singh, India's positive re-engagement with the Central Asian states is mainly due to new international and geopolitical realities. She maintains that India's attempts to establish 'good relations with them are a matter of pragmatism as India's neighbours and rivals, Pakistan and China, are interested in the region.'[12] Shahram Akbarzadeh explains India-Pakistan rivalry in Central Asia in terms of that region's vast energy reserves, its geostrategic importance in relation to Russia and China, and its potential role in the Kashmir dispute. He believes the Indian government has woken up to the role that Central Asia can play in advancing New Delhi's regional ambitions.[13]

During the past decade and half, the biggest threat to India's and Central Asia's security and regional stability has originated from Afghanistan in the activities of radical extremists and drug traffickers. Islamic radicalism and its manifestations of separatism and extremism justifying terrorist methods of conflict create instability in Central Asia. India and Central Asia share this common threat as they share their borders with Pakistan and Afghanistan. In fact, a common threat unites them in combating the common adversary and strengthening future ties.[14] As mentioned earlier, powers like Russia, the United States, and China are consolidating or increasing their presence in the region through complex modes of relationships that promote cooperation as well as trigger competition. A kind of rivalry between Russia, on the one side, and the United States on the other, has been accelerating in the region. It is complicated by the worsening security situation in Afghanistan. As militant Islamists infiltrate from across the Afghan border into Tajikistan and other Central Asian states, regional stability is under threat. The result is a state of strategic uncertainty as a medium-term prospect. The need to seriously engage Russia, China, Iran, and the Central Asian states on issues of regional security as powers affected by extremism emanating from the Af-Pak is urgent and requires immediate attention.[15]

There are experts who believe that India's security interest would be best served if it broadens the operational scope of Central Asia to include Xinjiang as well. According to P. Stobdan, events in this sensitive Chinese province need to be closely monitored by developing networks of hard information. Indian Missions in Bishkek, Almaty, and Dushanbe should be used as listening posts for Uyghur affairs. He is of the view that India enjoys certain advantages if it chooses to broaden its policy options in the region. It has religious and cultural links with the region going back to ancient times. It shares deep historical and civilizational linkages with the Uyghurs. India had thriving trade relations with Xinjiang until a few decades ago. The Indian Consulate in Kashgar was closed down only in the 1950s. Thus, a good number of intellectual and institutional resources capable of reviving the lost linkages exist in the country. He maintains that India should re-establish its old ties with this region. New Delhi needs to engage with moderate Uyghur groups which will give it leverage in that conflict and influence in the region.[16]

Central Asia is also an arena for India for global extension by asserting its presence and influence in the Asian region. There is a desire to reclaim the influence and cultural relations India has enjoyed with the nations of Central Asia before the advent of colonialism. 'India seems determined that if Central Asia is to be the scene of renewed great power rivalry, it will be a leading player.'[17] Most of the Central Asian states are not very comfortable with the great power competition in the region. According to a Kyrgyz Member of Parliament, 'as if it was not enough that Central Asia is squeezed by China, Russia and the Muslim World, now we also have an American eagle flying over it.'[18] Another commentator suggested the creation of a new vector—a new 'troika' consisting of Germany, Japan, and India as one of the solutions. The Central Asian States support India's increasing global profile and its candidature in the expanded United Nations Security Council (UNSC).[19]

But in order to emerge as a prominent player in Central Asia, New Delhi needs a strategy and mechanism. As of now, India is not a part of any significant regional initiative or organization except the Kazakhstan-initiated Conference on Interaction and Confidence-Building Measures in Asia (CICA). In the Shanghai Cooperation Organisation (SCO) it is just an Observer. Joining the SCO would enhance India's existing bilateral economic and military ties with the Central Asian states and Russia. Increasing military and other cooperation with Iran, Tajikistan, Kazakhstan, Kyrgyzstan, and Uzbekistan is critical to India's strategic vision. Joining the SCO may also provide a forum to engage China and strive towards a permanent, stable relationship with it.[20]

India also has significant economic interests in Central Asia. Central Asia provides a market for India's emerging export industries. New Delhi intends to ensure reliable access to oil and gas sources originating in Central Asia and increase its trade and investment in the region. India wants cooperation with the energy exporting states of Central Asia, particularly Kazakhstan, Uzbekistan, and Turkmenistan. A great power competition in Central Asia will make it difficult for India to pursue its goals. Hence, India's interest is best served through major power cooperation to bring stability to Afghanistan and the larger Central Asian region.[21]

It is estimated that the Central Asian republics of Turkmenistan, Uzbekistan, and Kazakhstan have about 300 trillion cubic feet of gas and 90 to 200 billion barrels of oil. This is about the same as that of Saudi Arabia. India's energy requirements in the next 10 years are expected to triple. In addition, gas needs would jump from 60 to 90 million cubic metres per day. The domestic sources cannot supply even one-third of this requirement. The use of nuclear energy is an option, but remains in question due to political problems at home and outside. Although India is close to the Central Asian supply chain, and potentially could be one of the biggest consumers of Central Asian oil and gas, it currently has no toehold in the region. The United States would prefer a route via Afghanistan, but it would be a long time for peace to return there, making a pipeline viable. The Iranian route, therefore, may be the easiest and possibly the cheapest gateway for Central Asian oil and gas. It would travel some 1300 km to its warm water ports of Jask and Chabahar in the Arabian Sea. There is already a small scale oil terminal at Jask. The port of Chabahar is a cargo terminal with connections to Central Asia and Afghanistan. Hence, these are ideal trans-shipping points. However, this supply route can only succeed if Iran and the United States resolve their differences.[22]

India has been trying to gain a foothold in Kazakhstan's hydrocarbon sector since 1995. But it was only in 2009 that an agreement was signed between Heads of India's Oil and Natural Gas Limited (ONGC), Videsh Limited (OVL), and Kazkhstan's Kaz Munai Gaz (KMG). This was followed by an Exploration Contract between India's Ministry of Oil and Gas and the KMG in 2010. During the Indian Prime Minister's Kazakhstan visit, definitive agreements between the ONGC and the KMG were signed. The latest agreement will assign 25 per cent participating interest in the Satpayev Block to OVL as a strategic foreign partner in the project. Thus, the agreement is the first breakthrough for India in the Central Asian energy sector. It will also help India diversify its oil acquisitions. India is currently dependent on West Asia and North Africa for 67 per cent of its oil imports. By 2025, India's oil imports are likely to grow to 90 per cent of its requirements.[23]

India attaches immense importance to Kazakhstan in the field of energy security. After Russia, Kazakhstan is the only country which is endowed to help meet India's energy security. This includes nuclear fuel and hydrocarbons. It has huge reserves of uranium as well as oil and gas. Kazakhstan has the second largest deposits of uranium of 1.5 million tons, constituting approximately 17 per cent of the world's total It is poised to emerge as the number one supplier of uranium in the world. Astana is planning to raise uranium output capacity from the current 6673 metric tons uranium (MTU) to 30,000 tons MTU by the end of 2018. In 2008, the President of Kazatom Prom, the nodal national atomic company set up in 1997, announced that it aims to increase the share of uranium supply from the present 12 per cent to 30 per cent of total world uranium output by 2015. The nuclear agreement signed with Kazakhstan makes it the fourth country besides the United States, France, and Russia that would supply uranium to India for civilian energy purposes. Under the proposed agreement, the Nuclear Power Corporation of India will begin to import at least 120 tons annually of Kazakhstan's uranium.[24]

Another significant proposal with regards to India's energy security is the development and the successful implementation of the Turkmenistan-Afghanistan-Pakistan-India (TAPI) Gas Pipeline Project. During the last TAPI Summit held in Ashgabat on 11 December 2010, all the four sides reaffirmed their commitment to implement the gas pipeline project. The

Inter-Governmental Agreement (IGA) and the Gas Pipeline Framework Agreement (GPFA) were signed during the TAPI Summit. As per the plan, India will receive 38 million cubic metres of natural gas per day (mmscmd) for a 30-year period from the TAPI gas pipeline on its completion.[25] However, there are a number of imponderables in implementing this project, including the conflict situation in Afghanistan and the India-Pakistan tension, which mar the prospects of this project.

India's space programme is also getting a fillip from the agreement between New Delhi and Astana relating to space research. The Indian Space Research Organisation (ISRO) and the National Space Agency of Kazakhstan have signed an agreement to help and cooperate with each other in space activities. Kazakhstan hosts the famous Baikanur Cosmodrome. Despite being a major centre for space research, Kazakhstan has more or less remained a passive partner of Russia. The current agreement signed between India and Kazakhstan is expected to assist the Kazakh space programme in a big way. Kazakhstan expects technology transfers from India in the space arena.[26]

Conclusion

India's interests in Central Asia are substantial, and it will seek to maximize its power and influence in the region to the extent possible in the years to come. New Delhi's major concerns include terrorism, Islamic fundamentalism, energy security, and new export markets. However, its prospects are fluid and subject to relations with other powers and regions. India, to the extent possible, would like to be a balancer in the region. However, relationships with Pakistan, the United States, and the Asian great powers tend to constrain these ambitions. New Delhi's interest is best served if there is cooperation with different players in the region. The future direction of India's strategic relationships with Central Asia remains uncertain. But a policy of multifaceted cooperation with all the Central Asian states and in conjunction with multiple players in the region is the best way forward.

Notes and References

1. S. Nurul Hasan (1985), Inaugural Address at the Indo-Soviet Seminar on Scientific and Technological Exchanges between India and Soviet Central Asia in

Medieval Period, Bombay, 7–12 November 1981. Proceedings, B.V. Subbaray-appa (ed.), New Delhi: Indian National Science Academy, p. 6.

2. G.M. Bongard-Levin (1971), *Studies in Ancient India and Central Asia*, Calcutta: Indian Studies; Past and Present, p. 203.

3. Ibid., p. 197.

4. D. Devahuti (2002), 'Ancient Central Asia and India' in A. Rahman (ed.), *India's Interaction with China, Central and West Asia: History of Science, Philosophy and Culture in Indian Civilization*, New Delhi: Oxford University Press, pp. 45–120.

5. Sanjay Kumar Pandey (2010), 'The Rise and Decline of Indian Trading Community in Central Asia', in Mushtaq A. Kaw (ed.), *Central Asia in Retrospect and Prospect*, New Delhi: Readworthy Publications, pp. 315–26.

6. Mehmet Ozkan (2010), 'What Does Central Asia Mean to India?', at http://opinionasia.com/node/829

7. Rasheeduddin Khan (1992), 'Emergence of Central Asia and its Relevance to India', *Mainstream*, 30 (24), pp. 15–22.

8. Arun Sahgal and Vinod Anand (2010), 'Strategic Environment in Central Asia and India', URL: http://www.silkroadstudies.org/new/docs/publications/1004Joshi-V-Strategic.pdf

9. Stephen Blank (2003), 'India's Rising Profile in Central Asia', *Comparative Strategy*, 22, pp. 139–57, http://www.tandfonline.com/doi/abs/10.1080/01495930390202607

10. Evan A. Feigenbaum (2011), 'Can India and United States Cooperate in Central Asia?' *Business Standard*, at http://www.cfr.org /central-asia/can-india-united-states-cooperate-central-asia/p25140

11. Scott Moore (2007), 'Peril and Promise: A Survey of India's Strategic Relationship with Central Asia', *Central Asian Survey*, 26(2), pp. 279–91.

12. Anita Inder Singh (1995), 'India's relations with Russia and Central Asia', *International Affairs*, 71(1) pp. 69–81.

13. Shahram Akbarzadeh (2003), 'India and Pakistan's Geostrategic Rivalry in Central Asia', *Contemporary South Asia* 12(2), pp. 219–28.

14. Poonam Mann (2001), 'Fighting Terrorism: India and Central Asia', *Strategic Analysis*, 24 (11), pp. 235–54.

15. M.K. Bhadrakumar (2009), 'Indian Interests in Regional Security', *The Hindu*, at http://www.thehindu.com/opinion/lead/article10434.ece, accessed on 31 July 2011.

16. P. Stobdan (2004), 'Central Asia and India's Security', *Strategic Analysis*, 28 (1), pp. 54–82.

17. Scott Moore (2007), 'Peril and Promise: A Survey of India's Strategic Relationship with Central Asia', *Central Asian Survey*, 26(2), pp. 279–91.

18. Quoted in Boris Rumer (2002), 'The Powers in Central Asia', *Survival*, 44 (3), p. 65.

19. 'Visit of His Excellency Mr Askar Akaev, President of Kyrgyz Republic: 7 August 2002 KYRGYZ-INDIA Joint Press Statement', available at http://meaindia.nic.in/
For Kazakhstan's support of India's membership of Security Council see http://www.osw.waw.pl/en/publikacje/eastweek/2009-01-27/india-new-direction-kazakhstans-foreign-policy

20. Jefferson Turner (2005), 'What is Driving India's and Pakistan's Interest in Joining the Shanghai Cooperation Organisation?', *Strategic Insights*, 14 (8). http://www.nps.edu/Academics/centers/ccc/publications/OnlineJournal/2005/Aug/turnerAug05.pdf

21. Harsh V. Pant (2011), 'Why Central Asia matters to India'. http://www.rediff.com/news/column/why-central-asia-matters-to-india/20110425.htm

22. Hari Sud (2008), 'India Looks to Central Asia for Energy', Column: Abroad View, Published: at http://www.upiasia.com/Economics/2008/06/17/india_looks_to_central_asia_for_energy/5733/

23. Meena Singh Roy (2011), 'IDSA COMMENT: Prime Minister Manmohan Singh's Visit to Kazakhstan', http://www.idsa.in/idsacomments/PrimeMinisterManmohanSinghsVisittoKazakhstan_msroy_270411

24. Zakir Hussain (2009), 'IDSA COMMENT: India and Kazakhstan: New Ways Ahead', http://www.idsa.in/idsastrategiccomments/IndiaandKazakhstan_ZHussain_180209

25. http://meaindia.nic.in/mystart.php?id=500417371

26. Zakir Hussain (2009), 'IDSA COMMENT: India and Kazakhstan: New Ways Ahead', http://www.idsa.in/idsastrategiccomments/IndiaandKazakhstan_ZHussain_180209

2

Silk Route
Transcendental Values in Time and Space

Ranjana Mishra

Genesis of the Silk Road

The Silk Road or Sichou Zhilu in Chinese is a convenient name for the Trans-Asian trade routes. It is the most famous and longest trade route of human history.[1] At one point, it was viewed as a road along which silk from China was brought to Turkey and sold to Europeans. The term Silk Road was coined by German geographer, Ferdinand von Richtofen in 1877. But the history of this route goes back to the days of yore, as far as the third to second millennium BC. There are bodies of existence of some roads directly connected with Tajikistan before the Silk Road. 'The Silk Road' is a bit of a misnomer. First, it was not a single road but a number of interconnecting caravan routes over which trade was conducted. It was rather a wandering network of trails linking the Far East to Europe, Persia, and northern Africa. Second, the Silk Route is much older as silk was but one of a considerable number of valuable commodities traded along the route and sericulture only dates back a few thousand years.[2]

It was this route which became a conduit where Hellenistic, Persian, Indian, and Chinese influences were able to intermix. In particular, Greco-Buddhist art represents one of the most vivid examples of this interaction.[3] The transmission was launched from north-western India to modern Pakistan, Afghanistan, Central Asia, Xinjiang (Chinese Turkistan), China, Mongolia, Korea, and Japan. Buddhism not only affected the lives and cultures of those regions but also left behind a world of wonders in art and literature.[4] It is commonly believed that it started with the journey of China's emissary, Zhang Qian, in the second century BC during the Han Dynasty (202 BC–AD 220).[5] The political contact with the many kingdoms of Central Asia opened up the great East-West trade route. The continental Silk Road was divided into north and south routes to avoid the great Central Asian deserts, the Taklamakan, the Gobi, and the Lop Nur deserts.[6] Among the network of routes, the first was the Lapis Lazuli route via which Lapis Lazuli was extracted in the mountains of Badakhshan (Modern Tajikistan). It was delivered to Mesopotamia, Egypt, and India in the third to second millennium BC. However, later on, in the first millennium BCE, this road turned east toward China. Parallel to this route was Nephrite road.[7] This second road was in the upper stretch of Yarkent Darya in Khotan (present day Xinjiang in China).[8] The third road was Sogdian which runs from Samarqand, the second-largest city in Uzbekistan, to Kokand in Uzbekistan, through Penjikent in northwest of Tajikistan, Varz (Aini), Bundjikat (Shahristan), Ura-Tyube, Khojand (southern bank of the river Jaxartes, modern day Syr Darya), Kanibadam (Tajikistan), and Isfara.

The fourth road was Karategin (Tajikistan) which branched off from Karategin and headed southward through Nurek, Barban (Dangara), Meizic (Khobvaling), Hulbuk, Parkhar, Kabadian, and Balkh (northern Afghanistan). The second, third, and fourth branches of the route could be called the Bactrian (south of the Amu Darya), (Oxus), and west of the (*Abasin*) Indus river road. The fifth route was the Pamir road, which went through Balkh to Barpanja and Khorog and Murghab and up to Tashkurgan in China. These roads were of great importance as the Sogdiana, or North Road, connected Samarkand and Kashgar; the Karategin Road connected Termez and Kashgar; and the Pamir Road linked Balkh and Tashkurgan. The trade on the Silk Road was a significant factor in the development of great civilizations and helped lay the foundation of the modern world in several respects.

In this essay, an attempt has been made to find out the immortal importance of the Silk Route in economic development and its cultural contribution which took place in several cultural regions along the Silk Route from seventh to the twelfth centuries. The volleys of literary and archaeological sources like scrolls, paintings retrieved from various grottos, found in Hejing County Museum as exhibited by Clark Centre for Cultural News at California have helped in constructing the paper. Various artefacts of museums of Xinjiang reveal multifaceted cultural interactions and changes in the regions along the Silk Route. An attempt has also been made as how to revive the old Silk Route, which remains to this day a treasure trove of heritage and monumental legacy of the yore.

Economic Corridor of the Past

The long route was divided into areas of influence, both political and economic. The Chinese traders escorted their merchandize probably as far as Dunhuang, where it was sold or bartered to Central Asian middlemen such as Parthians, Sogdianas, Indians, and Kushanas, who carried the trade on to the merchants in cities of Persia, Syria, and Greece. Each transaction enhanced the cost of the end product, which reached the Roman Empire through the hands of Greek and Jewish entrepreneurs. The Han-dynasty Silk Road took traders westwards into Gansu Province and along the Hexi corridor to the giant barrier of the Great Wall. From there, many caravans favoured the northern route through the Jade Gate Pass (Yumenguan) which is north-west of Dunhuang, along the southern foothills of the Heavenly Mountains (Tien Shan) and, skirting the northern rim of the Taklamakan desert, past the rich oasis towns of Hami (Kumul), Turpan, Yanqi, Korla, Kucha, and Kashgar. Others chose the more arduous but direct route through Yangguan Pass south-west of Dunhuang, and along the northern foothills of the Kunlun Mountains.[9] The earliest trade commodity on the route was rock salt which was mined in Afghanistan 5500 years ago. Salt was necessary for life and had a number of uses. Salt could help preserve meat and shepherds would salt their herds so that they might survive mountain forage or desert crossings without water for longer than they could otherwise. Another important item was the semi-precious stone called Lapis Lazuli. The only source of Lapis was the mines in Badakshan Province in Afghan-Tajik borders. Divine horses too was a major item of trade along the Silk Route. In ancient times, the best horses in the world were a breed that the Chinese called the Heavenly Horses. These horses, which were raised in the Ferghana valley, were the predecessors of today's Achal Teke and were the primary bloodstock for today's thoroughbred horses. If we compare the Achal Teke with the Heavenly Horses, we see a match in conformation, particularly in the pronounced withers. There are historical evidences that Han dynasty people purchased these horses sometime around 200 BC. With a view to preserving the pure breed of those horses, modern Turkmenistan has a special ministry of Horse Breeding and India's Prime Minister Narasimha Rao was presented with such a horse. Another item of trade was silk. Silk became sacred when used for religious purposes, especially for relic worship. The Buddhist relics gained commercial value when there was a market demand for them. They played a special role in the silk trade. It was through silk textile, China became popular to the outside world. In the Han dynasty (202 BC–AD 220), silk was already a major element in the Chinese economy. At that time, the Chinese were the only people who could weave silk. They exported silk to other countries, which were eager to obtain this fine fabric. The Chinese were deft in many different textiles, arts including gauze, quilt, embroidery, and damask. The embroidery was only done by hand with a needle. Large quantity of embroideries was transported to Europe through the Silk Route.

Some historians claim that the Chinese were the first to weave rugs as early as the Hsia dynasty (around 2205 BC). In a treasure trove of the Tang dynasty in Japan, there were many fine examples of Chinese rugs of the eighth century, with greyish white ground, brown border, and designs worked in brown and indigo blue. It proves that the idea of rug weaving originated from China, but some time later, perhaps during the Yuan dynasty, when China was ruled by the Mongols, the weavers exchanged their skills with those in Persia and the Chinese substituted the use of the Persian knot for their own use. Tajik myths tell stories that not only were lapis lazuli and spinel brought from Ferghana and Shugnan (Tajikistan) to China, but also musical instruments and herbs (dog-rose) for medical purpose.

Channel for Styles, Fashion, and Music and Art

The people of Central Asia—Sogdianas, Bactrians, Sakas, Scythians, and Turks—played a major role in providing contact and mutual cultural understanding between West (Europe) and East (China and India). The rich culture along the Silk Road has enabled art historians to research Indian, Kushana, Iranian, Syrian, and other influences on the painting and sculpture of Miran, Bamiyan, Kucha, Penzhikent, Khotan, Turfan, and Dunhung. There is no doubt that Central Asia was the melting pot of different civilizations. It was also the point of departure of stylistic influences on the art of Central China. The multiculture wave from Central Asia had reached China under Tang dynasty. The ornamental designs on the bronze bangles showing animals facing each other had reached China from Central Asia. The artistic aspects from Central Asia had affected the life-style of China in the areas of clothing, cooking, music, etc. Orchestras of Central Asia played the music of Kocho, Kashgar, Bukhara, Samarkand, and India, with their distinctive instruments such as flutes, percussion (gongs and drums), stringed instruments, and harps such as lutes and pipa. There are figurines of dancing girls and orchestras discovered in the tombs dating from Tang dynasty. This exotic culture soon spread out to other regions such as Japan and Korea, in the Tang period. Several traces of the influences still exist there. The evidence could be seen with the objects, instruments, and textiles preserved as treasure in Todaiji temple at Nara in Japan.

The technique of making porcelain was believed to be mastered by the potters in the Tang dynasty between 206 BC and AD 220. The skills of making porcelain were introduced to Central Asia through the Silk Route during the ninth century. There are evidences of porcelain products in the ruins of the Abbasid city of Samarra in Iraq. That city was once a summer residence of the Muslim leaders from AD 836 to AD 883. Later, porcelain was brought to Europe during the fifteenth century by the Arabs and it reached Japan after 1600. Marriages of various economic and cultural activities on the Silk Road were prominent, leading to mixed marriages in the social life as a very common phenomenon. People from different walks of life had come together in the Silk Road for trading, nay exchanging entrepreneurial skills, religious ideas, and friendship.

Buddhism along the Silk Route

The most significant innovations carried along the Silk Road to China were the belief system and religious arts of India, Central Asia, and the Middle East. Buddhism began its evolution as a religious doctrine in the sixth century BC. According to Chinese chronicles, Buddhism came to China in 147 from the country of the 'big yue dzhi', and thanks to the Kushana missionaries Buddhism was adopted as the official religion of the court of the Chinese emperor, Khuan-Di (147 BC–67 BC). During the Kushana period, various religious systems were widespread in Central Asia. These were the local cult of Mithra and Anahit, Zoroastrian pantheon (Ormuzd, Veretzanga, etc.), the Greek pantheon (Jupiter, Heliosis, Celen, etc.), and the cult of local heroes (Siyavush in Khorezm and Sogd). The followers of Buddhism had been banished from Persia in the second and third centuries, who found support in Central Asia, where Buddhism was widely practised. Buddhism did not enter Central Asia as an evangelical faith and did not supplant any other religion.

According to Professor A. Litvinskii, Buddhism had reached Merv (Turkmenistan) and Parthia (Khorasan in Iran) as early as Achaemenid times.[10] The *Mahavamsa*, the Great Chronicle of Ceylon described that Parthian and Alexandrian delegates were in attendance at a Buddhist Council held by King Dutthagamani, the Sinhalese king of Sri Lanka (161–137 BC).[11] Parthian's Buddhist faith was also confirmed by the Chinese records of the missions of the Parthian Buddhist preachers, An-Shih-Kao and An Hsuan during the second century.[12] Fa-hien and Xuan Zang appeared to indicate that most of the kingdoms such as Kashgar, Kizil, Karashahr, and Kucha on the northern Silk Route followed the Hinayana Vehicle, whereas Mahayana flourished along the southern Silk Route including the kingdoms of Khotan and Yarkand.[13] About the spread of Buddhism in Central Asia the *Encyclopaedia Britannica* writes, 'The spread of Buddhism into Central Asia is still not completely understood. However murky the details may be, it is clear that the trade routes introduced Buddhism to Central Asia for many centuries and the Buddhist culture flourished there.'

In the opinion of E. Rtveladze, Buddhism was prevalent in all five former Soviet Central Asian Republics that constitute Turkmenistan, Uzbekistan, Tajikistan, Kyrgyzstan, and Kazakhstan. By the first century AD, Buddhism had penetrated deeper into West Turkistan, spreading from Bactria to Sogdia. These five Central Asian countries together with Afghanistan and Pakistan are home to 'Istan Buddhism,' as termed by Chris Stanford.[14]

During the second century BC, Buddhism reached the northern rim of the Tarim Basin as well, passing from Bactria to the Tocharian people of Kucha and Turfan.[15] According to some sources, the Tocharians were descendants of the Yuezhi, a Caucasian people who spoke an ancient western Indo-

European language. In the second century BC, one group of the Yuezhi, later known as the Tocharians, had migrated to the west and settled in Bactria. The Zoroastrian elements appeared both in the Sarvastivada form of Hinayana Buddhism that flourished in Bactria, Sogdia, and Kucha, as well as in the Mahayana Buddhism that came to predominate in Khotan. The sixth century Chinese pilgrim Xuanzang (Hsüan-tsang) reported two huge Buddhist monasteries at the Sogdiana capital at Samarkand.[16] Long before the Arabs brought Islam to Central Asia in the mid-seventh century AD, Buddhism had flourished there for hundreds of years. In terms of current geographical areas, the early Buddhist regions of Central Asia included at various times:

1. Indian- and Pakistani-administered Kashmir (historical name Kashmir)
2. Northern Pakistani mountain valleys such as Gilgit (historical name Gilgit)
3. Pakistani Punjab, including the Swat Valley, and eastern Afghanistan south of the Hindu Kush Mountains (historical name Gandhara)
4. The Amu Darya River Valley to the north of the Hindu Kush, including both Afghani Turkistan to the south of the Amu Darya and southern West Turkistan (south-eastern Uzbekistan and southern Tajikistan) to the north of the river (historical name Bactria)
5. North-eastern Iran and southern Turkmenistan (historical name Parthia)
6. The areas between the Amu Darya and Syr Darya rivers, namely central West Turkistan (eastern Uzbekistan and western Tajikistan) (historical Sogdia)
7. The areas to the north of the Syr Darya, namely north-west Turkistan (Kyrgyzstan and eastern Kazakhstan) (historical name Suyab)
8. Southern Xinjiang (Sinkiang) in the Peoples' Republic of China, namely southern East Turkistan, both to north and south of the Taklamakan desert around the periphery of the Tarim Basin (historical name Dunhuang)
9. Northern Xinjiang, between the Tianshan (T'ian-shan) and Altai Mountains (historical name Dzungaria)
10. The Tibetan Autonomous Region, Qinghai (Ch'ing-hai), south-eastern Gansu (Kan-su), western Sichuan (Sze-ch'uan), and north-western

Yunnan (Yün-nan), all in the Peoples' Republic of China (historical name Tibet)

11. Inner Mongolia, in the Peoples' Republic of China, the Republic of Mongolia (Outer Mongolia), and the Buryat Republic in Siberia, Russia (historical name Mongolia).[17]

Extensive contacts and the missionary efforts of a great number of Central Asian Buddhist monks led to its popularization.[18] It expanded further along the southern part of Europe as suggested by the Buddhist settlement discovered at Airtam, 18 km north-west of Termez.[19] Buddhism reached its zenith in the eighth and ninth centuries in Afghanistan before it fell to the Arabs. In Kazakhstan, Buddhist culture can be found in many cities along the valleys and mountains close to the Chinese border and beyond. Turkmenistan provided an interesting mix of Persian, Turkic, and Islamic cultures in synthesis with Gandhara Buddhist culture. Buddhists in Turkmenistan took to the use of caves for isolation and for facilitating meditation.

In Samarkand, the Magok-I-Attari mosque was built upon a Zoroastrian temple that in turn was constructed on a Buddhist monastery. This gives us a view of the evolution of religious practice in Samarkand. Buddhism has a long history in that area. The greatest flux of Buddhism into China occurred during the Northern Wei dynasty, in the fourth and fifth centuries AD.[20] This was at a time when China was divided into several different kingdoms, and the Northern Wei dynasty had its capital in Datong in present day Shanxi Province. The rulers encouraged the development of Buddhism, and more missions were sent towards India. The new religion spread slowly eastwards, through the oases surrounding the Taklamakan, encouraged by an increasing number of merchants, missionaries, and pilgrims. In AD 569, two beautiful princesses converted the Tibetan king to Buddhism; one was a Nepalese and the other a Chinese. The king ordered monks to create a Tibetan writing, as they had no alphabet system and to go to Kashmir, Swat valley, Gilgit, and Taxila in order to search source documents on Buddhist philosophy and practice.[21] From there, Tibetan Buddhism blossomed and flourished in the sixth and seventh centuries AD with the translations of Indian Sanskrit writings, Chinese translations, and other Central Asian translations of Buddhist writings. All these led to the developments into what we know and recognize today. During the time of Kublai Khan, the Mongols who controlled the Silk Route clearly showed their preference for Buddhism even though most of the Mongol kingdoms converted to Islam. Marco Polo has written in his account that Kublai Khan accorded a magnificent ceremonial reception to the relics of the Buddha, sent to him by the king of Ceylon. Most of Kublai's successors were equally fervent Buddhists. Khaishan Khan (1307–11) had got many Buddhist texts translated into Mongolian.[22]

Preserving the Legacy of the Silk Route

With the rapid spread of Buddhism along the Silk Route, elaborate cave complexes and monasteries were built in and around the oasis towns, generously supported by powerful local families and merchants to ensure the safe passage of their caravans. Many of the cave frescoes portray these benefactors in pious positions, sometimes by name, since these gifts were believed to help them in their quest for nirvana. Pilgrims from China continued to travel westward searching for original manuscripts and holy sites, over the Karakoram Range to Gandhara and India. Some devotees were sufficiently inspired by the new ideas that they started to build monasteries, grottos, and stupas.[23] The development of the grotto is particularly interesting; the hills surrounding the desert are mostly of sandstone, with any streams or rivers carving cliffs that can be relatively easily dug into; there was also no shortage of funds for the work, particularly from wealthy traders, anxious to provide protection or give thanks for a safe desert crossing. Surviving Buddhist grottos in the area of the Silk Road are of particular significance. Famous sites such as the Mogao Grottos at Dunhuang, the Yulin Grottos at Anxi, Mt. Tianshui's Maiji Grottos, the Yungong Grottos at Datong, and the Longmen Grottos at Luoyang all represent the merging of Eastern and Indian art forms and Buddhist spirituality.[24] Dunhuang has 492 caves, with 45,000 square metres of frescoes, 2415 painted statues, and five wooden-structured caves.

Till today, Magao Grottos are a popular tourist attraction. These grottos specially consist of around a thousand caves, carved into the sandstone rocks by monks between the fourth and twelfth centuries. They were decorated with wall-paintings and statues of the Buddha. A large amount of scrolls, paintings, and important texts were stored in these grottos. Copying and painting religious images was believed to be one way of acquiring merit on the path to enlightenment, which was the reason that almost all the caves were so richly decorated. Central Asian Buddhist monks from the Tarim Basin and East Asian Buddhist monks appear to have maintained strong contacts until around the tenth century, as shown by frescoes from the Tarim Basin. Since the advent of Buddhism in Central Asia, each of these regions has ended up having strong remnants of existence of a Buddhist community. Buddhism has a long history in that area. Southern Uzbekistan has fragments of Buddhist temples, Buddhist stupas, and many Buddhist shrines.[25] In addition, the largest reclining Buddha in Central Asia was found in Tajikistan. Buddhism also set roots and thrived in Kyrgyzstan as Buddhist remnants can be seen along the rivers and lake of north-eastern Kyrgyzstan. In Kazakhstan, different sites of Buddhist culture can be found in many cities along the valleys and mountains close to the Chinese border and beyond. Turkmenistan provided an interesting amalgam of Persian and Turkic cultures in synthesis with Gandhara Buddhist culture. The remains of each of the two Parthian Buddhist stupas have been found in Turkmenistan at Merv (modern Mary) and near Ashgabat. The remains of Bactrian Buddhist monasteries have been found near Termez in southern Uzbekistan at Kara Tepe, Fayas Tepe, and Dalverzin Tepe, and the remains of a stupa at Zormala and of Buddhist wall murals at Balalyk Tepe, both in the Surkhan Darya region. Remains of a Buddhist monastery have been excavated at Ajina Tepe in southern Tajikistan. Buddhist remains from the Sogdiana culture have been found near Samarkand at Yerkurgan, Uzbekistan, Panjikent, and Tajikistan. They have also been discovered at Kuva in the Ferghana valley of eastern Uzbekistan. The remains at most of the Bactrian sites mentioned above extend into the Sogdiana period too. Findings have been made in the Talas River valley at Sayram Kelye (Sayirram) near Chimkent and Tektur Mas and Balasagun in the Dzhambul region. Archaeologists are hopeful of finding Buddhist remains also at Kos Tobe near Dzhambul. Buddhist sites have been found along the Chu River valley at Kyzyl Uzen near modern Cholpon Ata on the north shore of Lake Issyk-Kul, and at Ak-Beshim near Tokmak as well as along the Krasnaya River tributary of the Chu River. Around Lake Issyk-Kul, some 'mani' stones have been found underwater near Karakol (Przhevalsk) and along the southern shore at Tamga Gorge, as well as at

the Julku and Barskaon passes to the south and Issykata Pass to the north of
the lake. Mani stones have been found from this period at Tanglaly-Tas in
Semirechiye, at various sites near Almaty and at Zanka Gorge on the south
shore of Lake Issyk-Kul.

Elsewhere, Buddhist monasteries have been found all around the
Balkhash lake in Kazakhstan: at Almalik, along the Ili River to the east
of Lake Balkhash near the Kazakh/Chinese border, at Kyzyl-Kent near
Dzhezkazgan, along the Sary Su River to the west of Lake Balkhash, along
the Irtysh River, north of Lake Balkhash near the Kazakh/Russian border,
etc. There was a great Buddhist monastery in Semipalatinsk and the remains
of another have been found at Ablaiket near Ust Kamenogorsk. To the east
of Almaty, along the northern face of the Zailisky Ala Tau Mountains that
separate Kazakhstan from Lake Issyk Kul, there were Buddhist monasteries
all the way to the present Chinese border, with remains at Talgar, near
Almaty, and at Sumbe in the Narynkol region on the border.

The latest of them, a wooden monastery, was constructed at Medeo
near Almaty in the early nineteenth century. Kashgar had hundreds of
monasteries and 10,000 monks, while in Bactria the numbers were more
modest. The main monastery on the Kabul side of the Khyber Pass, Nagara
Vihara, just south of modern-day Jalalabad, housed the skull relic of the
Buddha and was one of the holiest pilgrimage sites in the Buddhist world.
The greatest monastery of the entire region was Nava Vihara (Nawbahar,
Nowbahar) in Balkh, the main city of Bactria. It served as the principal
centre of higher Buddhist learning for all of Central Asia, with satellite
monasteries in Bactria and Parthia, also called Nava Vihara. It ran like a
university and admitted only monks who had already composed scholarly
texts. It was famous for its stunningly beautiful Buddha statues, draped
with luxurious silk robes and lavishly adorned with magnificent jewel
ornaments as per local Zoroastrian custom. It had particularly close links
with Khotan, to which it sent many teachers. According to Xuanzang,
Khotan at the time had a hundred monasteries with 5000 monks. It is
natural to talk about Buddhism without mentioning its profound impact
on the development of Central Asian art. It is through those artworks that
a fusion of eastern and western cultures was demonstrated. Furthermore,
the contact with the Hellenized Gandharan culture resulted in the
development of a new art form. The earliest Buddha images resembled the

Greek god Apollo. From Gandhara, Bamiyan, Kumtura, Kizil, to Bezeklik and Dunhuang, the Buddhist artists, with arduous labour, created the most impressive wall-paintings of cave temples dedicated to Lord Buddha, his saints, and his legend. They present us an astounding pageant of local societies with kings, queens, knights, ladies, monks, and artists. Aside from their artistic values, those cave temples provide us with an immense amount of historical information. The portraits of Kizil donors with light complexions, blue eyes, and blond or reddish hair explain to us that they were more Indo-European than Mongoloid in appearance. The processions of an Uyghur prince and princess from Dunhuang illustrate how Uyghurs dressed themselves in the ninth century. It is from these wall-paintings that we can have a glance at the lives and cultures of these fascinating, but vanished ancient peoples. The image of the Buddha, originating during the first century in northern India in areas of Gandhara and Mathura was transmitted progressively through Central Asia and China until it reached Korea in the fourth century and Japan in the sixth century. However, the transmission of many iconographical details is clear, such as the Hercules inspiration behind the Nio guardian deities in front of Japanese Buddhist temples, and also representations of the Buddha reminiscent of Greek art such as the Buddha in Kamakura.[26] Another Buddhist deity, Shukongoshin, is also an interesting case of transmission of the image of the famous Greek god Herakles to the Far-East along the Silk Road. Herakles was used in Greco-Buddhist art to represent Vajrapani, the protector of the Buddha, and his representation was then used in China, Korea, and Japan to depict the protector gods of Buddhist temples.[27]

Cultural Borrowing on the Silk Route

There was a Persian cultural presence in many of these regions of West and East Turkistan, particularly in Bactria, Sogdia, Khotan, and Kucha. Consequently, Central Asian Buddhism came to incorporate Zoroastrian features to varying degrees.[28] The Zoroastrian elements appeared both in the Sarvastivada form of Hinayana Buddhism that flourished in Bactria, Sogdia, and Kucha, as well as in the Mahayana Buddhism that came to predominate in Khotan. Throughout the region, there are many indications of cultural borrowing between Buddhism and Islam. For instance, Kazakh Sufis not only believe in rebirth, but also identify reincarnations of past

Sufi masters like the Tibetan and Mongol Buddhists do of their teachers. The Sufis build shrines as graves for their masters, circumambulate them and light butter lamps, reminiscent of Buddhists practice around stupas of deceased masters. Sufi meditation includes recitation of the Islamic equivalent of mantras, often combined with the breathing cycle, as well as visualization of the Prophet and spiritual masters. Buddhism supplied a religious function for kings and emperors and created a shared political ideology for most of the states of medieval eastern Asia. Buddhism also facilitated the exchange of language, culture, and technology throughout eastern Turkistan, Central Asia, and India. Tang leaders used the Inner Asian tradition of Buddhism and commercially used the trade networks of Inner Asia to connect China. Central Asian and north Indian monks helped the Han Chinese translate Sanskrit and Gandhari Prakrit texts into Chinese, although the Central Asians themselves at first preferred these original Indian versions for their personal use. Han Chinese Buddhism took on many Daoist (Taoist) and Confucian cultural traits. All these embody a single cultural space and borderless cooperation without any barrier.

Saving History from Extinction

The Silk Road transmission of Buddhism essentially ended around the seventh century as it rose as a popular religion in Central Asia. The decline of Buddhism along the Silk Road was due to the collapse of the Tang dynasty in the East and the invasion of Arabs in the West. The conversion to Islam started in the eighth century in Central Asia.[29] Since Islam condemned iconography, most of the Buddhist statues and wall-paintings were damaged or destroyed. Buddhist temples and stupas were abandoned and buried beneath the sand. By the fifteenth century, the entire Central Asia had been converted to Islam. In March 2001, the Taliban of Afghanistan who were religious fanatics destroyed two very large Buddhist statues created over 1500 years ago in the Bamiyan valley.[30] The larger one was about 56 metres tall and the smaller one was 35 metres tall. Both icons represented in a subtle manner an evolution of not only an art form but also of a philosophical belief system. The Buddha has become less human and more superhuman. An age-old culture and heritage got destroyed on the altar of religious fanaticism. A similar example could be witnessed during the

Afghan civil war in the 1980s, when the Russians invaded Afghanistan. The most regrettable and irreparable casualties were the destruction of a rare Sanskrit manuscript collection housed in the Kabul museum. Both sides in the conflict bombed the museum and destroyed valuable artefacts housed therein. Cultural vivisection has overtaken unified feelings of Buddhist heritage in the entire Central Asian space.

Imperatives of Silk Route Revival

The Silk Route is once again growing in importance after what could perhaps be called an extended hibernation. Cultural sites embody a legacy of meaning and worldview from which contemporary people can draw strength. The construction of modern roads and railways, the discovery of oil reserves, and the industrialization of surrounding areas have led to the reopening of parts of this route to some extent. International efforts are under way to protect the legacy of the Silk Road. In Turkmenistan, the archaeological treasures of Merv, a city by some estimates believed to be the world's most populous in the mid-twelfth century, are didactic. The Islamic architecture of Bukhara and Samarkand in Uzbekistan are some of the riches of the Silk Road that are already protected by their inclusion in UNESCO's World Heritage list. Burana Tower, an important trade city on the Silk Road in Kyrgyzstan should be saved from decay and efforts ought to be made to include it in the World Heritage list.

Since 1943, the Dunhuang Art Institute, the predecessor of the current Dunhuang Academy, has been working with very limited resources, on the environmental monitoring of the caves along the Silk Route. They are working on the analysis of the colouring dye of the murals; research on the mechanism of the weathering of the rock structure, the deteriorations of the murals, and conservation techniques. At the last, many of these projects have been taken in collaboration with foreign institutions, such as the National Institute for Cultural Properties, Tokyo, Japan; the Getty Conservation Institute, USA, the Australian Heritage Council; the Andrew W. Mellon Foundation, USA; the Northwest University, USA; Tokyo University of the Arts, Japan; Osaka University, Japan; etc. The digitization project will help achieve a proper balance between tourism and conservation. The Asian Development Bank (ADB), the Islamic Development Bank, the Japan

International Cooperation Agency, and other international institutions are working on revamping of the entire highway by 2013 as they are heavily damaged in places by erosion, earthquakes, landslides, and avalanches. The M41, known informally and more commonly as the Pamir Highway, is a road traversing the Pamir ranges through Afghanistan, Uzbekistan, Tajikistan, and Kyrgyzstan in Central Asia. It is the only continuous route through the difficult terrain of the mountains and serves as the main supply route to Tajikistan's Gorno-Badakhshan Autonomous Region. The route has been in use for millennia, as there are a limited number of viable routes through the high Pamir mountains. The road formed one link of the ancient Silk Road trade route. Agartala Oil jointly with ONGC is planning to build a new 'Silk Route' via Bangladesh. It will be a 50 km road connecting India's landlocked north-eastern states with neighbouring countries, that is, Bangladesh, Myanmar, Bhutan, and China.[31] The old 'Silk Route' between India and China is accessible only after crossing West Bengal's Siliguri district. This new 'Silk Route' would not only benefit all the eight north-eastern states, but also boost the trade and economy between the region and the neighbouring countries. On 6 July 2006, the Nathula Pass between India and China has been opened once again. It used to be an important point on one of the many subsidiary paths of the Silk Road.[32] Over the centuries, the old trading routes had lost their connections. The most recent snapping of links was during the communist era. But after the break-up of the Soviet Union, several countries including some in the European Union have been making an effort to revive the overland route across Central Asia. China has also been making efforts to build railways from its Pacific coast via Central Asia to connect it with the Berlin-Baghdad rail link with an onward ambition of extending it through other countries to the Atlantic coast. More than 150 million Euros have been spent since 1993 to develop roads under the aegis of the Transport Corridor Europe Caucasus Asia Project, because ultimately transportation of goods via the New Silk Road promises to be a whole lot faster than via the sea route. A renaissance seems imminent.[33] It is the kind of place, stretching across Eurasia, which is rich in history and cultural legacy, surrounded by imposing geography, with people of diverse minorities and relatively untouched by mainstream tourist machinations.

Conclusion

The crying need of the day is to overcome national barriers in order to preserve this treasure trove of various cultures and civilizations. In today's consumer-driven world where one witnesses the dwarfing of the human consciousness, it is also essential to develop the past culture to manifest positive value. To be human in the full sense of the word is to lead a creative life and preserve the glorious past for future generations. The insecurity and politicization has resulted in destruction of a large number of treasure troves from the Silk Route preserve. This is high time that one should make concerted efforts to make this conduit once again a hub of cultural exchange despite of all geographical boundaries.

Now, focused efforts are being made to revive the heritage of the Silk Road. During the rule of the Taliban, there was a movement to retrieve every single Sanskrit manuscript from Afghanistan. One of these collections is housed at the University of Oslo in Norway. It is called the Schoyen collection. It consists of 1400 Sanskrit manuscripts and is for sale. One can buy the entire collection for 100 million US dollars. The route can pave the way for extensive amicable economic and cultural exchanges among widely separated regions and ethnic groups. It can bridge the gulf that has been created among various ethnic and religious groups, and in turn, bring harmony and peace in the world which electronic media alone cannot do sans personal touch. But aside from their architectural and archaeological value, the Silk Road sites also represent a chance for the people of Central Asia to rediscover their identities. The preservation of the Silk Road does not only mean respecting the past, but also means looking toward the future of Central Asia.

Notes and References

1. Janos Harmatta (ed.) (1994), 'History of civilizations of Central Asia', Volume II, in *The Development of Sedentary and Nomadic Civilizations: 700 BC to 250 BC*, Paris: UNESCO Publishing, pp. 101–4.
2. Daniel Waugh (2007), 'Richtofen's "Silk Roads": Toward the Archeology of a Concept', *The Silk Road*, 5 (1), Summer, p. 4.
3. Richard C. Foltz (1999), *Religions of the Silk Road: Overland Trade and Cultural Exchange from Antiquity to the Fifteenth Century*, New York: St. Martin's Griffin, pp. 109–12.

4. Ibid., pp. 113–17.
5. Roy Andrew Miller (1959), *Accounts of Western Nations in the History of the Northern Chou Dynasty*, Berkeley, CA: University of California Press, pp. 89–94.
6. Vadime Elisseeff (ed.) (2000), *The Silk Roads: Highways of Culture and Commerce*, Paris: UNESCO Publishing, (reprint), pp. 29–30.
7. Ibid., pp. 36–9.
8. Ibid., pp. 40–1.
9. John E. Hill, *The Western Regions according to the HouHanshu*, http://depts.washington.edu/silkroad/texts/hhshu/hou_han_shu.html
10. B.A. Litvinsky (ed.) (1996), 'History of civilizations of Central Asia', Volume III, in *The Crossroads of Civilizations: 250 to 750*, Paris: UNESCO Publishing, pp. 178–90.
11. Chen Yan (1986), 'Earliest Silk Route: The Southwest Route', *China Reconstructs*, XXXV (10), pp. 59–62.
12. Sogdiana Trade, *Encyclopedia Iranica*, (retrieved 15 June 2007) http://www.iranica.com/newsite
13. Felix Chami (2008), 'The Egypto-Graeco-Romans and Paanchea/Azania: Sailing in the Erythraean Sea', http://en.wikipedia.org/wiki/silk_road#cite_ref-9#cite_ref-9.
14. Vadime Eliseeff (2000 [1998]), 'Approaches Old and New to the Silk Roads', in *The Silk Roads: Highways of Culture and Commerce*, Paris: UNESCO, Reprint: Berghahn Books, pp. 1–2.
15. Susan Whitfield (2004 [1999]), *Life along the Silk Road*, (reissued), London, pp. 42–4.
16. Samuel Beal (2001 [1911]), *The Life of HiuenTsiang*, New Delhi, (reprinted), pp. 108–12.
17. Saan Hallikainen (2002), *Connections from Europe to Asia and How the Trading was affected by the Cultural Exchange*, Columbia University Press, pp. 150–5.
18. Aurel M. Stein (1990), *Ruins of Desert Cathay: Personal Narrative of Explorations in Central Asia and Westernmost China*, 2 Vols. Delhi: Low Price Publications (reprint), pp. 135–6.
19. Aurel M. Stein (1999), *On Ancient Central Asian Tracks: Brief Narrative of Three Expeditions in Innermost Asia and Northwestern China*. Reprinted with Introduction by Jeannette Mirsky. Book Faith India, Delhi, pp. 39–46.
20. http://www.iranica.com/newsite
21. Aurel M. Stein (1981 [1928]), *Innermost Asia: Detailed Report of Explorations in Central Asia, Kan-su and Eastern Iran*, Vol. 5, Clarendon Press, New Delhi: Cosmo Publications (reprint), pp. 87–9.
22. Killion Ulric (2006), *A Modern Chinese Journey to the West: Economic Globalization and Dualism*, Nova Science Publishers, p. 66.
23. Peter Hopkirk (1992), *The Great Game: the Struggle for Empire in Central Asia*, New York: Kodansha International, pp. 98–100.

24. Viktor Sarianidi (1985), The *Golden Hoard of Bactria: From the Tillya-tepe Excavations in Northern Afghanistan*, Harry N. Abrams, New York, pp. 23–67.

25. B.N. Puri (1987), *Buddhism in Central Asia*, Delhi: Motilal Banarsidas Publishers, p. vii.

26. Luce Boulnois (2004), *Silk Road: Monks, Warriors & Merchants on the Silk Road.* Translated by Helen Loveday with additional material by Bradley Mayhew and Angela Sheng. Airphoto International, p. 23.

27. Richard W. Bulliet (1995), *The Camel and the Wheel*, Harvard University Press, pp. 56–7.

28. Jonathan Tucker (2003), *The Silk Road: Art and History*, Timeless, pp. 364–6.

29. Edward C. Sachau (2002), *Alberuni's India*, New Delhi: Rupa and Co., pp. 201–3.

30. Sogdiana Trade (2007), *Encyclopedia Iranica*, 15 June, http://www.iranica.com/newsite

31. Rehman Sobhan (2000), *Rediscovering the Southern Silk Route*, Mohiuddin Ahmed, Bangladesh: The University Press Limited, pp. 2–12.

32. *Hindustan Times*, 'Indo-China to Revive Part of Silk Route', Anirban Choudhary, 22 March 2007, p. 9.

33. In an article in GEO on Myths and Legends of the Imperial Road by Sushmita Arp, June 2008, pp. 25–6.

3

Kashmir and Central Asia
Past Legacy and Future Continuum

MUSHTAQ A. KAW*

A deep political crisis overtook Kashmir over the last two decades,[1] which, besides affecting its vertical and horizontal growth, created the unfortunate impression that Kashmir was always a fragile zone and its people were habitually violent and unfriendly albeit the fact is the other way round. Historically speaking, Kashmir symbolized not only a 'paradise on earth',[2] but also a celebrated space of 'cultural pluralism'. Consequently, its people were imbued with symbiotic traditions of universal brotherhood, communal harmony, and mutual coexistence antedating the pre- and post-Islamic times:[3] courtesy soft borders, free trade and people-to-people contacts, and Kashmir's remarkable exposure to and multilateral collaboration with South and Central Asian countries. The influence of her multilateral connections with the outer world has been so profound that Kashmir is often called as the 'Iran-i-Saghir' [Small Iran].

However, unfortunately,[4] such connections nosedived in the aftermath of the partition of Indian subcontinent in 1947 and the de-facto division of thitherto 'Greater Kashmir' into what constitutes India Administered Kashmir or J&K State [J&K] and Pakistan Administered Kashmir [PAK].

* Professor and Director, Area Studies Programme, *Centre of Central Asian Studies*, University of Kashmir, Srinagar, J&K, India. He can be mailed at: mkaw@ rediffmail.com and kawm_06@yahoo.ac.in

This was followed by a number of Indo-Pakistan and Indo-China wars in 1960s and 1970s, which eventually led to the emergence of LoC and the rigid borders between India and Pakistan, cessation of cross-cultural fertilization and people-to-people contacts, and, above all, closure of India's direct trans-surface access to South and Central Asian neighbourhood across Kashmir with inestimable trade loss. Currently, however, efforts are afoot to resuscitate such historical linkages for larger economic, security, cultural, and civilizational interests.

Legacy of the Past

HISTORICAL CONNECTIONS

From the days of antiquity, connections were maintained over a cluster of routes and sub-routes transcending Kunlun, Pamirs, Hindu Kush, and Karakoram mountains via Ladakh and Gurais-Bandipora in J&K [India] and Gilgit and Muzaffarabad in PAK [Pakistan].[5] True prehistoric records are deficient to support such connections. However, archaeological finds from several Paleolithic and Neolithic sites in Kashmir, Xinjiang [China], and Tajikistan in modern Central Asian space vindicate these connections since remote past.[6] Even the ancient literature lends adequate support to such connections along the Grand Silk Road to which Kashmir, India, China, Afghanistan, and Central Asia were significant contributors.[7] Despite the discovery of the sea route to India in the fifteenth century, these trans-surface connections thrived till recent past notwithstanding geographical, territorial, and national hassles.[8]

CONTRIBUTORY FACTORS

Several factors contributed to such connections, and one among them was the political integration of Kashmir, north India, Afghanistan, and Central Asia under the Indo-Bactrian Greeks (190 BC), Scythians (early BC), Sakas and Parthians (90 BC–AD 64),[9] Kushanas (first to second century AD), Hunas (fifth century AD),[10] Karkotas (eighth century Kashmir),[11] and Mughals and the Afghans (sixteenth to nineteenth centuries).[12] It is true that such a centralized politico-administrative structure was, at times, plagued with centrifugal tendencies which led to its fragmentation and emergence of separate political entities on its debris. But this did not affect the continuity of age-long connections between Kashmir and Central Asia. These were instead cemented by ancient Indian faith of Buddhism, and in whose transmission from India to Soghdiana, Bactria, Gandhara, Farghana, Samarqand, Bukhara, Xinjiang in China, Kyrgyzstan, and Southeast Asia, Kashmir played a major role, which pronounced further with the hosting of a largest Buddhist conference (commonly believed as the third or fourth) by Kushana King Kanishka in Kashmir in the second century AD. According to Hsüan-tsang, the conference was attended by many of holy priests from far and near to explore the hidden secrets and existential realities of Buddhism. The discourses of the holy assembly were engraved on sheets of red copper 'enclosed … in a stone receptacle …' and the king then 'raised over it a stupa with the Scriptures in the middle …'[13] The said event recognized Kashmir as the undisputed abode for a peaceful and meaningful dialogue on religio-cultural issues on the one hand[14] and hooked her to a wider Buddhist world on the other.[15] The two-way connections were nurtured during the process of ideological transformation from Buddhism to Islam: the latter was transported to Kashmir from Central Asia.[16] True Buddhism and Islam were ideologically incompatible,[17] but both complemented each other in cultural terms. Quite precisely, Islam in Kashmir lost its Arab character and instead emerged as the hand mix of the innate and alien customs and traditions of the pre- and post-Islamic times.[18] In sequence thereof, Kashmir registered progressive thought in art, letters, values, traditions, beliefs, and practices:[19] thanks to the noble and unflinching endeavours of Buddhist monks and pilgrims, Kashmiri Brahmans and Muslim priests, Sufis and saints together. However, the role of the merchant community was in no way insignificant. While withstanding man-made and God-made hazards, they kept going; supply-consumer relationship in both high-bulk and low-value; and low-value and high-bulk commodities between Kashmir and Central Asia.[20] Likewise, the contribution of the professionals, artisans, craftsmen, litterateurs,[21] physicians, and poets who accompanied religious missionaries from Central Asia to Kashmir and vice versa, cannot be underestimated in this regard. As a matter of fact, they boosted bilateral bonds through mutual diaspora,[22] marital ties and socio-economic pro-activism,[23] and thereby assumed the role of 'cultural diplomats' and stimulants of regional peace and prosperity and cross-cultural and ideological fertilization.[24] However, as argued above, such historical connections were severed with the Partition of the Indian subcontinent in 1947. Consequent events were tragic enough to adversely affect border-free trade, human mobility, and disconnection of India's direct overland access to Central Asia to the detriment of her wide-ranging interests, trade, and security in particular.

Future Continuum

INDO-CHINESE RELATIONS: REVITALIZING TRADITIONAL LINKAGES

The restoration of such traditional trans-surface connections is quite demanding in view of the rapidly transforming economic world order. The shift to market economy, integration of local, regional, and global economies, advancement in communication and transportation technology, massive foreign investment in the developing countries and sharing of expertise and resources between the developed and developing countries, are such factors that demand forthwith flexible borders to ensure equitable human growth and development in a world often termed as a 'global village'.[25] Restoring traditional links is equally warranted to build confidence among the otherwise unfriendly neighbours like India, Pakistan, and China to jointly fight global terrorism, to jointly fight the non-state forces and avoid further damage to the rich systems, structures, values, and traditions of the region. Such a threat may aggravate in case the stake-holders fail to evolve a common strategy, resolve long-pending issues through dialogue and consultation and pursue Confidence Building Measures (CBMs) including the restoration of their traditional links. Few Eurasian countries, if not all, have already reopened rigid borders, settled border disputes, pooled resources, established power and energy grids, etc.[26] India, Pakistan, and China, in their own interests and that of the region as a whole, need to vigorously pursue CBMs for they have a major role in shaping South Asian destiny and brave the security stakes as a potential threat to their overall growth and development. They have abounded responsibility to evolve common mechanism while keeping aside their individual differences; and in that, they need to restore traditional transmission channels to build mutual beneficial relationship for posterity and the future of their majority young population in South Asia. Indeed, in this behalf, trade can serve as the most useful instrument to forge strong ties on zero sum principle.

To recall, India's trade potential was quite significant prior to the partition of Indian sub-continent in 1947. She had a share of 20 per cent in global GDP in 1820, and had a fair amount of trade with China, Central Asia, Middle East, and Europe across Kashmir in the north and Afghanistan in the west. In the process, the Ladakh route in J&K offered an effective bridge to sustain such relations over the centuries together. The Multani, the Punjabi, and the Kashmiri merchant communities had their systematic settings in Yarkand, Kashghar, and Khotan in what currently constitutes Chinese part of Central Asia [Xinjiang] and Khiva, Khokand, Bukhara, and Samarkand in what once formed Soviet Central Asia, for trade in felts, carpets, shawls, silk, cocoons, tobacco, tea, saffron, hemp, grains, herbs, teapots, porcelain, dry fruits, and shoes.[27] Such commodities hold relevance even now, and hence, can be exchanged together with industrial products, hardware, electronics, automobiles, pharmaceuticals, textiles, etc., over the Ladakh Route. This is not unlikely in view of the already existing informal trade in cloths, dress materials, electronic goods, medicines, crockery, porcelain, footwear, craft products, tea, saffron, jewellery, etc., on the Indo-Chinese cross-border points in Ladakh. Even the existing well-built roads and telecommunication systems from two sides of the Karakoram in Xinjiang and Ladakh in J&K indicate a great deal of optimism in the foreseeable future. However, Indo-Chinese relations went through rough weather on account of their border disputes over Indian states of J&K, Himachal Pradesh, and Arunachal Pradesh, and China's continued support to Pakistan in building her military capabilities and her stand on Kashmir and Kashmiris for secessionism from New Delhi. This was compounded lately by China's objection to Indian Prime Minister Manmohan Singh's visit to the Indian state of Arunachal Pradesh and her criticism of India's waiver in the meeting of the 45 nations' Energy Suppliers Group at Vienna.

Nevertheless, both crave for mutual partnership to further their individual economic agendas. China has, beyond doubt, emerged as a robust economy over the past few decades, which United States finds as a potential threat to her future interests in South Asia in particular and elsewhere at large. On the other hand, 1990s crisis-ridden India due to imbalance of payments which forced her to mortgage even her gold reserves abroad, has successfully re-emerged as a comparable partner to China: thanks to her policy to end License Raj, shift to free market economy, liberalize investment (FDI) regime, and enter into partnership with the regional trade organizations like South Asia Preferential Trade Agreement (SAPTA) in the 1990s and South Asia Free Trade Area (SAFTA) in 2006. Pursuant to these types of reforms, India currently contributes almost 80 per cent to South Asia's economic structure.

Perhaps because of their being comparable economies, India and China sustain their regular official and diplomatic meetings for economic, educational, security, and scientific cooperation despite border disputes and diverse stand on Kashmir. In fact, both realized the stark reality of resolution of border conflicts, [28] and abstained from any further war after 1962. Instead, tension over Sikkim was neutralized with the reopening of the traditional Nathula Pass in 2006. The said route opens every year from May to November to cut short the distance between India and China, reduce transport costs on goods entering into and exiting from India and to offer a viable alternative to shipment of goods between the two countries.

Given this two-way optimism, the restitution of traditional Ladakh Route over Karakoram in J&K is imminent in the coming years. In fact, the Governor of Xinjiang Province had long back outlined the need of direct aerial and trans-surface connection between Kashghar and Delhi over Ladakh in J&K to marginalize the dependence of the two countries on transportation of merchandise through shipment via Bay of Bengal. The need has still great potential of benefit to both countries: it would shorten distances, reduce transport costs by around 30 per cent and boost Indo-China trade volume from US$ 40 billion in 2010 to US$ 100 billion by 2015; it was only US$ 11.4 billion in 2007.[29] So, it is obvious that it would increase India's industrial exports to China and Central Asia; the reopening of Ladakh Route would facilitate India's energy imports from Central Asia over Xinjiang and J&K;[30] and thus bail her out from the deep energy crisis emanating from her unceasing population growth, depleting traditional energy resources, and staggering Gulf supplies.[31] China may, at the moment, be disinclined to the oil and gas pipeline idea to India as she too is plagued with energy deficiency. However, she may gradually appreciate the idea to earn regular transit fees, gain regional influence, boost trade volume with India, and above all, build mutual trust and confidence to jointly address fundamentalism and secessionism in the fragile spaces of J&K and Xinjiang, where the Kashmiris and Uyghurs, the two Muslim identities, though ethnically divergent, make a common case of 'secessionism' from New Delhi and Beijing, the two post-colonial regimes in Asia.

INDO-PAKISTAN RELATIONS: REVIVING TRADITIONAL ROUTES

Srinagar-Muzaffarabad and Srinagar-Bandipora transmission channels towards Peshawar and Gilgit served as the major trans-surface links between India, Pakistan, Afghanistan, China, and Central Asia before 1947. Large number of pilgrims, missionaries, adventurers, traders, and the ilk regularly treaded these routes for fame, fortune, adventure, and religious pursuits. However, in this case too, the partition of Indian subcontinent and the periodic Indo-Pak wars proved a misfortune. Rigid borders surfaced which eventually axed India's direct connections with the Central Asian space. Further, it impeded the process of cross-cultural fertilization, free trade and human movement and divided not only the people of the same ethno-historical descent but also the nations of the same Asian civilization, rendering India and Pakistan as traditional enemies.

> Of late, however, the Indo-Pak enmity has narrowed down, but not ended. Seemingly as friends, both have their wide military agendas against each other, which have correspondingly impacted their indicators of social and economic development, more so in case of Pakistan because of unceasing political instability in the country and violence along the Pak-Afghan borders. Consequently, both India and Pakistan have been annually increasing their budget on defence; hence, rank fourth and the seventh respectively as regards their military manpower. India's expenditure on defence and development is 2.7 per cent and 6.2 per cent respectively of GDP, whereas that of Pakistan is 3.8 per cent of GDP. In other words, Indian expenditure on defence is 34 per cent and that of Pakistan as 50 per cent.[32] Consequently, there has been little respite in India's fiscal deficit though in case of Pakistan it is as alarming as Rs 1.3 trillion were spent by 2010 as reported in *Indo Asian News Service* from New Delhi.[33] As a matter of fact, the defence factor has impeded the growth of human development in both the countries. According to the Human Development Report (2003) of the United Nations Development Programme, out of 191 countries, India and Pakistan figure at 127 and 144 respectively in terms of human development,[34] which is not a healthy trend at all.
>
> Both countries should recognize each other's national integrity, and explore possibilities of better economic cooperation through the medium of trade, other fields aside. Despite their varying scales of population, territory, growth and development, both have a reason to exploit economic diplomacy as a means to address common security threat. After all, India's growth is subservient to the stability in Pakistan and South Asian neighbourhood and vice versa. Thus,

bilateral trade through multilateral means can push up their annual volume which has been significantly as low as US$ 1.85 billion in 2009–10 with trade benefit to India by US$ 1.3 billion for many reasons including lack of mutual trust and formal trade agreement which has scaled down their range of merchandise in exchange. More so, while India has since granted Pakistan the Most Favoured Nations status, Pakistan has not yet done so, and she still keeps a list of around 1938 importable items from India for levy of duty under what is called as the 'positive List'.[35]

However, trade having assumed a key role in integrating developed, developing, and otherwise unfriendly nations across the region, India and Pakistan need to reconcile their varying interests and ideologies by pursuing non-reciprocal openings in South Asian trade for which the creation of a conducive atmosphere through dialogue and mutual consultation is mandatory. Their traditional enmity on J&K and its allied war history had started receding due to the international pressure to avoid Kashmir becoming a flash point and a potent threat to regional peace, stability, and development. Several elite groups, social, political, cultural, and diplomatic including electronic and print media, also built up pressure on the two countries to resume 'peace process' and 'sustained dialogue' in 2007–8 for the settlement of the long standing conflicts. In sequence thereof, the trust level between them increased to such an extent that both nations conceded to share lists of nuclear installations, exchange specific information, and conduct joint investigation on terrorist incidents. Pakistan went a step further by holding back support to militants in Jammu and Kashmir, and organizing systematic military campaigns against the non-state forces in the North West Frontier Province (NWFP).[36] She manoeuvred to marginalize their support of the tribal chiefs[37] and dissuade the youth from joining the Taliban and Al-Qaeda ranks in Waziristan and the areas adjoining NWFP bordering India.[38] Having felt complacent, Arthur Hermann reported in the *Wall Street Journal* that 'Pakistan tension with India on Kashmir has eased'.[39]

Quite jubilantly, they reopened traditional links, Srinagar-Muzaffarabad and Poonch-Rawalakot over India Administered Kashmir (J&K) and Pakistan Administered Kashmir (PAK) to begin with on 21 October 2008 for restricted traffic and tariff-free and permit-based truck trade albeit the mounting pressure of the Kashmiris on two governments during June agitation in 2008 could not be underestimated. They forcibly tried to cross the LoC to abstain from the intensity of often-caused blockade to their incoming supplies from Punjab along the Banihal Road and symbolically explore markets for their agricultural, horticultural, floricultural, and craft products in Pakistan and onwards in Afghanistan and Central Asia.[40]

Unluckily, while both nations had sincerely started treading the path of reconciliation and mutual understanding through CBMs, the Indian city of Mumbai experienced a dreadful terrorist attack in November 2008, which India believed Pakistan had a hand in it. It brought both the countries almost on the verge of war, which, however, was averted, courtesy external pressure and maturity of the Indian and Pakistani leadership. Nevertheless, both countries lost trust in each other and stayed away from further peace talks for resolution of their long-pending conflicts notwithstanding Pakistan's reassurances to India for her friendship and innocence in Mumbai attack purportedly for regional peace and stability. To quote the Pakistan Foreign Minister, Shah Mehmood Qureshi, 'The most important thing is that India and Pakistan have to live as good neighbours. Our government … started on a policy of normalization and we were doing fairly well until the unfortunate Mumbai incident that has caused a hiccup and there is a pause in the composite dialogue. We want to … resume dialogue with India because we feel that if we want regional peace, then normal friendly relations between Pakistan and India will play a significant role.'[41] Pakistan evenly carried out military onslaught against the Taliban in Swat, Waziristan, and NWFP; no matter it culminated in the change of government in Pakistan and brought the whole of Pakistan face to face with huge human and infrastructural loss during retaliatory attacks.[42] Nevertheless, due to internal and external pressure from United States, United Nations,[43] European Union, OIC, etc., limited trade and traffic obtained over aforementioned Srinagar-Muzaffarabad and Poonch-Rawalakot routes, presupposing two-way optimism.

Lately, however, the visit of Pakistan Foreign Minister, Hina Rabbani Khar, to India and her meetings with her Indian counterpart S.M. Krishna on 27 July 2011 created new hopes of 'continued dialogue' for settlement of outstanding issues including Jammu and Kashmir. Both announced new CBMs on Kashmir which included increasing cross-LoC trading days for trade, religious, and other type of tourism, allowing multi-entry Permit for six months to people of Jammu & Kashmir to PAK, starting weekly bus service, holding regular meetings of cross-LoC traders, re-opening Kargil-Iskardu-Gilgit route for trade and traffic and involving Kashmiri leadership in talks for the settlement of Kashmir issue. Many viewed the ministerial-level parleys positively. United Nations Chief, Ban Ki-Moon welcomed the talks and wished their continuation for regional interest and resolution of all disputes including Kashmir.[44] Indian Foreign Minister S.M. Krishna expressed satisfaction on the outcome of talks: 'while being cognizant of the challenges ahead, I am confident about our future ... relations ... for peace, progress and prosperity.'[45] Pakistan Foreign Minister also expressed optimism about the ministerial-level talks. She claimed a 'forward movement'... over the past few months and called for leaving the baggage of history behind as a key to 'proactive, productive and result-oriented' engagement with India on all issues including Kashmir.[46] The US Secretary of State, Hillary Clinton, expressed joy on the new beginning for which she believed regional integration through the medium of trade is immensely useful to the South Asian countries. To quote her according to the *Press Trust of India* from Chennai, 'Promoting trade links in violence-hit South Asia will bring prosperity and peace not only to India, but also to countries like Pakistan and Afghanistan.' She impressed upon India to do more in this regard.[47] On the other hand, on 27 July 2011, Foreign Minister S.M. Krishna urged upon the Pakistan government to grant Most-Favoured Nation (MFN) status to India to boost bilateral trade and set up non-discriminatory trade regime and transform her policy from the present 'positive' to the 'negative' list by 2011. Perhaps in this backdrop, Pakistan is conferring the MFN status on India by the end of 2011 to reduce tariff and non-tariff barriers and broaden the trade basket between the two countries. The commerce secretaries of the two countries also met in November 2011 to finalize the proposal on the trading partnership.[48]

Importantly, the grant of the MFN status by Pakistan to India would be beneficial to Afghanistan as well because absence of direct trans-land access inhibits India-Afghanistan trade structure to grow. True Pakistan allows Afghan goods, especially dry fruits, to India on its soil. But she does not permit Indian goods to enter Pakistan for onward transmission to Afghanistan. Consequently, India thrives on Iran's port Chabahar for connectivity with Afghanistan, which, however, was upgraded onward by India through the construction of a 218 km trans-surface Zaranj-Dilaram highway, connecting landlocked Afghanistan and its three bordering Central Asian states, Turkmenistan, Uzbekistan, and Tajikistan with the Persian Gulf. It is a part of US$ 2 billion Indian aid for the reconstruction projects in Afghanistan in the post-9/11 scenario presupposing continuity in the bilateral relations of the erstwhile two Silk Route partners of South Asia. Such a partnership has been reaffirmed to continue in future too as was admitted by President Hamid Karzai during his two-day visit to India from 5 October 2011. According to the *Press Trust of India* the two countries sealed a strategic partnership pact in the fight against international terrorism, organized crimes, illegal drug trafficking, and money laundering. They further agreed that Afghanistan's economic integration with India and South Asia as a whole is beneficial to the Afghan people; they realized it can be achieved by promoting 'closer trade, investment and transit links.'[49] No doubt the Zaranj-Dilaram Highway serves as a viable Indo-Afghanistan transmission link; there is, nevertheless, an immediate need to open similar links across Pakistan, and, in that, the restoration of ancient trans-Kashmir land routes shall fetch multiple benefits to all stakeholders of the region.

Reaping Benefits

As regards security, it shall build trust and confidence between India and Pakistan as both brave the odds of terrorism and fundamentalism, which pose a serious threat to their invaluable systems, structures, and values. Further, such a reopening would rehook the countries of Asian civilization as was underscored by the members of Shanghai Cooperation Organisation (SCO) at its different meetings.[50] In the same manner, it would forge economic and regional integration and transcend geographic, national, and territorial hassles as is warranted under the norms of new world economic order[51] and the dynamics of regional peace, security, and development as was underscored by the US Secretary of States Hillary Clinton in July 2011.

Benefits to South Asian Countries

INDIA

Other than general benefits, the restoration of trans-Kashmir traditional routes is not without benefits to the individual nations. India would immediately find a direct overland access for her industrial exports in hardware, IT, pharmaceuticals, chemicals, petrochemicals, textiles, railways, steel and iron, etc., to the neighbouring South Asian countries. Her exports to Pakistan in sugar, dyes, plastic and petroleum products, machinery, tyres, chemicals, tea, cotton, etc. together with her imports from there in edible oils, spices, dry fruits, nuts, cotton, yarn and fabrics, organic chemicals and pulses would sequentially increase. [52] The Indo-Pak trade volume from US$ 251 million in 2000–1 and US$ 2233 million in 2008[53] shall accordingly leapfrog to US$ 12 billion as is targeted for 2015, and the same would still enhance once the cross-border trade in smuggled goods worth US$ 10 billion is formalized[54] though trade balance would remain in India's favour for her strong industrial base and production.[55] India's trade volume with Central Asian states from US$ 100 million in 2000–1 to US$ 230 million in 2005 to US$ 518.49 million in 2008 and US$ 481.64 million in 2009[56] with Kazakhstan contributing more than 50 per cent of the share would correspondingly swell. Currently, the share of foodstuffs, mineral products, chemicals, hides and skins, precious metals and stones[57] in Indo-Central Asian trade is just 1 per cent of the total regional trade,[58] with energy having just little or no share in it. The reason is obvious enough as whole trade in merchandize between India and Central Asia is conducted by air-lifts from Dubai and Delhi airports and shipped through the deep water channels of Bay of Bengal and Bandar Abbas at Chabahar in Iran.

Importantly, such a reopening would enable India to directly import energy from energy-abundant Central Asian states, and thereby bail her out of the deep energy crisis characterizing periodic power cuts and black outs in villages, cities, and towns, indisputably a common characteristic of Pakistan, Afghanistan, and whole South Asia. Indeed, India can offer to be the biggest market for Central Asian energy resources[59] owing to her ever growing population, presently more than 1.25 billion, and depleting traditional energy resources. While Devendra Kaushik supports the restoration of Xinjiang-Karakoram route for transportation of Central Asian gas and oil to India across Ladakh in J&K,[60] Suryakant Bal favours the relinking of Gilgit and Wakkhan Corridor for carrying Tajik hydroelectricity and Central Asian oil and gas to J&K and Punjab in India.[61] During empirical studies in Xinjiang, Tajikistan, Kyrgyzstan, etc., this researcher found a great substance in the aforementioned argument of Kaushik and Bal keeping in view geographical proximity and modern means of transportation and communication.[62]

PAKISTAN, AFGHANISTAN, AND CENTRAL ASIAN STATES

Pakistan and Afghanistan would earn regular transit fee with which to strengthen their otherwise feeble economies.[63] They can even pool their trade products with the merchandize-laden truckloads set from India to Pakistan, Afghanistan, and onwards to Central Asia. As argued above, Pakistan has already allowed the passage of Afghan goods to India under the terms of the Afghan Transit Trade (ATT). Similarly, both countries can become partners to the Indo-Central Asia energy trade if they wish so in consultation with the energy producing Central Asian states. It is to be emphasized that PAK and J&K offer a viable trans-land alternative for energy transportation from Central Asian states to energy-deficient South Asian countries including India, conditioning peace and stability in the region. Such a pipeline arrangement is cost-effective and involves less security threats than are anticipated in the proposed energy transportation Turkmenistan-Afghanistan-Pakistan-India (TAPI) and Iran-Pakistan-India (IPI) gas pipeline projects. While former is cleared for funding by Asian Development Bank (ADB), the latter is being funded by the Iranian government: Pakistan and Iran have already settled terms of trade on IPI; whereas, the United States is supportive of TAPI in preference to IPI given its hostility with Iran and the economic sanctions there against her.

Central Asian states would be exposed to new South Asian energy transportation corridors on the reopening of trans-Kashmir traditional roads for regional and economic integration. They can bargain their energy on better terms than offered to them traditionally by Russia and Iran and lately by Turkish oil companies. It would finally re-engage ancient trade and civilized South Asian partners.[64]

JAMMU&KASHMIR STATE

As far as J&K state is concerned, such an arrangement can expose her to the northern world for integration with the competitive and progressive world communities, seek to soothe, if not satisfy, its restive Kashmiri population, ease their energy crisis and help them find additional markets for their fruits, carpets, rugs, chain stitch, wall hangings, shawls, embroidery, silk cloths, shawls, spices, flowers, saffron, Kashmiri cuisine (*wazw'aan*), timber, furniture, aromatic and fruit bearing plants in the South and Central Asian countries. Besides, the reopening towards Pakistan across Muzaffarabad and Gilgit would serve as an alternative transportation channel to the Srinagar-Jammu Banihal national highway, which has proved arduous due to complex road structure and its often-recurring road blocks or blockades due to political complications and ideological incompatibility between the Kashmiris and Jammuites on the issue of union with India. In addition, it would be more effective for disaster management like in the 2005 earthquakes.[65] Since the whole valley falls within the seismic zone, the researchers in the United States Institute of Peace (USIP) in Washington DC, recommended the reopening of five cross-LoC points, resumption of transportation along the Jhelum River and construction of railways between Sialkote and Jammu, and Rawalpindi, Muzaffarabad, Abbotabad, Uri, and Srinagar for effective disaster management and promotion of people-to-people contacts. One may recall that these routes were optimized for relief during the massive earthquake in the area in 2005. Thus, multiple access points across J&K in India and PAK in Pakistan yield numerous benefits to all participating parties.

Summing up

In short, Kashmir and Central Asia were closely knitted with each other since ancient times via a cluster of routes traversing Kashmir over the Karakoram, Pamirs, and the Hindukush mountains. The archaeological and literary evidences support such connections and the role played by the State and the private individuals/organizations in their promotion amid political convulsions, dynastic wars, geographic, and other disorders. Such connections had multiple benefits to India for she was directly hooked to Central Asia through Kashmir in the north and Afghanistan in the west. Several religious, cultural, and ideological movements radiated into and across these routes from time to time.

However, with the partition of the Indian subcontinent in 1947 and following emergence of two new nation states of India and Pakistan, contacts along both sides of the India-Pakistan borders became remote despite their immense ethno-cultural closeness. Soon, both states fought wars with each other on J&K which led to closure of porous borders and free trade and human mobility along the borders and rendered villages and towns desolate and subjected tens and thousands of peoples to unemployment. Yet, one finds great scope for their restitution in view of a rapidly transforming regional and global scenario. Over the last few decades, India, China, and Pakistan view the reopening of traditional roads with adequate benefits, and. to this effect, India and China have already made a smooth beginning in Sikkim and so have India and Pakistan in PAK and J&K. However, they require carrying forward their efforts ahead of challenges for it is not devoid of multiple benefits to them, for trade and security in particular and regional peace and development in general.

References and Notes

1. Tens and thousands of people including the security personals were killed and injured during the two-decade strife, unprecedented damage to precious systems and structures apart. Many were rendered homeless and still many migrated including Kashmiri Pandits to Indian States for survival. The number of the orphans and destitute is equally innumerable. The given crisis also impinged upon the Indo-Pak friendly relations and the South Asian security and development. Though the militancy stands marginalized, yet the two-decade strife following Kashmir conflict continues till date.

2. Father Xavier (1927), 'Letters from Kashmir, Sept., 1597', H. Hosten, Eng. tr. from Spanish, *Journal of the Asiatic Society of Bengal*, XXIII (1), pp. 115–17; Khafi Khan, Muntakhab-al Lubab, Mehmud Ahmad Farooqi, Urdu tr. from Persian (Karachi, 1963), pp. 301–4; Birbal Kachroo, Majmu'at Tawarikh, Per. ms., Research and Publication Department of the J&K State Libraries, J&K, India (hereafter R&P Deptt., Srinagar), pp. 148–9; Mushtaq A. Kaw (2001), *The Agrarian System of Kashmir, 1586–1819 AD*, Srinagar: Aiman Publications, p. 1.

3. Mushtaq A. Kaw (2010), 'Central Asian Contribution to Kashmir's Tradition of Religio-Cultural Pluralism',*Central Asiatic Journal*, Giovanni Starry (ed.), 52(2), Autumn, pp. 237–55.

4. Mushtaq A. Kaw (2009), 'Restoring India's Silk Route Links with South and Central Asia across Kashmir: Challenges and Opportunities', *The China and Eurasia Forum Quarterly*, 7(2), May/June, *The Central Asia-Caucasus Institute*, Paul H. Nitze School of Advanced International Studies, Washington DC, USA or The Silk Route Studies Programme, Institute for Security and Development Policy, Stockholm, Sweden, pp. 59–74.

5. For details, see S.L. Shali (1989), 'Cultural Ecology of Prehistoric Kashmir', in B.K. Kaul Deambi (ed.), *Kashmir and Central Asia*, Srinagar; H.de Terra and T.T. Paterson (1939), *Studies in the Ice Age in India and Associated Human Cultures*,

Washington DC; Masson and Sarianidi (1972), *Central Asia: Turkmenia Before the Achaemenids*, London; Allchin and Hammond (eds) (1978), *Archaeology of Afghansitan*, London.

6. Iqbal M. Shafi (1988), *Silk Road to Sin Kiang*, Lahore: Wajidalis Publication; Richard C. Foltz (1999), *Religions of the Silk Road: Overland Trade and Cultural Exchange from Antiquity to the Fifteenth Century*, London: Macmillan Press; Jonathan Trucker (2003), *The Silk Road-Art and History*, New Delhi: Timeless Books; Lal and Gupta (1984), *Frontier of the Indus Civilization*, New Delhi.

7. C. Wessels (1921), *Early Jesuit Travellers* (1603–1721), Hague, pp. 30–1; C.P. Skrine (1926), *Chinese Central Asia*, London, pp. 74–5; File no. 771/S.1935-36 (1878–9), His Highness Government, J&K, Persian/General Records, *Jammu Archives*.

8. W.W. Taran (1951), The *Greeks in Bactria and India*, Cambridge, p. 155. Kalhana (1979), *Rajatarangini*, eng. tr. M.A. Stein, *Chronicle of the Kings of Kashmir*, Vol. I, Delhi, (reprint), p. 116; *Rajatarangini*, Vol. I, pp. 109–47; R.C. Kak (1933), *The Ancient Movements of Kashmir*, London.

9. The archaeological finds of Semthan Kashmir and copper coins of Kajula Kara Kadaphises including few Huna coins dug at Tarakpur on way to Sopore-Bandipora link road, support Kushana occupation of Kashmir. This is besides few post-Kushana finds retrieved on way from Gurais, AstoreBhunji, Gilgit, Chitral and Yasin valleys in the Dard country to Central Asia: G.S. Gaur (1987), *Semthan Excavations in Archaeology and History*, B.M. Pande et al. (eds), New Delhi, pp. 327–37; S.L. Shali (1993), *Kashmir: History and Archaeology Through the Ages*, New Delhi, p. 122. Percy Brown (1959), *Indian Architecture (Buddhist and Hindu Periods)*, Bombay, p. 34.

10. For details, see *Kalhana's Rajatarangni*, Chapter III, Verses 486–97; Chapter IV, Verses 8, 132, 150, 163, 186, 207, 216, etc., eng. tr. M.A. Stein (1989), *A Chronicle of the Kings of Kashmir*, Vol. I, Delhi; B.K. Kaul Deambi (ed.) (1989), *Kashmir and Central Asia: Cultural Contacts and Interactions*, Centre of Central Asian Studies, University of Kashmir, Srinagar.

11. For details, see Mushtaq A. Kaw (2001), *The Agrarian System of Kashmir, 1586-1819 AD*, Srinagar: Aiman Publications.

12. SI-YU-KI (1884), *Buddhist Records of the Western World*, Part I, eng. tr. from the Chinese of HIUEN Tsiang (AD629) by Samuel Beal, London, reprint Delhi, Motilal Banarasidas, 1981, pp. 150–3 and 156.

13. Jean Nauduu (1980), *Buddhists of Kashmir*, Delhi, p. 10.

14. *Chronicles of the Kings of Kashmir*, Vol. I, Chapter I, Verse 173, pp. 30–1 .

15. Sayyid Ali, *Tarikh-i Sayyid Ali*, Ms. Research & Publication Division of the J&K State Libraries (R&PD), ff. 2–4; *Baharistan-i Shahi*, (Anonymous), Ms. R&PD, ff. 9–10. Also see, *The Agrarian System of Kashmir, 1586-1819 A.D.*, pp. 295–301; Muhammad Ashraf Wani (2004), *Islam in Kashmir (Fourteenth to Sixteenth Century)*, Srinagar, pp. 55–8.

16. Caroline Hodges, *Understanding Society: Introduction to Sociology*, USA, Harper and Row, p. 448.

17. Mushtaq A. Kaw (2010), 'Central Asian Contribution to Kashmir's Tradition of Religio-Cultural Pluralism',*Central Asiatic Journal*, Giovanni Starry (ed.), 52(2), Autumn, pp. 237–55.
18. Utpal K. Banerjee (1998), 'Role of Cultural Diplomacy', *Indian Democracy: Agenda for the 21st Century*, Konark Publications, New Delhi, pp. 397–412.
19. Mushtaq A. Kaw (2006), 'Trade & Commerce in the Chinese Central Asia (19th–20th Century)', in Kaw and Bandey (eds), *Central Asia: Introspection*, Centre of Central Asian Studies, University of Kashmir, Srinagar, pp. 47–61.
20. Jonaraja (1898), *DvitiyaRajatarangini*, eng. tr., J.C. Dutt, *Kings of Kashmira*, Calcutta, p. 58.
21. W.H. Wathen (1834), 'Memoir on Uzbek State', *Journal of the Asiatic Society*, *JAS*, No. 32, August, Calcutta, p. 372; W.H. Wathen (1835), 'Memoir on Chinese Tartary and Khotan', *Journal of the Asiatic Society*, 48, December, Calcutta, p. 654.
22. Srivara (1898), *Jaina Rajatarangini*, eng.tr., J.C. Dutt, *Kings of Kashmira*, Calcutta, pp. 134–50; *Tarikh-i Sayyid Ali*, ff. 16–17; *Baharistan-i Shahi*, ff. 23–4.
23. 'Restoring India's Silk Route Links with South and Central Asia across Kashmir: Challenges and Opportunities', *The China and Eurasia Forum Quarterly*, 7(2), May/June 2009, pp. 59–74.
24. Mushtaq A. Kaw (2008), 'Profiling the Impact of Globalization on Central Asian Republics: A Perspective', *Contemporary Central Asia*, XII(3), Centre for Russian & Central Asian Studies, School of International Studies (Hereafter SIS), Jawaharlal Nehru University, New Delhi, December, pp. 1–14.
25. 'Restoring India's Silk Route Links with South and Central Asia across Kashmir: Challenges and Opportunities', *The China and Eurasia Forum Quarterly*, 7(2), May/June 2009, pp. 59–74.
26. Mushtaq A. Kaw (2006), 'Trade and Commerce in Chinese Central Asia (19th–20th Century)', in Mushtaq Kaw and AijazBandey (eds), *Central Asia: Introspection*, Kashmir: Centre of Central Asian Studies, University of Kashmir, Srinagar, J&K, India, pp. 47–61.
27. Yongnian Zheng and Sow Keat Tok (2005), 'China's Peaceful Rise: Concept and Practice,' Discussion Paper 1, China Policy Institute, University of Nottingham, November: http://www.nottingham.ac.uk/cpi/research/ research_impact.php.
28. *The Straits Times*, Singapore, 18 June 2007.
29. Devendra Kaushik (1970), *Central Asia in Modern Times*, Moscow.
30. In fact, centrality of energy in India's foreign policy agenda was explicitly underscored by then-Petroleum Minister, Mani Shankar Aiyer, in a meeting with his Pakistani counterpart on 5–7 June 2005, '... any country could become part of any project in the process of contacts of South Asia with West, East, and Central Asia in the hydrocarbon sector': Ashok K. Behuria, 'Politics of Pipeline', p. 11.
31. M. Ashraf, 'Peace in South Asia', Greater Kashmir, Srinagar, J&K, India, 22/02/2009.

32. *Greater Kashmir*, Srinagar, J&K, India, 1 October 2011, p. 15.
33. Manjrika Sewak (2005), *Multi-Track Diplomacy between India and Pakistan: A Conceptual Framework for Sustainable Security*, New Delhi: Manohar Publications, p. 20.
34. 'India's Trade Initiatives in South & Central Asia', Lecture delivered by Sudhir Devare, Director General, Indian Council of World Affairs, New Delhi, in the Centre of Central Asian Studies, University of Kashmir, Srinagar, on 20 August 2011.
35. *Kashmir Uzma* [in Urdu], Srinagar, JUK, India, 17 June 2007.
36. Ismail Khan (2007), 'The Game is Up for Uzbeks,' *Dawn*, Pakistan, 16 April; B. Raman (2007), 'Anti-Uzbek Anger in South Waziristan,' International Terrorism Monitor-South Asia Analysis Group, Paper No. 215, 8 April, http://www.saag.org/common/uploaded_files/paper2200.html (1 December 2008).
37. SENLIS Council, *Afghanistan Five Years Later:The Return of the Taliban*, Spring/Summer 2006: http://www.icosgroup.net/documents/Afghanistan_5_Years_Later.pdf (21 May 2006)
38. *Greater Kashmir*, Srinagar, J&K, India, 16 June 2007.
39. The June agitation, 2008, and the march of the restive Kashmiris towards Muzaffarabad followed the act of the J&K state to transfer 800 acres of forest land in Kashmir to the Hindu Shrine Board. It evoked a sharp reaction from Kashmiri Muslims in Kashmir division. Under public pressure, the State revoked the transfer order, which, however, agitated the Jammuites in another division of J&K State. For the first time in more than 50 years, the Kashmiris and the Jammuites locked horns with each other and took opposite stand on Kashmir's accession with India, one for and another against it: for further details see the English daily, *Greater Kashmir,* Srinagar, J&K, India, from June to August 2008.
40. *Greater Kashmir*, Srinagar, J&K, India, 8 January 2009.
41. 'Briefing Pakistan: A general state of disarray,' *The Economist*, 19 May 2007, pp. 28–30.
42. UN involvement in Kashmir issue was the outcome of the 18 resolution that it passed in favour of right of self-determination of the people of Jammu and Kashmir after India herself took and got Kashmir issue registered as a dispute in UN on 1 January 1948. On UN mediation, the Indo-Pak War on Kashmir ended on 1 January 1949: *Press Trust of India*, 'UN Welcomes Indo-Pak Thaw, Secretary General Encourages Resolution of Outstanding Issues Through Dialogue', *Greater Kashmir*, 31 July 2011, Srinagar, J&K, India, p. 12.
43. *Press Trust of India*, 'UN Welcomes Indo-Pak Thaw, Secretary General Encourages Resolution of Outstanding Issues Through Dialogue', *Greater Kashmir*, 31 July 2011, Srinagar, J&K, India, pp. 1 and 12.
44. 'India, Pak to Continue Talks on J&K, Terror', *Kashmir Times*, Srinagar, J&K, India, 28 July 2011, p. 1.
45. 'Pak FM in India, Stakes in Welfare of Each Other', *Kashmir Times*, 27 July 2011, Srinagar, J&K, India, p. 1.

46. 'US pitches for enhanced trade links in South Asia: India has to do more to Integrate Economically with Its Neighbours', *Greater Kashmir*, Srinagar, J&K, India, 21 July 2011, pp. 1 and 12.

47. 'Pak to name India "most favoured trading partnership by year end"?' *Greater Kashmir*, Srinagar, 3 October 2011, p. 13.

48. 'India, Afghanistan Ink Strategic Partnership Pact: Afghan Army to be Trained by Indian Army', *Greater Kashmir*, Srinagar, J&K, India, 6 October 2011, p. 6.

49. See author, 'Reassessing the Role of SCO in the South & Central Asian Context', *Journal of South Asian and Middle Eastern Studies*, XXXIII(2), Winter 2010, Pakistan American Foundation, Villanova University, Villanova, USA, pp. 34–49.

50. 'Profiling the Impact of Globalization on Central Asian Republics: A Perspective', *Contemporary Central Asia*, XII(3), New Delhi, December, 2008, pp. 1–14.

51. Tajamul Hussain (2008), 'Of Self-sufficiency and Cross Border Trade', *Greater Kashmir*, Srinagar, J&K, India, 20 September, p. 7.

52. Data from the Export Import Data Bank, Department of Commerce, Ministry of Commerce and Industry, India: http://commerce.nic.in/eidb/default.asp (7 February 2009).

53. Arjimand Husain Talib (2008), 'Re-thinking Loc-Trade,' *Greater Kashmir*, Srinagar, J&K, India, 14 September, p. 9.

54. In that event, India's export would be US$ 9.2 billion and that of Pakistan US$ 2.2 billion: Data from the Export Import Data Bank, Department of Commerce, Ministry of Commerce and Industry, India: http://commerce.nic.in/eidb/default.asp (7 February 2009).

55. *Export-Import Data Bank, Region-wise* (New Delhi: Ministry of Commerce & Industry, Department. of Commerce, Government of India): *http://commerce.nic.in/ejdb/default.asp* (Last updated 17/8/2010).

56. 'Direction of Trade Statistics,' International Monetary Bank (hereafter IMF) Year Book, Washington, Yearly Issues; 'Key Indicators of Developing Asian and Pacific Countries,' Asian Development Bank, Yearly Reports; United Nations (UN), Statistical Yearbook.

57. *Export Import Data Bank, Country-wise*, New Delhi: Ministry of Commerce, Government of India, 2005.

58. The Central Asian States and Russia have largest global reserves of gas and oil which are transmitted to China and Europe though at a high cost. Russian oil and gas company Gazprom produces around 90 per cent of Russian gas and has a monopoly on its export despite US endeavours to de-monopolize it through a newly built pipeline project across Turkey which bypasses Russia and Iranian pipeline corridors. No doubt, China has its own oil and gas dumps especially in Xinjiang, it nonetheless looks directly to Russia, its major SCO counterpart, for the gas supplies followed by the newly-born Central Asian republics.

59. Devendra Kaushik (1970), *Central Asia in Modern Times*, Moscow.

60. Suryakant Nijanand Bal (2004), *Central Asia: A Strategy for India's Look-North Policy*, New Delhi, p. 361.

61. Indian entrepreneurs have since invested in Tajik hotel industry and are in the process of making investment in Tajik power sector much like on the investment pattern of Russia, Iran, and China on some major hydro-power projects like 'Sangtuda-I', 'Sangtuda-II', 'Rogun', and 'Anzob Tunnel' in Tajikistan. These economic initiatives justify India's chance of becoming a permanent member of the Shanghai Cooperation Organisation(SCO).

62. Jeremy Breacher and Tim Costello (1994), *Global Village or Global Pillage: Economic Reconstruction from the Bottom Up*, Cambridge, MA: South End Press, pp. 1–9.

63. For details, see Mushtaq A. Kaw (2009), 'Restoring India's Silk Route Links with South and Central Asia across Kashmir: Challenges and Opportunities', *The China and Eurasia Forum Quarterly*, 7(2), May/June, pp. 59–74.

64. Kashmir being a highly seismic zone is exposed to high intensity earthquakes.

4

India-Central Asia Energy Cooperation

Nirmala Joshi

By the turn of the century, one of the distinct trends that emerged in international politics was the tremendous attention the post-Soviet space drew, especially the vast Eurasian landmass. Apart from the perceived rise of China and India as pivotal players of the future, the huge natural resources of Eurasia including energy resources—oil, natural gas, and hydrocarbons—attracted immense global attention. By the mid-1990s, the issue of ensuring energy security had come to occupy the centre-stage of international politics. In the past, it was largely the industrialized nations of the West that were the chief consumers of energy. Today, it is both the industrialized and developing countries whose demand for energy resources is rising at a phenomenal rate. The Joint Statement on the New US-Russian Energy Dialogue of May 2002 succinctly put the issue of energy security in a contemporary perspective. It stated, 'Successful development of the global economy depends on timely and reliable energy delivery.'[1] In addition to the rising demand, it is the politicization of the issue that has complicated the demand. Securing this vital resource shapes a nation's policy and conduct.

Located in the centre of Eurasia, the five Central Asian Republics (CARs) are richly endowed with natural resources including energy resources. There has been a virtual scramble to secure and control this vital resource. In Eurasia, the search for new energy resources has got entangled with geopolitics that gives the Central Asian region a geostrategic character. All of them being landlocked, and Uzbekistan doubly so, the issue of constructing pipeline infrastructure to access the energy resources soon acquired a competitive aspect among the major and regional powers. This competition is often referred to by analysts and observers as the new version of the nineteenth century 'Great Game' between the British and Tsarist empires. In the context of the twenty-first century, the issue of ensuring energy security became one of the factors that brought a shift in international politics from Europe to Asia.

Viewed against this background of rising demand for energy by the global community, Indian search to ensure energy security is no exception. Indian demand for energy has grown phenomenally. India's rising international profile, rapid growth of the economy and industrialization, and the rising expectation of its population have all combined to make ensuring energy surety a top priority in Indian foreign and security policies. Though domestic production of energy is increasing, it is unable to keep pace with the growing demand. Consequently, India is dependent on imports and this dependence has assumed enormous proportions. The bulk of Indian imports of energy are from the Middle East and Persian Gulf. It is imperative for India to diversify its sources of energy. In this context, though Central Asian energy reserves are not comparable to that of the Middle East and Persian Gulf, they nevertheless do constitute a significant alternative. A significant factor in accessing Central Asian energy is their landlocked status and India has no common border with any of the CARs. Hence transporting energy will depend on an efficient and excellent export pipeline infrastructure that will have to pass through third countries. In view of this geographical limitation, what are the prospects for India to access Central Asian energy? A brief survey of Central Asian energy resources would be in order.

Central Asian Energy Scenario

The CARs as mentioned have abundant natural resources. Kazakhstan and Turkmenistan are well endowed with oil and natural gas respectively. Uzbekistan has modest quantity of natural gas, but the possibility of new finds is high. Kyrgyzstan and Tajikistan have plenty of water resources which they are trying to convert to hydel power. Various studies offer different estimates of the total energy reserves in the region. According to Ariel Cohen, a well-known scholar at the Heritage Foundation, the region has possible deposits of 170.5 billion barrels of oil, while natural gas is estimated at 15.3 trillion cubic metres.[2] The Scottish firm Wood Mackenzie estimates the proven reserves at 26.01 billion barrels and 56.64 billion barrels of possible reserves.[3] In Kazakhstan, proven oil reserves are 10 billion barrels and potential reserves are estimated as high as 85 billion barrels. The discovery of the Kashagan offshore oil field in 2002 often referred to as the 'elephant' as it is considered to be one of the largest in Asia and the expansion of the giant Tengiz oil should push Kazakh production toward 2.35 million barrels per day (b/d) by 2013. Similarly, the Karachaganak gas field is estimated to contain vast quantities of gas. The Kurmangazy, a joint venture of Kazakhstan, Russia, and France in the sphere of gas and expected to go on stream by 2016, would radically change Kazakhstan's energy picture. The Kurmangazy is estimated to contain vast quantities of gas. Incidentally, initially, India was a preferred partner to this joint venture. Finally, however, France replaced India. From the long term perspective, Kazakhstan would have surplus energy, despite the expansion of the existing pipeline systems. While the climate for foreign investors in the energy sector is friendly as compared to other Central Asian countries, the passage of an amendment to the law on subsoil resources could be a dampener in future. The amendment, approved by the Parliament in September 2007, empowers the authorities to amend terms of contracts with investors where Kazakhstan's economic interests or national security are deemed to be in jeopardy.[4]

Turkmenistan is the fifth largest depository of natural gas in the world. Its proven oil resources at 1.5 billion barrels and possible resources are estimated at 32 billion barrels. Gas resources including proven and possible deposits are at 8.9 trillion cubic metres (tcm).[5] After assuming office in February 2007, President Gurbanguly Berdymukhammedov announced ambitious production targets of extracting 80 billion cubic metres (bcm) of natural gas and 10.4 million tons of crude oil. But these targets can be fulfilled only if Turkmenistan is able to attract foreign investments. So far Turkmenistan has succeeded in attracting Chinese investment. In December 2009, a natural gas pipeline from Turkmenistan to Western China via Uzbekistan and Kazakhstan has become operational. Plans are afoot to construct a second major pipeline infrastructure to China and to Western Europe. The Turkmen sector of the Caspian Sea is equally rich in energy resources. The legal status of the Caspian Sea has still to be fixed. In the absence of any such agreement among the littoral states, exploration and extraction of energy resources has become difficult.

Uzbekistan's energy wealth is modest. It has confirmed oil deposits of 0.2 billion barrels and possible deposits estimated at 1 billion barrels. Natural gas deposits, both proven and possible, are estimated at 3.1 tcm.[6] The possibility of new finds, both oil and natural gas, in Uzbekistan are as high as very little prospecting has been done. The business climate in Uzbekistan is difficult and repatriation of profit from that country is still more difficult.

Kyrgyzstan and Tajikistan are well endowed with perennial rivers—Syr Darya and Amu Darya. Attempts to harness the hydel potential of these countries have already been launched. In Kambrata of Kyrgyzstan, one and two Hydel Power Projects (HPP) have the capacity to generate 2.2 billion kWh of electricity, which is sufficient to meet Kyrgyzstan's domestic demand as well as to export to neighbouring countries via high transmission lines. In Tajikistan, the Rogun Hydro Power Project on the river Vakhsh is one of the biggest such projects. Rogun is expected to generate 3600 kilowatts per hour (kWh) of electricity, but it has run into controversy with neighbouring Uzbekistan opposing Rogun on Vakhsh. Meanwhile, the issue at hand for these countries is how to attract foreign investment.

While estimates of various studies about the Central Asian energy resources may vary, they all, however, agree that reserves are substantial to make a difference, 'if Central Asian energy could play a significant role as a marginal supplier in arresting a jump in the price of oil in a high price environment and diversifying supplies.'[7] Similarly, if Kyrgyzstan and Tajikistan are able to overcome their investment difficulties, Afghanistan, Pakistan, and India could benefit immensely from the electricity trade.

India-Central Asia Energy Cooperation

By the mid-1990s, the issue of ensuring energy security had acquired serious dimensions among the nations of the world. It had become a key element in the foreign policies of States. In Eurasia, a competition among major and regional powers to secure and control the energy resources of Central Asia had already commenced. An element of geopolitics had become evident which gave a sharper edge to the competition. India was a latecomer on the energy scene of Central Asia. Although the Oil and Natural Gas Corporation (ONGC) had set up an office in Almaty in the 1990s, it did precious little to advance India's interests. It was only by the turn of the century that the issue of energy security began to receive serious attention from Indian policy makers. Several factors were responsible for this turn in Indian thinking. By the turn of the century, India's international profile had risen considerably. Its rapid economic growth, knowledge-based industries and overall industrialization, and the rising expectations of its population combined to push India to the position of being sixth largest consumer of energy in the world. If India has to maintain its high level of growth, then it could become the fourth largest consumer of energy. 'The Hydrocarbon Vision 2025' published by the Government of India in February 2000 clearly highlighted the predicament faced by the country in ensuring energy security. India's oil self-sufficiency declined from 63 per cent in 1989–90 to 30 per cent in 2000–1. India's demand for oil is expected to increase from 122 million tons in 2001–2 to 364 million tons in 2024–5. Domestic production during this period would increase but would not be able to keep pace with the demand. It is predicted that oil sufficiency would be a mere 15 per cent. Similarly, India's requirement for natural gas would increase and is expected to rise from 49 bcm in 2006–7 to 125 bcm in 2024–5.[8] The Integrated Energy Policy Report of the Indian Planning Commission called for an energy regime that ensures supply, manages demand, and balances pricing to enable growth.[9] The volatility and uncertainty in the Middle East and the Persian Gulf, the need to search for new sources of energy, acquired a new urgency.

Another dimension was the rise of non-traditional threats and challenges to a nation's security. This phenomenon raised the apprehension that forces of extremism and terrorism could interdict with energy supplies. Hence, the search for secure and predictable sources of energy was an urgent need. The need to diversify sources of energy supplies was apparent. In the words of Prime Minister Manmohan Singh, 'The quest for energy security is second only in our (India's) scheme of things to food security ... the quest for energy security had become an important element of Indian diplomacy and shaping India's relations with a range of countries across the globe.'[10] The India Oil Corporation (IOL) and Gas Authority of India Limited (GAIL) have been permitted to acquire stakes. After Prime Minister Manmohan

Singh's visit to Kazakhstan in April 2011, India has acquired a 25 per cent stake in Satpayev—an offshore oil block in the northern part of the Kazakh sector of the Caspian Sea.

In view of India's high dependence on oil imports, the urgent need for diversification of sources is obvious. How does India access Central Asian energy? An impediment for India is the landlocked status of the CARs. Earlier, as part of the Soviet Union, there were two pipelines—one for oil and second for natural gas. These two pipelines were connected with Moscow carrying Kazakh oil and Turkmen gas. After the radical geopolitical change of 1991, the CARs have been in search of pipeline infrastructure that would help them diversify their markets and overcome their landlocked status. However, the search for new routes has got entangled in geopolitical considerations.

For India in the prevailing situation, the following are the options. First, the biggest and much talked about pipeline project is a natural gas project called TAPI, spanning four countries—Turkmenistan, Afghanistan, Pakistan, and India. TAPI has been under discussion for many years. In the early years of the TAPI project, India was not at all enthusiastic about it. In the Annual Report of the Ministry of Defence for the year 2000–1, it was clearly stated that 'energy co-operation and sharing arrangements are only with countries whose actions do not undermine India's security and which have demonstrated a willingness to co-operate meaningfully with India.'[11] The geopolitical change in India's neighbourhood and partly the increasing urgency to ensure energy security made India see the situation differently. Since TAPI is strongly backed by Asian Development Bank (ADB), India formally joined the project in November 2007. Negotiations for the project are slow. Perhaps the unstable security situation in Afghanistan and Pakistan is a daunting challenge, especially to those who would be part of the TAPI consortium. Presently, the TAPI consortium is being negotiated. In spite of the delays, there are hopeful signs and it is expected that TAPI would go on-stream in 2016. The proposed pipeline will have a capacity of 33 bcm of natural gas. Once TAPI gets operational, there is a possibility that Kazakhstan may also join it. The TAPI project is a win-win one for all concerned. It would enhance the region's economic prosperity by way of transit revenues that would accrue to the countries and at the same time help Turkmenistan and Kazakhstan to overcome their landlocked status.

The second option for India is the Iran-Pakistan-India (IPI) pipeline project. The IPI project was launched in 1994. The 2600-km long pipeline is expected to transport Iranian gas to Pakistan and India. Contrary to prevailing views, India has been interested in the project. Prime Minister Manmohan Singh said in reply to a question whether the pipeline was a good idea, 'We are in dire need of energy and we are keen on carrying out this project. The negotiations are proceeding.'[12] If the project comes on board then probably Turkmenistan and Kazakhstan could also be associated with it. The third option is to build pipeline infrastructure through China. The pipeline route would be via Xinjiang and then across the Karakorum and Himalayan mountain ranges, and thereafter across Aksai-Chin into India. This does not appear as a feasible proposition because of the technological and geographical challenges it poses, and Aksai-Chin is a disputed area between India and China.

Apart from the above mentioned pipeline projects, other attempts were launched by Mani Shankar Aiyar as India's Minister for Petroleum. During his tenure, India made a proposal for Asian gas grid—the objective being to link energy producing and consuming countries and regions to one another. Accordingly, a meeting was held in New Delhi in November 2005. India unveiled an ambitious US$ 22.4 billion Pan Asian grid and security pipeline system. It seems that the objective was to forge some kind of an understanding with China on the energy issue. Such an approach came in the wake of the Indian fiasco in the Petro Kazakhstan deal which was lost to China. Nothing further was heard about the Asian grid idea, after Mani Shankar Aiyar moved out of the Petroleum Ministry. India has shown interest in the Ashkelon-Eilat pipeline, an extension of the Baku-Tbilisi-Ceyhan pipeline. The pipeline is from Turkey to Israel and from the Israeli port of Eilat, oil would be transported by super tankers to Mumbai. Indian interest seems primarily because the Ashkelon-Eilat pipeline would cut down transportation time from 40 to 19 days.

Earlier, India had entered into swap deals with Kazakhstan. Kazakh oil would be delivered to Iran, and in return, Iran would send the equivalent oil to India by tankers. Subsequently, Iran was not satisfied with this arrangement as Iran thought Kazakh oil had a high quantity of sulphur, whereas Iranian oil was clean and of good quality. This arrangement came to an end by 1997. Perhaps, the Reliance Industries who have the capability and reputation to refine oil ranging from the heaviest to the lightest could solve this difficulty, if given an opportunity.

Another area of interest is the electricity trade. In this regard, India has already transmitted Uzbek electricity to Kabul by building transmission lines across the northern Afghanistan from Uzbekistan territories. It is not clear why the Russian initiative of a quadrilateral agreement between Russia, Tajikistan, Afghanistan, and Pakistan did not include India. One of the objectives of the agreement is electricity trade. India could be a market for such electricity generated especially when the mega Hydro Power Projects come on stream.

Challenges for India

Hence, Indian attempts to access Central Asian energy have met with limited success. Probably, Indian attempts were earlier not as vigorous as they should have been though the trend has now been considerably reversed in favour of an active engagement. Nevertheless, India faces numerous challenges in Central Asia and these have to be overcome. First, apart from the landlocked status of the CARs, India's lack of geographical contiguity with the Central Asian region is an impediment. The construction of a new pipeline infrastructure highly depends on third countries, and the prevailing political and geo-political considerations. From the Indian perspective, it limits India from establishing a credible presence in Central Asia, including on the energy scene. A complimentary factor could be to establish transport connectivity with the region. A related factor is that Kazakhstan and Turkmenistan are located in a region that is also rich in energy resources. Russia and Iran are leading producers of oil and natural gas. Therefore, 'Turkmenistan's two easiest routes to markets are through large gas producing states—Russia and Iran—and both these countries have a strong interest in harnessing Turkmenistan reserves only insofar as they amplify the value of their own gas assets.'[13]

Second, Central Asia has been caught in the vortex of international politics. The competition to control this vital resource has already intensified between the United States and the European Union (EU) on the one hand, and Russia on the other. Construction of new pipeline infrastructure has become a tool in the hands of both sides. The energy issue has provided the Western countries with an opportunity to advance not only their economic interests, but geopolitical as well. The Western strategy is to ensure that these countries are independent, prosperous, and secure. Such an approach would widen the area of stability. Consequently, in Western energy strategy, plans to construct new pipelines should skirt Russia. This would reduce the dependence of CARs on Russia. The Baku-Tbilisi-Ceyhan pipeline which bypasses Russia is a step in the direction of independence. While planning transport routes of energy, efforts are to reduce Russian influence and challenge its monopoly. Another factor that has given edge to Western strategy is the war on terror that began in 2001. Western military presence has undoubtedly altered the geopolitical situation in the region, but it has substantially increased the strategic significance of CARs. It remains to be seen how the situation in the region evolves after the withdrawal of Western military presence in 2014.

On the other hand, Russia has abundant energy wealth. It ranks second after Saudi Arabia in terms of oil production and reserves. Apart from using its energy sources to bolster its economy, Russia has also been using this factor to advance its objectives in Central Asia and the region. Russia's emergence as 'Energy Super Power' has helped it to deal with major Western powers from a position of strength. As President Putin stated 'it's a seller's market'. A seller's market implies that the countries must guarantee stable income to the supplier. Hence, in order to retain its 'energy super power' status, Russia has to ensure that the energy strategy of the CARs is in tandem with its own. It does not like them to chart independent course. The Russian Administration under Putin made it quite clear that it hopes to gain complete control of Central Asia's gas supplies. Turkmen gas is critical to Russia's plans for the development of a unified gas system—the 'Eurasian Gas Alliance'.

Third, although not a party to the on-going competition, Indian presence was marginal in the beginning. It was only by the turn of the century that the issue of ensuring energy security became a priority in Indian policy. By then, the major and regional powers had already established their presence on the energy scene. What is important now is to establish a credible presence. Areas of cooperation are in the construction of pipelines and the expansion of the existing ones. In this regard, Punj Lloyd is involved in building pipelines in Kazakhstan, besides pipeline maintenance and repair where Indian expertise can be utilized. From various reports, it appears that the Caspian Sea has unexplored findings. Besides downstream activities, such as petrochemical plants, upgradation of existing refineries is an area of promise. Importantly, the ONGC Videsh Limited (OVL) and GAIL should open their offices represented by high level officials. Similarly, Indian banks should open their branches so as to facilitate faster implementation. It would be beneficial for India to set up a Joint Working Group (JWG) on energy with the energy producing countries. It would lead to comprehensive dialogue on energy. Given India's vast skills and expertise in the energy sector, India could be involved in capacity building and cooperate in research and developmental activities. Since Indian energy security also involves acquiring stakes, it would be worthwhile to explore this in Central Asia. During Prime Minister Manmohan Singh's visit to Kazakhstan in April 2011, India acquired a 25 per cent equity stakes in Satpayev. Finally, a proactive diplomacy is absolutely essential. An active presence of India in Central Asia would generate tremendous goodwill. Enhanced good will could lead to the growth of Indian influence in the region. This is important in view of India's heavy stakes in Afghanistan. India is perceived as a friendly country and the rich legacy of past contacts and interaction would certainly enhance India's engagement with the CARs. India should rid itself of the common refrain often heard in Central Asian countries that it is slow in implementation. India needs to explore the possibility of cooperation with the United States, the EU, and Russia in order to launch cooperative ventures.

Fourth, the CARs also need to create an investor-friendly environment. Attempts to minimize delays should be undertaken. As an example, when a pipeline passes through more than two or three countries, securing each country's concurrence is by no means an easy task. According to a pre-feasibility study conducted on 'North South Energy Corridor Kazakhstan-Iran-India' by the ORF Centre for Resources Management in April 2006, the Baku-Tbilisi-Ceyhan (BTC) pipeline which involved inter-governmental agreements between four countries took all of four years to get 17,000 signatures (one signature for every ten metres of the pipeline) required for financial closure of the project.[14] All the CARs being landlocked it is necessary that differences among themselves, especially ethnic discord and border disputes, are resolved. Regional cooperation among themselves would contribute to their goals of being truly independent. It would give their multi-vector policies substance and content.

Fifth, lack of consensus among the five littoral states of the Caspian Sea to determine their respective sectors has stalled activity in the Caspian Sea basin. Kazakhstan is very keen for the Trans Caspian Pipeline which envisages laying pipelines on the floor of the sea. The Trans Caspian Pipeline would facilitate the transport of Kazakh oil to the BTC. However, Russian objection has stalled the construction of this pipeline because the legal status of the Caspian Sea has not been resolved and environmental reasons have overwhelmed the issue. Till the status of the Caspian Sea is determined, Kazakhstan would have to depend on tankers to transport its oil to Baku. A legal settlement of the Caspian Sea among the five littoral states would have a salutary effect on all the countries. The hydrocarbon wealth of the Caspian Sea is enormous and the potential for reserves is also high. Many believe that it is the hydrocarbon wealth that is at the heart of major and regional powers' rivalry.

Conclusion

The energy reserves of Central Asia are undoubtedly significant and could to a certain extent address India's growing demand for energy. However, geography, geopolitics, and security in India's neighbourhood are challenges that India has to overcome. A meaningful and a cooperative relationship with the Central Asian countries can be established by adopting an innovative approach coupled with regular high level diplomatic exchanges.

Notes and References

1. 'Bush-Putin Joint Statement on New US-Russian Energy Dialogue', 24 May 2002, Issued by the International Information Programme of the US Department of State.
2. Ariel Cohen (1999), 'Testimony before the Sub Committee on Asia and Pacific, United States House of Representatives', 17 March.
3. R.H. Dekmejian and Hovann H. Simonian (2001), *Troubled Waters: The Geopolitics of the Caspian Region*, London. IB Tauris, p. 32.
4. The Economic Intelligence Unit (EIU) London, 'Country Reports—Kazakhstan', October 2007, p. 27.
5. Ariel Cohen, No. 2.
6. EIU, 'Country Reports—Uzbekistan', September 2002, p. 28.

7. Kapil Kak (2007), 'India's Strategic and Security Interests in Central Asia', in N. Rao and Mohammad Monir Alam (eds), *Central Asia: Present Challenges and Future Prospects*, New Delhi, Academic Foundation, p. 218.

8. Talmiz Ahmed (2007), 'Oil Diplomacy for India's Energy Security', in Atish Sinha and Madhup Mohta (eds), *Indian Foreign Policy: Challenges and Opportunities*, New Delhi, Academic Foundation, p. 1093.

9. Harsh Pant (2008), *Contemporary Debates in Indian Foreign and Security Policy*, London: Palgrave, p. 154.

10. Quoted by Manjeet Pardesi and Sumit Ganguly (2009), 'India's Energy Security: A Foreign Policy Priority', in Harsh Pant (ed.), *Indian Foreign Policy in a Unipolar World*, London.

11. 'Annual Report of the Ministry of Defence', Government of India, 2000–01, p. 11.

12. *The Hindu* (Chennai), 17 February 2007.

13. Martha Brill Olcott (2006), 'International Gas Trade in Central Asia: Turkmenistan, Iran, Russia and Afghanistan', in David G. Victor and others (eds), *Natural Gas and Geopolitics from 1970 to 2040*, Cambridge University Press, p. 227.

14. Quoted in a meeting with Kaz Munay Gas, October 2005 '*North South Energy Corridor: Kazakhstan-Iran-India*', A Pre-Feasibility Study, April 2006, ORF Centre for Resources Management, Delhi, p. 12.

5

China-Led Multilateralism in Central Asia
Strategic Implications for India

Swaran Singh

With the collapse of former Soviet Union, and especially since 9/11, international relations have witnessed various innovations in existing concepts and paradigms. Amongst these, the first decade of the twenty-first century has witnessed multiple genres of multilateralism being debated across the world. Especially, the emerging Asian powers have found multilateralism useful for organizing their rapidly evolving new equations. The last epoch of contemporary genre of multilateralism is normally traced to the early 1960s and it was triggered by the tumultuous process of decolonization amongst Afro-Asian nations. It was then understood primarily in terms of expanding 'numbers' and 'forums' involving newly independent nations; not necessarily newer themes and formulations. But thanks to the rise of two superpowers and their coming together from early 1970s, these efforts were soon overshadowed by power-driven multi-polarism and finally ended as rigid bi-polar system dominated by the United States and former Soviet Union.

No doubt, the twenty-first century conceptions of multilateralism continue with several of the traits of multilateralism of 1960s. For instance, it is still seen primarily in its negative connotations with regard to its traits of anti-imperialism or anti-isolationalism in international relations.[1] But more recent debates have begun to provide it a positive spin; contrasting it not only with the cold war multi-polarism but also with polycentrism and minilateralism of 1990s.[2] Although these paradigms had respectively evolved out of strategic studies and international political economy, yet these have been adopted into mainstream international relations and Six Party Talks have lately been one apt example of this hybridization of multilateralism. Scholars now describe contemporary multilateralism as a far deeper and complex mix that not shuns but blends with extremes like isolationism and hegemony to produce 'a dynamic relationship that changes overtime'.[3]

It is in this emerging complex of evolving new frameworks in international relations that this essay seeks to underline the contribution of China-led multilateralism in Central Asia that marks one important alternative paradigm. It will also then explore its strategic implications for India's foreign policy.

Shanghai Five to SCO

Shanghai Cooperation Organisation (SCO) remains writ-large on most recent debates around Asian multilateralism. It is not only projected as one of the most effective, efficient, and credible alternative paradigms on regional security but one that comprises of the world's four nuclear weapons powers (Russia, China, India, and Pakistan) and nearly half the world's population.[4] It is since expanded both in its themes as well as participants. Originally created as the Shanghai-Five in 1996, this Chinese initiative was able to make impressive progress in its original agenda—of ensuring peace with Russia and other newly liberated Central Asian Republics (CARs) through evolving confidence-building measures (CBMs) and accelerating the process of border demarcation—within a short span of time of initial two-three years. Since then, it has expanded its strategic focus to larger Eurasian issues like energy security and countering terrorism which have since become their top priority.

In the spirit of widening its footprint, the most visible has been SCO's expansion of participants' list. It had first invited Uzbekistan to join as its sixth member as the Shanghai-Five reorganized themselves into SCO in 2001. Since then, though the working language of the SCO remains Chinese and Russian, yet it is as part of projecting 'greater confidence that the SCO could expand its strategic and economic interests beyond

Central Asia'.[5] The SCO conferred Observer status to Mongolia at its 2004 Tashkent Summit and to India, Iran, and Pakistan during July 2005 Astana Summit. Sri Lanka and Belarus were conferred status of Dialogue Partner at the Yekaterinburg Summit of 15–16 May 2009. Beginning the 2006 Shanghai Summit that completed ten years of this initiative, President Karzai has often been invited as special guest to their meetings. From SCO's March 2009 special conference on Afghanistan in Moscow, Afghanistan has emerged as an important concern of these countries. At their 2011 Astana Summit, coming in the wake of sharpening hype about the 2014 exit-date for international security forces from Afghanistan and on the heels of the killing of Osama bin Laden in Pakistan, the deliberations had witnessed both India (Observer) and Afghanistan (Special Guest) emerging as strong contenders for full membership of SCO.[6] This has clearly heightened both stakes and interest of New Delhi in keeping tab on SCO initiatives.

Moreover, given the impressive track-record of SCO, all Observer and Dialogue Partners, (even the United States), have shown keen interest in acquiring full membership of this organization. Experts assume that SCO accepting more members is not any longer a matter of 'if' but 'when'.[7] Meanwhile, SCO has agreed, in principle, to open itself for new members. And it in this context that membership of emerging India has elicited considerable speculations both inside India and outside. However, official India has shown only occasional and subdued enthusiasm in making its case; its official position being that New Delhi expects to be formally invited instead of lining up with its application, or even campaigning for its membership. At the same time, India is often seen working hard to dispel the impressions that New Delhi's close relations with the United States perhaps explain its lack of enthusiasm about SCO membership.[8] It is in this evolving complex of multiple pull and pressures that flow from SCO's expanding footprint across Eurasia that India's academics and policy makers have become increasingly conscious of India's own policies as also of India's future role in SCO.

India's Interests and Limitations

The current chapter of Central Asian story begins only after the collapse of former Soviet Union. There are experts who believe today that India would have had far more easier relations with Central Asia via Moscow, that is, if

Soviet Union had not collapsed. In the collapse of Soviet Union, India had lost its time-tested and long-standing friend. New Delhi was to gradually redefine its foreign policy and evolve its Central Asian policies. In this, India was soon to evince strong interest in its Buddhist links with Central Asian countries, as it 'did not want this region to become a hotbed of radical Islam by becoming an extension of Pakistan-sponsored Taliban and Al-Qaeda, which could further undermine the security situation in Kashmir.'[9] This needs to be viewed in the context of India's complicated relations with Pakistan and the latter's participation in the raising of Mujahideen forces in Afghanistan during the 1980s with an aim to ensure the exit of the Soviet forces from there that finally happened in 1989.

Meanwhile, during the 1990s, radical Islamic forces were to remain suspect of consolidating themselves in these countries which had raised a spectre in view of 9/11 events and initiatives. With this backdrop, though its participation in SCO remains driven mainly by India's interest in Central Asia, the main focus in India's interest in SCO has other drivers as well that include (a) India's general commitment to Asian multilateralism, especially of the community-building typologies and (b) its considerable interest in being part of any pan-Asian arrangements for energy security and countering terrorism. Starting from India's Asian Relations Conference of April 1947 that started Afro-Asian and non-aligned moments, these have been India's time-tested ideals for ensuring regional peace and security.

Second, the last ten years of SCO have coincided with the unprecedented rise of China followed by the gradual rise of India. In particular, China's success in engaging, accessing, and exploiting the vital energy sources of Central Asia and Beijing's sustained influence on Central Asian regimes have further ignited India's curiosity about using SCO for staging an engagement with CARs. Besides, it is also true that India's 'interest in SCO is a recent phenomenon and it has resulted in India becoming an "Observer" in the SCO in 2005'.[10] However, even after becoming Observer at SCO, India's engagement with this SCO remains all but lukewarm. Central Asia has also not been very high on India's foreign policy agenda, whereas United States and Southeast Asia (positively) and China and Pakistan (negatively) have been the main focus. To some extent, this again is sought to be explained in terms of India's relations with Beijing which has been recently sceptical of its friendship with India and which remains a major influence in SCO decision-making process. Clearly, the fact that the last few years have witnessed downtrends in India-China relations make China further reluctant in endorsing India in multilateral forums, especially SCO.[11]

As regards SCO perspective on India, other than China, most of the other member-states have not only welcomed but pursued India's participation considering New Delhi as a crucial strategic partner, especially in countering terrorism. Some even speculate that this is driven by their desire to ensuring restraint on an extremely well-endowed rising China.[12] Starting from the year 2005, Russia was the first to express a desire to hold even multi-country military exercises (involving Russia-China-India) within the SCO framework where India is now routinely invited as Observer. What makes it particularly interesting is that Russia, China, and India have also been holding trilateral strategic dialogues which had moved to their stand-along trilateral foreign ministers' meetings since 2001 which have even facilitated India's participation in SCO military exercises. To quote Thrassy Marketos:

> ... any long-term quest for full membership [by India] is negatively viewed by Beijing, partly because of historical animosity between the two Asian giants and because Washington, which views the SCO as an attempt to forge a rival power centre, wouldn't welcome any such move from New Delhi, at a time when the US-India nuclear deal is under consideration of the US Congress.[13]

Why is India So Reluctant?

Prima facie, in spite of a fair amount of sustained engagement, India is not seen as most enthusiastic about SCO proceedings. At the bilateral level, of course, other than India's traditionally close friend former Soviet Union and now Russian Federation, New Delhi has also evolved closer cooperation with the CARs, especially Kazakhstan, Uzbekistan, and Tajikistan. Even with China, India has sustained an intense economic and diplomatic engagement though there have been fluctuations from time to time. As regards SCO, however, there remains certain perceptible reluctance in New Delhi being seen as too enthusiastic about their activities. Therefore, India's pursuit of SCO membership has not been as aggressive or as sustained as by some of the other aspirant contenders like Belarus, Iran, or Pakistan. This lukewarm approach of India is often explained by citing some of the following factors:

- First, India remains reluctant given its traditional preoccupation with autonomy; ensuring that it does not get into any such binding relationships that may circumscribe its future policy options. And the fact that SCO is often viewed as parallel to NATO makes India cautious.

- Second, India's continuous rivalry with Pakistan, and China's close ties with Pakistan, act against India's desire to show intense interest in joining the SCO as India does not wish to be seen competing with Pakistan. This is also likely to increase SCO's influence in India-Pakistan mutual policies.

- Third, SCO has been especially sceptical of US overtures to be part of SCO initiatives and western experts criticize SCO for being exclusivist economic, if not military, forum. They even call it a camouflage to cover for totalitarian regimes. The bottom-line is that, given India's growing closeness to the United States, India would not like being seen siding with forums trying to exclude United States.

- Fourth, China—which has been the main force behind the evolution of the SCO—remains wary of allowing India any influence in the region whatsoever, and especially so when it comes to SCO. This is partly driven by India's rising profile and its long-standing close ties with Moscow and its growing acceptance amongst major powers.

- And last but not the least, in more practical terms, lack of easy and direct access for India to Eurasian landmass is often cited as something that discourages Indian initiatives. India has to access CARs through troubled states of Afghanistan, Pakistan, or Iran that very often becomes a non-starter in considering and implementing specific projects.

At the same time, however, there is no doubt that SCO promises to provide India with an effective model and platform of Asian multilateralism which has been making rather visible contributions towards ensuring peace and stability in its region as also facilitating rapid development across various sectors. Given India's growing interest in gas and oil of CARs, India was represented by the Petroleum Minister in SCO summits during 2006–8 which resulted in an improvement in relations with several CARs. This was followed by the Indian Prime Minister's participation at the Yekaterinburg SCO Summit in May 2009 and, in his speeches, Manmohan

Singh underlined the need for evolving an innovative means to strengthen people-to-people contacts and exchanges of business delegations to expand bilateral trade, investments, and technology transfers. However, the June 2010 and June 2011 summits at Astana were attended by India's foreign minister that is seen as lowering of the SCO in India's list of priorities.

Given SCO's unique selling point being its attempt to evolve innovative strategies, India also sees a special role for itself in making important 'value addition' to SCO functioning as also to its evolving aims and initiatives. New Delhi especially sees opportunities for itself in helping CARs in specific sectors like agriculture, pharmaceuticals, food distribution, and security as also in building material and social capital and infrastructure development across Central Asia. Similarly, CARs can also offer India energy sources like oil, gas, uranium, and the two can cooperate in such resource explorations to develop a mutual beneficial relationship. At the multilateral level as well, given that most of SCO Observers are 'regional powers with claims to global status ... will undoubtedly turn the SCO into a major regional organization to be reckoned with'.[14] But there remain serious challenges in operationalizing some of these visions and in overcoming the historical baggage of China and India equations that remain the most difficult hurdle that continues to persist and circumscribe India's opportunities.

China-India Equations in SCO

For understandable reasons, of all the SCO member-states, China had been the last to endorse India any positive role in the SCO framework. Beijing remains unconvinced as yet if India deserves to be given full membership of the SCO.[15] Other SCO leaders, by comparison, have been making such endorsements from the early 2000s. Other than India's old friend Soviet Union/Russia, President Nazarbayev of Kazakhstan had put on record his desire to persuade India to join SCO during his February 2002 visit to New Delhi. The Joint Declaration at the end of his visit said that India's membership in the SCO 'would add to the strength of that organization'.[16] Similarly, India has also had its constituencies that have been sporadically campaigning for taking initiatives to joining SCO and using it as India's springboard to launch itself across Eurasia.

It was only after some coaxing and cajoling that China had finally agreed in 2005 to grant India the status of Observer in SCO. This, of course, was also linked to India agreeing to invite China as Observer in South Asian Association for Regional Cooperation (SAARC). Normally, China waits till its reluctance to India becomes too glaring a reality and Beijing is the only one not supporting India's candidature or proposals. So just as in case of other such proposals—like granting India a permanent seat at the UN Security Council or waiver for India for nuclear commerce at Nuclear Suppliers Group—it will take lots of efforts to get China to support India's full membership of SCO. Given the nature of India-Pakistan rivalry, Pakistan's close relations with China and India's close relations with Russia, the membership issue of India remains tied to the membership for Pakistan. Even in ideal circumstances of both India and Pakistan becoming acceptable to join SCO as full members, experts opine that 'their membership will likely be simultaneous to avoid alienating one or the other'.[17]

However, India's rapidly growing participation in international relations in general and across Asia in particular is impacting on both sides. The hallmark of this new approach has been India's participation in two simultaneous conferences on Afghanistan: one called by SCO in Moscow on 27 March 2011 and the other sponsored by the United States in Geneva three days later. Time and again, the Moscow conference has been underlining the fact that SCO was not merely a clearing house for the Caspian hydrocarbon reserves but a regional security organization squarely placing SCO in a key role especially in post-INSAF-exit Afghanistan. The case of Afghanistan and experience of rather limited success by the United States and North Atlantic Treaty Organization (NATO) forces here plus the fragility of Karzai government have brought Russia, China, and India closer on regional security issues though there remain serious differences yet on good and bad Taliban. But the larger context of India becoming acceptable to SCO has witnessed a visible improvement and reorientation.

India's Half-hearted Engagement

Amongst SCO's impressive structures that make India particularly interested in this forum, a Regional Anti-Terrorist Structure (RATS) was created as a permanent organ of SCO at their Tashkent Summit of June 2004. Located at Tashkent, it serves as a secretariat to promote cooperation amongst member states to fight against the three evils of terrorism, separatism, and extremism. By April 2006, RATS had begun expanding its domain to include its plans to fight cross-border drug crimes under the framework of counter-terrorism. By October 2007, SCO had signed agreements with the Collective Security Treaty Organization (CSTO) of ex-Soviet republics to further broaden its regional cooperation paradigm to include issues like security, crime, and drug trafficking and both organizations have since chalked out detailed plans in these fields.[18] As a result, though SCO has repeatedly clarified that it does not expect itself to emerge as a military block, it now holds regular joint military exercises amongst its members and is often viewed as counter to the eastward expansion of NATO.[19] Such interpretations make India cautious though it feels that it can contribute to counter-terrorism measures and mechanisms.

It is important to underline that India's own approach to SCO has, therefore, been cautious and lukewarm though it continues to engage SCO and this is equally true for the period since 2005 when India was conferred Observer status in SCO. This reluctance is also explained to be there partly for reasons of Indian political and diplomatic elite being busy engaging the United States during this period but they have also been conscious of its implications for their equations with both Beijing and Moscow. Even after becoming Observer, India's lukewarm posture was clearly visible from New Delhi sending only junior ministers to SCO summits against other Observer states represented by heads of state/or government at these meetings. This has allowed experts to make insinuations that by doing so India was projecting itself as part of the United States 'Great Central Asia' that had led to South and Central Asian bureaus at US State Department being merged into one in January 2006.

The United States has also been seen as seeking India's assistance to sustain its access to Eurasian strategic landscape and strategic resources. This strategy is also seen as driven by the United States' desire to sustain its military presence in the immediate periphery of both Russia and China. As a result, SCO in its 2007 summit had asked the United States to vacate its forces from CARs. All this was to only further re-enforce earlier insinuations about India playing the United States game of counterbalancing traditional Russian (and increasingly Chinese) influence in this region.[20] Some of the Indian experts were to go as far as to allude how the 'growing strategic partnership between India and the United States would dilute the importance of the SCO'.[21] It is only more recently that New Delhi has begun making efforts to seriously contest some of these perceptions and India's participation in SCO as also in several other multilateral forums have become far more proactive. Especially, initiatives like Steel Authority of India's proposal to set up a steel plant at Hajigak in Central Bamyan Province of Afghanistan—which is also known as one of the largest iron ore reserves—presents a shift towards hands-on strategy that can sustain India's engagement with Afghanistan, and from there with larger Eurasia.[22]

Again, even such a proactive approach of India is sometimes seen and interpreted as driven by evolving India-US equations. Since the change of guard in White House since January 2009, initial months had witnessed serious apprehensions amongst India's policy makers about President Obama's India policy and his insistence on arms control and nuclear weapon-free world using old tools like nuclear non-proliferation treaty, comprehensive test ban treaty, and fissile cut-off ban treaty which had been the bane of Indo-US ties. This, as if, triggered India's proactive approach to SCO summits with India's Prime Minister joining these since the Yekaterinburg summit of May 2009. Now, the improved chemistry between Indian and the United States' political leadership seems to have relaxed those pressures to engage SCO as part of posturing; but this has not been replaced yet by genuine engagement efforts, the need for which can never be over-emphasized.

It is too early to expect this evolving hands-on approach of India in Afghanistan to even begin to show any immediate signs of making China friendly towards the issue of India's SCO membership. To some extent, its impact can be seen in terms of warming up in India-China ties which, of course, has its own pace and grammar. Starting from several heads of state and government visiting India during December 2010, one has witnessed a series of high-level China-India interactions—many of these in multilateral forums like SCO—and just like these are having a positive impact on India-China equations, their better resultant bilateral relations are expected to facilitate China's change of heart on India's SCO membership in due course of time. But, all these remain too tentative and long-term trends to even suggest any broad, let alone conclusive, trajectories in equations between SCO and New Delhi, especially when the latter has not been very active in seeking this engagement.

Strategic Implications for India

Though India has had long, close, and direct relations with Russia, China, and CARs, India's interest in SCO has been primarily in engaging the relatively younger CARs. This is partly so because with both Russia and China, India has had active bilateral interactions. It is from this perspective on seeking engagement with CARs that India sees itself making a value addition to the SCO's multilateralism. India's participation in SCO, although, is expected to have a positive spin-off on the nature of New Delhi's bilateral interactions with CARs and even with both Beijing and Moscow. It is interesting to note that whereas SCO remains China-driven, India's bilateral relationships with CARs have failed to convince Beijing for a dependable partnership and failed to grow out of peculiar visions of flowing from India's original engagement via Moscow. Even India's interest in participating in regional and multilateral arrangements towards ensuring energy security and counter-terrorism remain at wide variance with China's own needs for energy security as also given its close relationship with Pakistan that India sees as the main culprit for terrorism.

But the nature of SCO multilateralism across CARs has also had its limitations. Its functioning has generated an extreme opposite analysis making New Delhi cautious and suspect about appearing over-enthusiastic, especially given its tag of being a China-led initiative. Experts like Marc Lanteigne see structures of SCO borrowing heavily from secured community-building practices in Northeast and Southeast Asia. These include use of informality and consensus-building and focus on open-regionalism, inclusiveness, and non-discrimination. This was impelled by the need to accommodate different power levels and political orientations amongst its members and was further strengthened by inclusion of new Observers and Dialogue Partners.[23] But, on the other hand, while SCO and especially China boasts of inclusiveness and non-discrimination, there are equally strong counterviews to what seems to be SCO's reality. Gill Bates of SIPRI, on the other hand, cites the example of East Asian Summit where China is known to have been reluctant to allow any participation to the United States. On India's reluctance in campaigning for its SCO membership, he says:

India has been reluctant to endorse the Chinese agenda on excluding 'external powers'. ... India has not backed the SCO's call for withdrawal of US and other foreign troops from Central Asia. Such a withdrawal, India is aware, would only benefit the extremist forces in the region, including the Taliban.[24]

In the end, it is in these continuing dichotomous perceptions about China-led SCO that lay the roots of India's strategic challenge. The bottom-line is that in spite of these limitations, India cannot ignore engaging SCO. But India remains equally bound to its influential traditions of promoting norm-based multilateralism which will continue to guide India's foreign policy initiatives. And it is essentially from this perspective that, even if piecemeal and painfully-slow moving, India would be able to make any useful contribution to SCO's multilateralism. At the same time, there is no denying that some of the support to India's candidature for SCO membership is often driven by expectations that entry of India will strengthen global and regional efforts at 'socialising' and 'balancing' rising China. More than its campaign to enter the SCO, India has tried hard to contest any such speculations.

Notes and References

1. Thomas F. Keating (2002), *Canada and World Order: The Multilateralist Tradition in Canadian Foreign Policy*, London: Oxford University Press, p. 13; also Zhou Enlai (1964), *Afro-Asian Solidarity Against Imperialism: A Collection of Documents, Speeches and Press Interviews from the visits of Chinese Leaders to Thirteen African and Asian Countries*, Beijing: Foreign Language Press.

2. Tim Groser (2000), 'Multilateralism and Minilateralism: On a Collision Course? Or Can Trade Policy Practitioners Walk and Chew Gum at the Same Time', in Martin Richardson (ed.), *Globalisation and International Trade Liberalisation: Continuity and Change*, Cheltenham: Edward Elgar Publishing Limited, p. 135.

3. Charles Doran (2010), 'The two sides of Multilateral Cooperation', in I. William Zartman and Saadia Touval (eds), *International Cooperation: The Extent and Limits of Multilateralism*, New York: Cambridge University Press, pp. 40–1; Amitav Acharya (2009), 'Multilateralism, Sovereignty and Normative Change in World Politics', in Edward Newman, Ramesh Thakur, and John Tirman (eds), *Multilateralism Under Challenge?: Power, International Order and Structural Change*, New Delhi: Academic Foundation, p. 108.

4. Swaran Singh (2009), 'China's Quest for Multilateralism', in Anjali Ghosh et al., *India's Foreign Policy*, Delhi: Dorling Kindersley, p. 200; Pan Guang (2009), 'The SCO's Success in Security Architecture', in Ron Huisken (ed.), *The Architecture of Security in the Asia-Pacific*, Canberra: ANU E Press, p. 38.

5. Marc Lanteigne (2010), 'Security, Strategy and the former USSR: China and the Shanghai Cooperation Organisation', in Shaun Breslin (ed.), *Handbook of China's International Relations*, London: Routledge, p. 170.

6. Sandeep Dikshit (2011), 'India poised to join Shanghai grouping', *The Hindu* (New Delhi), 16 June, p. 1; Vladimir Radyuhin, 'Afghanistan may join SCO', *The Hindu* (New Delhi), 16 May 2011, p. 10; Erica Marat (2011), 'Afghanistan: NATO Out, SCO In?', *Eurasia Daily Monitor*, The Jamestown Foundation, 8 (98), 20 May.

7. Hooman Peimani (2009), *Conflict and Security in Central Asia and the Caucasus*, Santa Barbara, Ca.: Greenwood, p. 320.

8. 'India keen to become member of SCO', *The Times of India* New Delhi, 1 June 2010 at http://timesofindia.indiatimes.com/india/India-keen-to-become-member-of-SCO/articleshow/5995619.cms

9. G.V.C. Naidu (2009), 'India and East Asian Multilateralism', in Anjali Ghosh, Tridib Chakraborti, Anindyo Jyoti Majumdar, Shibashis Chatterjee (eds), *India's Foreign Policy*, New Delhi: Dorling Kindersley, p. 445.

10. Ibid., p. 445.

11. Lisa Curtis and Dean Cheng (2011), 'The China Challenge: A strategic vision for U.S.-India relations', *Expert Zone* at Reuters, 19 July, at http://blogs.reuters.com/india-expertzone/2011/07/19/the-china-challenge-a-strategic-vision-for-u-s-india-relations/

12. Zheng Yongnian (2010), 'Organizing China's Inter-state Relations: From "*tianxia*" (all-under Heaven) to the Modern International Order', in Zheng Yongnian (ed.), *China and International Relation: The Chinese View and the Contribution of Wang Gungwu*, New York: Routledge, pp. 316–17.

13. Thrassy N. Marketos (2009), *China's Energy Geoplotics: The Shanghai Cooperation Organisation and Central Asia*, New York: Routledge, p. 64.

14. Hooman Peimani (2009), *Conflict and Security in Central Asia and the Caucasus*, Santa Barbara, Cali: Greenwood, p. 320.

15. S.D. Muni (2004), 'September 11: The Asian Giants get Closer', in Marika Vicziany, David Wright-Neville, Pete Lentini (eds), *Regional Security in the Asia-Pacific: 9/11 and After*, Cheltenham, UK: Edward Elgar Publishing Limited, p. 91.

16. Ajay Patnaik (2005), 'Central Asia's Security: The Asian Dimension', in R.R. Sharma (ed.), *India and Emerging Asia*, New Delhi: Sage, p. 223.

17. Hooman Peimani (2009), *Conflict and Security in Central Asia and the Caucasus*, Santa Barbara, Cali: Greenwood, p. 320.

18. Bobo Lo (2008), *Axis of Convenience: Moscow, Beijing and the New Geopolitics*, London: Royal Institute of International Affairs, p. 113; Emilian Kavalski (ed.) (2009), *China and the Global Politics of Regionalizatioin*, Farnham, Surrey: Ashgate, p. 75.

19. Gregory Chin (2010), 'China's Rising Institutional Influence', in Alan S. Alexandroff and Andrew F. Cooper (eds), *Rising States, Rising Institutions: Challenges for Global Governance*, Baltimore: Brookings Institution Press, pp. 88–9.

20. M.K. Bhadrakumar (2009), 'India begins uphill journey with the SCO', *Asia Times* (Hong Kong), 25 March.

21. Phunchok Stobdan (2009), 'Shanghai Cooperation Organisation and Asian Multilateralism in the Twenty-first Century', in N.S. Sisodia and V. Krishnappa (eds), *Global Power Sjhifts and Strategic Transition in Asia*, New Delhi: Academic Foundation, p. 240.

22. M.K. Bhadrakumar (2011), 'Getting the Regional Act Together', *The Hindu* (New Delhi), 27 August, p. 10.

23. Marc Lanteigne (2010), 'Security, strategy and the former USSR: China and the Shanghai Cooperation Organisation', in Shaun Breslin (ed.), *Handbook of China's International Relations*, London: Routledge, p. 170.

24. C. Raja Mohan (2009), 'India and the Asian Security Architecture', in Michael J. Green and Bill Gates (eds), *China's New Multilateralism: Cooperation, Competition, and the Search for Community*, New York: Columbia University Press, p. 147.

6

Shanghai Cooperation Organisation
Hopes Amid Hurdles

MARLÈNE LARUELLE and SÉBASTIEN PEYROUSE

With the border issues resolved and the Uyghur question—at least temporarily—quashed, China reinforced its presence in Central Asia by investing massively in the Shanghai Cooperation Organisation (SCO). Created on the basis of a structure first established in 1996, called the Group of Five, or the Shanghai Group, the SCO has not gone unnoticed in the international community. It is probably one of the most discussed and most studied international organizations, a fact that stands in total disproportion to its real levels of activism. All the debates on the state of Chinese and Russian relations, on China's rise to power on the international scene, on the emergence of a new world order stamped by anti-American alliances, feel obliged to mention the SCO. This can be explained for the most part by the fundamentally new character of the organization. It is the only multilateral organization that has been set up by China; it gathers together regions of the world that were practically in open conflict only a few decades ago; it encompasses three-fifths of the Eurasian continent and a quarter of the world's population; and it gives off the image—whether true or false—of being an anti-Western organization, challenging US supremacy in the heart of the Eurasian continent.[1] Granting associated member status to Mongolia, Iran, India, and Pakistan in 2004–5 thrust the SCO even more into the media spotlight. However, beyond its rhetoric of cooperation and declarations of good intentions, the young organization is not without many difficulties. Its member states often have very divergent interests, some of which bring into question its mid- to long-term credibility.

The Security Paradigm: The Effectiveness of the SCO and of China

Created to settle border tensions peacefully and progressively demilitarize them, the Shanghai Group rapidly transformed into a more global platform for discussion between Russia, China, Kazakhstan, Kyrgyzstan, and Tajikistan. The series of destabilizations during the summer of 1999–2000, which saw incursions from the Islamic Movement of Uzbekistan across the Tajik and Kyrgyz borders, and the incapacity of the Kyrgyz army to regain control of its territory gave renewed impetus to the Shanghai Group, which then decided to go a step further in terms of institutionalization and became the Shanghai Cooperation Organisation. Without any common border with China, Tashkent's decision of joining the SCO in 2001 confirmed that it was no longer limited to settling border disputes, but was now concentrated on regional security stakes. Whereas until that point, Uzbekistan had been very reluctant to enter a regional organization, even more so one in which Russia was a key power, and whereas it made no secret of its support for United States' growing involvement in the region, the Islamist incursions changed profoundly the given situation, and highlighted the need for all the state actors to create a new multilateral platform.[2] The US-led 'global war on terror', which made it possible to add the East Turkestan Islamic Movement to the list of international terrorist movements, also partly legitimized the SCO's turn towards counterterrorism.

Security cooperation is conceived as the very core of SCO activity. The first joint military exercises began in 2003, and they are now repeated yearly in one of the member countries.[3] The main participants in them are the Russian, Chinese, and Kazakh forces. The participating troops sent by Kyrgyzstan and Tajikistan are minimal due to lack of means, while Uzbekistan remains reluctant to embark on any large-scale involvement. Simulations are carried out of terrorist attacks like those that took place in 1999 and 2000, including exercises in mountainous terrain and hostage scenarios. Since an agreement passed between the SCO and the Moscow-led Collective Security Treaty Organization (CSTO) in 2005, some exercises, called Peace Missions, now include both organizations (with Armenia being a member of the latter but not of the former).[4] These exercises have an impact on national and international public opinion, giving the impression of collective actions in sensitive domains linked to national sovereignty. However, they remain superficial: they are about parallel manoeuvres more than joint ones. While the general staffs may decide on common strategy together, the battalions involved often remain without any contact with their foreign colleagues. During the 'Peace Mission 2010', exercises held at the Kazakh firing range of Matybulak, the only combats necessitating real interaction between troops were by the Russian and Kazakh forces; whereas the Chinese forces led their own demonstration in parallel.[5] Operations organized in a bilateral manner, such as the Sino-Kazakh border drug-seizing operations, which have been ongoing since 2008,[6] are more effective than the SCO exercises in terms of interaction between Central Asian and Chinese soldiers.

The second element of the SCO security cooperation is linked to a larger but less militarized conception of security. The organization is particularly attached to the aspect of fighting against non-traditional threats, since it is the one where the interests of all the state members are the most similar and only elicit small divergences of opinion.[7] This security focus is supposedly embodied in the Regional Anti-Terrorist Structure (RATS), which was going to be opened in Bishkek but was ultimately 'offered' to Tashkent, in obligation for its joining and because this issue is dear to the regime of Islam Karimov. Active since 2004, RATS, by the nature of its activities, is not open to an outside view and lets hardly any information filter out about itself.[8] The structure is set up to promote common methods to fight against terrorist movements and to exchange information on suspicious individuals. It seems that on several occasions the Chinese authorities have asked their Central Asian partners to arrest and then to deport some Uyghur opponents, and when Islamists allegedly cross the border, they are followed by the RATS joint procedures set up to monitor them. However, it is difficult to say whether this type of information exchange has been made possible thanks to RATS and through it, or whether it took place in a bilateral framework. Truly sensitive matters, such as the expulsion of Uyghur opponents to China, are generally managed in very high-level bilateral relations.[9]

Even if the RATS and the SCO multilateral exercises enable doctrinal dialogue to take place, and promote better understanding between the security structures and the armies of member states, the organization's multilateral security dynamic remains embryonic.[10] Not having any mission to become a supranational organization that would infringe on its members' sovereignty, the SCO does not have a military structure like the CSTO, which in addition, involves the sale of technological material to member states. It does not project itself either as a military defence alliance in the image of NATO, or seek to create multilateral or police military units, and RATS cannot be considered a sort of Interpol for the SCO. The hesitations manifested by member states to embark on closer collaboration are several. All extol their right to sovereignty and criticize supranational logics. Russia has refused to participate in several exercises in which China has taken part and seems less and less committed to promoting the military aspect of the SCO. Neither Moscow nor Beijing is inclined to disclosing sensitive information about new technologies and their respective nuclear complexes. While the two capitals do not officially see themselves as potential enemies, traditional distrust and a sense of inevitable rivalry dominate.[11]

Despite its emphasis on security, the SCO has been helpless to react to any of the crises that have impacted upon the Central Asian region, such as 'the Tulip revolution' in Kyrgyzstan in March 2005, the overthrow of the Bakiyev government in April 2010, the interethnic pogroms of Osh in June 2010, the regular clashes between the security services and armed Islamist groups in the mountainous regions of Tajikistan (for the most part in the Rasht Valley), and so on. For the SCO, the worsening situation in two of its member states, Kyrgyzstan and Tajikistan, is not only disquieting at the level of security, but also revealing of the ineffectiveness of its mechanisms and its impossibility of undertaking concerted collective actions on subjects that significantly affect state sovereignty.

Afghanistan is also an indicator of the difficulties that the SCO has in advancing any collective management of global security. While there is great disappointment among the Central Asian states as regards the West's handling of the Afghan question—they all criticize NATO's focus on military solutions and, by contrast, endorse political solutions and economic reconstruction—the organization itself has not come up with any solution to end the stalemate of the international coalition. Afghanistan has already become a symbol of one of the SCO's first defeats in terms of image. In 2001, the US intervention, launched only a few weeks after the attack of 11 September, demonstrated the capacities of the world's premier superpower and its European allies to engage rapidly and massively in a new war theatre that the SCO deemed was more or less part of its 'sphere of influence'. The organization's members also reacted in their own separate ways to this event: Moscow's rapprochement with Washington and the opening of two US military bases in Kyrgyzstan and Uzbekistan displeased the Chinese authorities and weakened political confidence among member states.[12]

The SCO began to feel the need to develop a common policy on Afghanistan in 2004, and a few years later the organization's name cropped up regularly among the international protagonists of the Afghan theatre. In 2004, the SCO created a first contact group with Afghanistan, which was institutionalized in 2005. In 2006, Hamid Karzai declared that his country 'belonged to the region in which the SCO was situated. Afghanistan has no other solutions and cannot exist outside of this region.'[13] In 2007, the Afghan Vice-President, Ahmad Zia Masood, stated that he expected far greater cooperation with the organization, in particular in the economic sector. Ever since, the Afghan issue has become one of the major SCO discussion topics. In 2008, a conference devoted to this issue was held on the shores of the Lake Issyk-Kul, for the purpose of increasing the organization's profile as well as of making Iran a fully-fledged member. In 2009, it was made clear at the SCO meeting in Moscow, which included representatives from the G8 and other international organizations that Russia as well as China wished to be seen as essential partners in any Afghan solution.[14]

Nonetheless, despite its declarations of intention, the SCO has few means to be able to influence Afghan realities.[15] Its financial capacities as a multilateral organization are minimal. The idea of creating collective military forces is not included among its member's objectives. Even collective actions in the domain of reconstruction seem difficult to make a reality. While all the SCO member states play a role in Afghanistan— Russia due to its Soviet past,[16] China due to its massive investments in the exploitation of resources,[17] Kazakhstan thanks to its humanitarian aid and its cereal sales, and Uzbekistan and Tajikistan due to their co-ethnics in the northern Afghan provinces—there exists no attempt to unify these individual approaches into a collective action. In addition, Kabul clearly gives its priority to bilateral relations. Nikolai Bordiuzha, the CSTO General Secretary, acknowledged for instance that the CSTO-Afghanistan working group was only minimally effective and that the Karzai government had asked Moscow for bilateral and not multilateral cooperation.[18]

In the 10 years of Western initiatives in Afghanistan, the SCO has therefore often found itself in the margins: it has had no solutions to offer to the stalemate, unless this has been to criticize the ISAF's lack of success, and none of its members want to send its troops to Afghanistan; despite the insistence that it has made on the need for reconstructing the country and of finding a political solution, no collective action has been organized in this regard; all its members conduct bilateral politics with Kabul without any coordination between them. Eventually, thanks to the Northern Distribution Network,[19] the United States has succeeded in recreating networks for negotiations with the Central Asian governments, and giving life to some regional coordination related to transit to Afghanistan, something that the SCO has never succeeded in doing.

Even in a bilateral framework, China is unable to rival Russia's major role in military cooperation with the Central Asian states. Its aid is limited to electronic material, automobiles, and military clothes; but includes almost no military sales. Since 2000, Kazakhstan and China have signed multiple agreements under which Astana buys Chinese technical equipment.[20] In total, between 1997 and 2003, Astana has received US$ 4.5 million of US technological aid, and communications and transportation equipment from China. Astana has expressed its intention to obtain military material from the Chinese People's Liberation Army (PLA) and hopes to take advantage of free transfers of decommissioned military assets when the Chinese army modernizes its equipment.[21] Under the joint counterterrorism operations, Kazakhstan also wants to take advantage of the expertise and experience of China, which has strengthened its special forces in this area.[22] The 2007 Kazakhstan military doctrine attaches special importance to the bilateral security relationship with China, but without taking away Russia's prominent role.

Chinese aid to the other Central Asian states is more modest. During a meeting between the defence ministers of China and Turkmenistan in 2007, it was decided that Beijing would equip the Turkmen army with precision equipment and uniforms for officers and soldiers, offering a US$ 3 million loan for its military needs.[23] China is also trying to expand its military cooperation with its two immediate neighbours, Kyrgyzstan and Tajikistan. In 2005, an official visit of the Chinese minister of defence to Dushanbe led to the signing of several military cooperation documents; although limited in scope and mostly rhetorical, such as sharing of intelligence on terrorism, drug trafficking, and organized crime.[24] Between 1993 and 2008, Beijing has provided US$ 15 million in aid to Tajikistan,[25] and in 2009 it pledged US$ 1.5 million to Tajikistan's military; the latest in a series of financial aid packages for the region's armed forces. Under an agreement signed in 2002, in Bishkek, China has also provided technical military assistance to Kyrgyzstan worth US$ 1.2 million.[26] With Uzbekistan, relations are more complex. In 2000, China made a first step on to the Central Asian arms market, delivering sniper rifles to Tashkent. In 2009, the two countries signed a new agreement whereby Beijing will provide US$ 3.7 million to the Uzbek authorities to equip its border crossings with mobile scanning systems.[27]

Finally, training aid is attempting to develop, however modestly. Exchanges have been organized to train military cadres, but the language barrier hinders prospects. Courses for Central Asian officers in Chinese military academies are taught in Russian, as Chinese instructors are unable to speak Central Asian languages or Central Asian officers, Chinese. Between 1990 and 2005, only 15 Kazakh officers were sent to China for training. Yet this cooperation is growing: between 2003 and 2009, 65 members of the Kazakh military took courses in Chinese institutions.[28] Further negotiations in this area were organized between the two countries at the beginning of 2009. About 30 Kyrgyz officers also received training in China; and in 2008, 30 members of the Tajik army were trained in Chinese military academies. For the Central Asian governments, equipment and training from the Peoples' Liberation Army is a—still mainly theoretical—welcome balance to the supplies of outdated Soviet hardware which is sometimes offloaded by Moscow, but for the time being aid remains focused on non-military material and involves little training.

Quest for 'Shanghai Spirit'

Whereas it originally focused on security questions, the SCO has quickly formed many commissions and forums devoted not only to economic, financial, and investment questions, but also to the environment and cultural exchanges. This activism has earned not only its increased visibility, but has also worked to accelerate the dissolution of its security objectives while failing to yield any new, well-defined priorities.[29] Each member state, therefore, tries to promote its own interests, which are often very divergent from those of its neighbours. The differences in prospects for economic development, in domestic fragility, and divergences in the geopolitical strategies broadly influences the perceptions harboured by each of the states and their expectations of the SCO. For Russia, the organization obliges China to play the card of multilateralism and allows Moscow to curb Beijing's ambitions without directly confronting its growing influence in the Central Asian region. For China, the SCO has made it possible to institutionalize its legitimacy in the region. With this done, it can go about playing on the contradictions between member states and lobby groups without the risk of being accused of expansionism. For the Central Asians, the organization serves as a buffer: it can mediate disagreements peacefully and channel competition between the two dominant powers for more advantageous solutions.

An implicit hierarchy has therefore taken shape, despite discourses about equality among member states. At the first level, Russia and China dominate the SCO international visibility: through it both powers not only negotiate their relation to Central Asia but also their international positioning in favour of a multi-polar world, and the organization's relations with other regional and international institutions. At a second level, Kazakhstan joins this duo to form a dominant trio. The Moscow-Astana-Beijing trio is in charge of promoting the organization among the observer states, as well as the other parts of post-Soviet space through their overlapping membership in several regional organizations, such as the CSTO or the Eurasian Economic Community (EEC). It is also pushing the SCO to take a more economic focus; since Kazakhstan is one of the regions' energy leaders and constitutes the territorial link between Russia and China. Astana is at an advantage whenever the SCO seeks to promote a nuclear weapons free world. While Russia and China appeal for the world to avoid nuclear proliferation, neither country is ready to call its atomic status into question and the issue is a sticking point for the three main observer countries—Iran, Pakistan, and India. In Kazakhstan, on the contrary, denuclearization was a complete success. Astana plays this hand to its fullest, as it did, for example, during the Nuclear Security Summit in Washington in April 2010 or with Nursultan Nazarbayev's proposal to elaborate a universal declaration for a denuclearized world.[30] At the third level are Uzbekistan, Kyrgyzstan, and Tajikistan; the first for being a rebellious member against any collective activities, the other two for their internal weaknesses. The leaders of these three countries participate much less in the SCO activities that attract international visibility or in the large-scale energy projects, and appeal to the organization to return to its initial aims, namely regional stability, and the fight against terrorist threats.

China constitutes the main driver behind the SCO orientation towards economy, in which it sees, among other things, an opportunity for the development of the 'Far West' and the conquest of new markets. Since 2002, Beijing has proposed to make the SCO a free trade zone that would be the largest in the world with more than 1.5 billion people. At a 2003 summit, the SCO prime ministers signed an agreement for multilateral trade and economic cooperation. In 2004, four working groups were formed for electronic commerce, customs, inspection of goods and harmonization of standards, and cooperation in investment. However, this Chinese dynamic toward a common market is far from being unanimously accepted. Moscow as well as the Central Asian states fear that they will pass under a kind of Chinese economic protectorate given the development and growth differential. In the post-Soviet space, where transformative industries have never recovered from the collapse of the USSR, those that still exist cannot compete with the profitability of their Chinese competitors. Russia and Central Asia are thus not interested in forming a free market with China, but they privilege the energy sector and Chinese investment capacities, in which they see an alternative to their more demanding, Western partners. The setting up of a transport corridor between China and Europe via Russia and Central Asia, export agreements for electricity, and the transit of hydrocarbons thus elicits the interest of all member states,[31] even if Sino-Russian competition for Central Asian gas in particular is also growing.

Uzbekistan occupies its own specific position since it is the only member state to have declared its reluctance to engage in any multilateral cooperation and to refuse to envisage, even symbolically, any loss of sovereignty. Islam Karimov's regime regularly refuses to participate in SCO joint military exercises, and often only sends observers or a few participants from the security services, but not the regular army. Tashkent does not conceal its discontent at the SCO cautiousness: Moscow and Beijing are criticized for refusing to tackle basic problems, such as the question of water management, and for not voicing themselves in favour of the Uzbek stance. Only the activities of RATS, as they are based in the Uzbek capital city and centre on questions of anti-terrorism, seem to find Tashkent's favour. Uzbekistan's strategy is thus to use the SCO as a multilateral platform in which it requests a reinforcement of actions, which go in its own direction: the anti-terrorist struggle and the settling of tensions related to hydroelectricity. The other SCO components are discreetly put to one side, such as the debates on economic integration, as they go directly against Uzbek isolationist logics. Last, the Uzbek regime interprets the declarations which present the SCO as a 'rampart' against Western influence in accordance with its geopolitical strategy of the moment: either such pronouncements are deemed to be in line with its own anti-Western stance, or else they are denounced as Russian interference and American interest is solicited.[32]

Kyrgyzstan and Tajikistan have similar positions when it comes to their expectations of the SCO. During official meetings, Dushanbe and Bishkek complain of the growing disinterest in security questions; despite the centrality of these matters for both of them given their domestic instability. The Tajik and Kyrgyz governments could also barely hide their disappointment during their wrestling with Tashkent over water management, since neither Moscow nor Beijing openly took their side. The SCO anti-Western rhetoric has sometimes caused Bishkek difficulties, notably over pressures to close the US base at Manas, but this does not prevent the Kyrgyz government from negotiating directly with the United States or the European Union. Thanks to American and Russian presence on its territory, financial blackmail (the annual rent paid for the two bases) and symbolic blackmail (the change in status of the Manas 'base', which since 2009 has officially become a 'transit centre') now form part of the Kyrgyz foreign policy and guarantee it some room for manoeuvre. Dushanbe is more restricted than Bishkek since the United States has no presence there, Russia dominates on the security level, and neighbouring Iran makes debates on strategic evolutions even more complex. On the economic level, Kyrgyzstan and Tajikistan are enthusiastic SCO participants: They were the grateful beneficiaries of US$ 900 million in credit, offered to them by Beijing, and are able to take plenty of advantage of developments in cooperation over banking and finance, investments for large projects, and SCO study bourses and training—all essentially at China's initiative. Lastly, on the military plain, the supervision provided by the organization, even if it is more limited than that of the CSTO, offers unique possibilities for training and practical experience for the weak Tajik and Kyrgyz armies.

Kazakhstan, for its part, can allow itself both to be a key actor of the SCO and an autonomous, demanding partner. The organization is pointed up in Kazakh discourse, since it is part of its logic of promoting all the regional and international organizations, but Astana does not consider that this membership restricts its own foreign policy choices.[33] The partnership with Russia under the auspices of the CSTO is the more privileged, and Kazakhstan makes no secret of its preference for this institutional framework, which guarantees its low-price Russian military material, Russian investments in its military-industrial complex, the training of hundreds of officers, and so on.[34] Kazakhstan is also the most advanced Central Asian country in terms of cooperation with NATO, thanks to its Individual Plan of Action for the Partnership (IPAP).[35] It is furthermore the only Central Asian state to have created a peacekeeping force—namely the Kazbat battalion, which has been elevated to a brigade, Kazbrig, and was sent to Iraq from 2003 to 2008—which it has done in collaboration with NATO under UN mandate. In the years to come, Astana thus hopes to obtain interoperability status with NATO and this is in spite of its privileged partnership with Russia and its official enthusiasm toward the SCO.

On the economic level, Kazakhstan, like Russia, is pushing for the establishment of collective rationales in terms of hydrocarbons, electricity, and transit corridors, but rejects Chinese projects for a common market that would abolish customs barriers. Astana is also anxious about the possibility of the Yuan becoming the common currency for intra-SCO exchanges.[36] As a result, Kazakhstan has joined forces with Russia and Belarus to request joint entry to the World Trade Organization (WTO). This is to the great displeasure of China, which had been hoping for rapid, individual entry for Kazakhstan in order to boost economic exchanges without having to go through Kyrgyzstan, a member of the WTO since 1998. The new Russia-Belarus-Kazakhstan Customs Union which came into effect in July 2010 confirms that Astana's economic orientation privileges Moscow over Beijing, and that the SCO is not seen as the main engine of economic cooperation in the region.

Political Alliance: An 'Axis of Convenience'

Since its inception, the SCO has announced that it does not oppose any other organization or foreign state. However, it quickly emerged as a virtually anti-Western organization. It was founded during the NATO attacks against Serbia and the bombing of the Chinese Embassy in Belgrade, which raised the ire of Moscow and Beijing. In 2000, the Dushanbe Declaration asserted that the organization was against any intervention undertaken without UN approval and interference in internal affairs under the pretext of defending human rights, a direct reference to US policy in the region. This anti-Western orientation became clearer at the Astana Summit in July 2005, when the SCO demanded that the United States limit the duration of their military presence in Central Asia. After Andizhan, Tashkent insisted that Washington close the base at Karshi-Khanabad, which Washington did in November of that year.[37] Though Russia is often accused, in the West, of wanting to see the US Manas base in Kyrgyzstan closed, the Chinese authorities seem just as intent on ending the American presence on their borders. They allegedly offered financial compensation to the Kyrgyz state for any revenue loss incurred by the base's closure.[38]

China and Russia both share a similar commitment to fight against Western influence in Eurasia and claim that they are victims of a containment policy pursued by Washington through establishing friendly regimes via 'colour revolutions'.[39] They also have the same view of the dangers that they face in Central Asia, deemed a potentially unstable area with risks of Islamism, state failure, and drug trafficking. For this reason, Beijing, like Moscow, gives its support to local authoritarian regimes, arguing that they are the last guarantors of stability and secularism. They all adopted similar interpretations of the Chechen issue in Russia, the Tibetan and Uyghur issues in China, and the Islamist risk in Central Asia. Nevertheless, there have been several SCO policy fits and starts. After 11 September 2001, China was offended by Moscow and the Central Asian regimes' acceptance to cooperate with the United States in Afghanistan. Nonetheless, since 2003, the atmosphere once deemed conducive to cooperate with the West, has come to an end. Although SCO statutes formally prohibit any interference in the internal affairs of members, the shock waves sent into the post-Soviet space by the 'colour revolutions' and the Andizhan events in May 2005[40] helped to revive political ties between the SCO member states. However, Moscow's recognition of the independence of South Ossetia and Abkhazia in August 2008 caused confusion in China, and angered Central Asian authorities, which made calls for former Soviet borders to be preserved and for the propagation of secessionist movements to be curtailed. China and Central Asia's refusal to recognize the new states disappointed Moscow, which had sought the unwavering support of its SCO allies.[41]

The question of Chinese influence on the Central Asian political regimes ought to be discussed. Western observers often tend to overestimate Beijing's ability to direct Central Asian political choices. With the exception of the Uyghur diaspora, on which, indeed, the Chinese authorities bring their full weight to bear, the Central Asian regimes remain as impermeable as possible to Chinese political influence. Their choice in favour of increasingly authoritarian regimes, if it is evidently influenced by the regional situation, nonetheless cannot be explained by this proximity: it cannot be assumed that Kazakhstan, Tajikistan, Uzbekistan, and Turkmenistan are spontaneously more democratic but have become 'victims' of Russian and Chinese authoritarian pressures. The proof of this is Kyrgyzstan, a country which has managed to uphold a greater ideological liberty and authorizes the expression of a greater diversity of viewpoints, without Beijing's being able or wanting to prevent this. Even Moscow's influence, although more manifest in this domain than China's, is unable to explain the choices of the Central Asian regimes and the choices which are driven by domestic issues and local political culture. Though the SCO really is an alliance of authoritarian regimes, with the mitigated case of Kyrgyzstan, it is more a matter of an axis of convenience than of an influence of the stronger over the weaker.

Moreover, although the SCO undeniably attempts to counter Western influence in Eurasia, no member state wishes to pursue an aggressive policy aimed directly against US interests or a slowdown of its integration into the international community.[42] China cannot afford to be declared as a 'rogue state' by Washington, as its economy is now too dependent on its relations with the United States. The Central Asian states seek to keep contacts with the West in order to weaken both Moscow and Beijing. Despite the rise of anti-American sentiment among Central Asian elites, all consider Western presence in the region to guarantee stability and agree that the exclusive, dual grip of Russia and China is dangerous.[43] For its part, Russia seeks to signal to the West that it has geopolitical alternatives if the European Union and the United States oppose its objectives, without calling for a rupture of its partnership with the West. For Moscow, the SCO can be seen as an extension of the 'Primakov doctrine', which sought to reorient Russian foreign policy towards Asia, and to strike a balance between East and West. Given this state of affairs and the interests of its members, the Shanghai Cooperation Organisation does not appear to pose a direct threat to Western interests, despite the refusal of the US request to be granted the status of associated member.[44]

The issue of enlarging the SCO to new states has come up as well; but now it has become a subject of contradictory discussions related to the internal balance between member states and to the organization's international image. While four states were granted associate member status in 2004–5, the SCO's terms of membership were not defined until 2010.[45] They prohibited entry into the SCO for non-signatory countries to the Nuclear Non-proliferation Treaty or countries that are subject to UN sanctions, which makes it possible to block membership to India and Pakistan, on the one hand, and Iran, on the other. In the short term, the six members appear reluctant to make any wide overtures. Observer status is not considered to be a door leading to membership, and the two states that currently lack any formal status, Turkmenistan and Afghanistan, could potentially enter the organization before the observer states. In 2009, Belarus and Sri Lanka, the former advanced by Russia and the latter by China, have become 'discussion partners', which is a more informal status than that of associate member.

For the three main observer states—India, Pakistan, and Iran—the question of SCO membership constitutes part of a broader range of geopolitical issues. New Delhi and Islamabad want to find a new institutional framework to negotiate their competition in Central Asia.[46] The agreement reached between India and the International Agency for Atomic Energy in 2008 helped Delhi escape from its 'nuclear apartheid', which in principle could be used as a positive argument in case of a membership request. However, the border tensions between India and China have not been settled and could therefore cast a shadow over the SCO's main success, namely the peaceful resolution of the Sino-Soviet border disputes and their demilitarization, a gain that no member wishes to see undermined, not even symbolically. The state of Indian-Pakistani relations, in particular the situation in Kashmir, can also only disquiet the SCO member states, which do not want to manage 'hot conflicts'. The prospects for entry are thus limited so long as the SCO sees itself as a non-conflictive, regional platform. However, Russia has confirmed that it supports India's possible membership, probably in order to weaken China, and the strategic partnership signed between India and Kazakhstan in 2009 works to strengthen Indian ambitions toward the SCO.

Under the weight of international sanctions and US embargo, Iran is on the search for new allies and a means to enter the international arena as a regional power, rather than as an Islamic revolutionary state. Then, Tehran has been trying for several years to escape from its international isolation by emphasizing on its Asian identity and turning in the main toward China. The SCO is especially appealing given its repeatedly stated principle of non-interference in the internal affairs. Iran is also seeking cooperation in the energy sector. In 2006, Mahmoud Ahmedinejad hosted the leaders of the member states to discuss possible joint energy development.[47] However, Russia and China have already conveyed that they do not intend to share their influence over Central Asian oil and gas with other regional Asian powers, some of which, like Iran, are also energy producers. Moreover, the prospect of working closely with the Iranian regime would not be without consequences for the relations between member states and the West, particularly the United States.[48] Such cooperation would distinctly paint the SCO as anti-American and its members as a group of 'dissidents', which neither Moscow, Beijing, nor Central Asian regimes desire.

More globally, the Sino-Russian partnership in Central Asia, supposedly embodied in the SCO, remains ambivalent: not founded on a 'values base', it lacks resilience to political, strategic, or economic downturns, and could be tested by a change in the geopolitics of either actor. China has positioned itself as a faithful second to Russia and tacitly recognizes Central Asia as still being in the Russian 'sphere of influence'. Beijing, in actual fact, wishes to preserve Russian strategic domination, preferring to let Moscow pay the heavy costs of military security and of guaranteeing the survival of unstable regimes, while it focuses on economic involvement.[49] Russian military presence in the region does not raise any problems for China, which actually needs the Kremlin's support both to nip its own separatist movements in the bud and to act as a check on Western influence and growing competition with Washington. For Russia, the situation is more complex and ambivalent.[50] Russian policymakers are indeed increasingly concerned at the speed with which China is narrowing the strategic gap, and the Middle Kingdom awakens old identity fears what Bobo Lo rightly called the 'Mongol syndrome'[51] raising concerns about the territorial unity of the Russian Federation in the future. In Central Asia, economic competition between Moscow and Beijing is already palpable and it will become increasingly important in the years to come.[52] Any change in the overall balance between Moscow and Beijing may upset the Kremlin, which is unprepared to accept China as a top-notch political or cultural power. The Sino-Russian 'axis of convenience'[53] is all the more paradoxical as both Russian and Chinese elites are really geared towards the West, but geopolitical and economic imperatives call them to order in Central Asia.

A Summing Up

In its 15 years of existence, the SCO has allowed the Central Asian governments to familiarize themselves with their Chinese neighbour, a neighbour with which historical relations were partially ruptured in the twentieth century. This improved mutual knowledge has materialized in the framework of bilateral exchanges, but the SCO continues to be important in this regard: the proliferation of commissions, forums, and working groups has given rise to an intense diplomatic ballet throughout all sectors, from the more political to the more cultural. Thus, in addition to the official summits at which heads of state and ministers gather, and the military exercises for which officers come together, thousands of Central Asian state employees, experts, and academics have had the occasion to visit China, to be welcomed there with full honours, and to host their Chinese counterparts in return. With the numerous partnerships signed under SCO auspices, the Central Asians' degree of institutional, not to mention of personal, familiarity, with the Chinese world has grown exponentially within the space of a few years. It can thus be said that SCO positives include the gaining of knowledge about the 'Other', person-to-person relations, and the forming of—at least partial—relations of confidence.

The SCO and its precursor, the Shanghai Group, have undeniably been successful. They have helped to ease long-standing tensions between the Russian and Chinese worlds, to put in place cooperative mechanisms for the border management, and to establish a collective narrative on the common threats they face. But now that threshold of development and institutionalization has been reached and the organization faces new challenges. Despite its security rhetoric, it is relatively inactive in practice and unable to compete with Russian influence in strategic terms. It cannot be compared to the CSTO structure, which offers real interactions between the general staffs and army corps, along with the training of soldiers, arms sales, technological and logistical interoperability, and so on.[54] Shanghai Cooperation Organisation activities largely remain at the stage of declarations of intent. A lack of coordination between member states is evident, the desire to exchange information is restrained, the financial resources are far too few, and bureaucratic structures remain too weak. Furthermore, the absence of actual common jurisdiction in most areas and the lack of relay on important and related matters weaken considerably the scope for potential action. In economic terms, the SCO has failed to compete with the EEC or the Customs Union, to guide the development of trade relations between member states—which remain primarily bilateral—or to allay Russian and Central Asian fears of the impending 'invasion' of Chinese products. In the coming years, a growing Sino-Russian competition for Central Asian resources—mainly hydrocarbons and potentially uranium, but probably not electricity—could also impede SCO energy-related cooperation.

If the SCO is viewed as a mechanism to reinforce confidence, it has been an historical success. But if it is viewed as an organization that attempts to influence Central Asian security realities, for the time being at least it appears to be no more than a 'paper tiger'.[55] The gap between the organization's narrative about the fight against non-traditional threats and its mechanisms to enable collective, or at least concerted, action is immense. The SCO does not provide any military guarantees in case of domestic crisis, but neither does it offer any such structure as a 'rapid intervention force' or a collective troop force like that of the Ministry of Emergency Situations in Russia, able to intervene in situations such as natural and ecological catastrophes, sudden populations displacements, refugees, and so on. The SCO has never managed to react to a large-scale crisis within one of its member states: its silence during the Kyrgyz events of 2010 confirmed, as does its incapacity to offer anything collective to a state, that albeit a non-member is as strategic as Afghanistan.

The obsession for consensus and for maintaining the status quo has in fact hampered the effectiveness of the SCO, and risks delegitimizing it in the future. Since 2008, the organization seems to have entered into a growth crisis. It has no definite positive long-term goal, has no well-defined priorities, and refuses to discuss divergences in its members' priorities. The SCO seems, therefore, primarily to be a reflection of Chinese willingness to support so-called 'healthy Central Asian order', free from any of the three evils,[56] and devoid of pro-Western forces that might act to destabilize China. Even if the organization partially limits the room in which the Central Asian states have to manoeuvre, in particular relative to the West, it provides the established regimes with an ideological framework by which to shore up their legitimacy on both the domestic and international fronts.

Notes and References

1. S. Hanova (2009), 'Perspectives on the SCO: Images and Discourses', *The China and Eurasia Forum Quarterly*, 7(2), pp. 63–82.
2. B.F. Gonzalez (2001), *Charting a New Silk Road?: The Shanghai Cooperation Organization and Russian Foreign Policy.* Master Thesis, University of Oregon.
3. More details in M. de Haas (ed.) (2007), *The Shanghai Cooperation Organisation: Towards a Full-Grown Security Alliance?* Clingendael: Netherlands Institute of International Relations.
4. R.N. McDermott (2007), 'The Rising Dragon. SCO Peace Mission 2007', *Jamestown Occasional Paper*.
5. Information provided by an observer of the Peace Mission 2010, Adil Kaukenov, former director of the Center for Studies of Contemporary China at the Institute of Global Economics and Politics, and today editor in chief of an analysis webportal, *Today.kz*, Almaty, 28 September 2010.
6. For more details, see S. Peyrouse, 'Sino-Kazakh Relations: A Nascent Strategic Partnership', *China Brief*, 7 November 2008, http://www.jamestown.org/single/?no_cache=1&tx_ttnews%5Btt_news%5D=34142

7. More in de Haas, *The Shanghai Cooperation Organisation: Towards a Full-Grown Security Alliance?*

8. Interview with Irina Tchernykh, and Rustam Burnashev, experts from the Institute for Policy Solutions, Almaty, 27 September 2010.

9. Anonymous interviews with several Central Asian experts with access to the ruling circles.

10. H. Zhao (2005), *Kitai, Tsentral'naia Aziia i Shankhaiskaia Organizatsiia Sotrudnichestva*. Moscow: Carnegie Endowment for International Peace.

11. V. Shlapentokh (2007), 'China in the Russian Mind Today: Ambivalence and Defeatism', *Europe Asia Studies*, 59(1), pp. 1–22.

12. E. Wishnik (2009), *Russia, China, and the United States in Central Asia: Prospects for Great Power Competition and Cooperation in the Shadow of the Georgian Crisis*. Carlisle: U.S. Army War College.

13. A. Tarzi (2006), 'Afghan Leader Talks About China Ties,' *RFE/RL*, 14 June, http://www.russian-news.com/msg04848.html

14. 'Moscow Special Conference on Afghanistan', Permanent Mission of Afghanistan in the United Nations, 30 March 2009, http://www.afghanistan-un.org/2009/03/moscow-special-conference-on-afghanistan/

15. M. Singh Roy (2010), 'Shanghai Cooperation Organisation and Afghanistan: Scope and Limitation', *Strategic Analysis*, 34(4), pp. 545–61.

16. M. Laruelle (2009), 'Beyond the Afghan Trauma: Russia's Return to Afghanistan', *Jamestown Occasional Paper*, August.

17. K. Katzman (2010), 'Afghanistan: Post-Taliban Governance, Security, and U.S. Policy', Congressional Research Service, 20 April; A. Kuhn (2009), 'China Becomes a Player in Afghanistan's Future', *NPR*, 21 October, http://www.npr.org/templates/story/story.php?storyId=113967842

18. N. Bordiuzha (2008), 'ODKB gotova k sotrudnichestvu s Afganistanom', *Afghanistan.ru*, 19 November, http://www.afghanistan.ru/doc/13412.html

19. A. Kuchins, T. Sanderson, and D. Gordon (2009), *The Northern Distribution Network and the Modern Silk Road*. Washington, DC: CSIS, December.

20. O.G. Mirutina (2003), *Perspektivy razvitiia sotrudnichestva Kitaia i Kazakhstana i ego znachenie dlia Rossii*. Master Thesis, Omsk University.

21. Peyrouse, 'Sino-Kazakh Relations: A Nascent Strategic Partnership'.

22. R.N. McDermott (2007), 'Kazakhstan's Emerging Security Ties with China,' *Central Asia and Caucasus Analyst*, 9 May, http://www.cacianalyst.org/?q=node/4684

23. A. Paramonov, and O. Stolpovskii (2007), *Kitai i Tsentral'naia Aziia: sotrudnichestvo v sfere bezopasnosti*, Ceasia, 31 July, http://www.ceasia.ru/bezopasnost/kitay-i-tsentralnaya-aziya-sotrudnichestvo-v-sfere-bezopasnosti.html; see also *French Embassy in Turkmenistan News Digest*, 22 January 2009.

24. R.N. McDermott (2005), 'China quietly Increases Military Links with Tajikistan', *Eurasia Daily Monitor*, 2(176), 21 September, http://www.jamestown.org/single/?no_cache=1&tx_ttnews%5Btt_news%5D=30885

25. 'Kitai i Tadzhikistan rasshiriat voennoe sotrudnichestvo', *Ni-hao.ru*, 15 May 2008, http://www.ni-hao.ru/news/china/1916

26. 'Kitai okazal Kyrgyzstanu voenno-tekhnicheskuiu pomoshch' v razmere 4 mln iuanei', *Novosti Kyrgyzstana*, 13 August 2008, http://www.for.kg/ru/news/69727/; and Paramonov, and Stolpovskii, *Kitai i Tsentral'naia Aziia: sotrudnichestvo v sfere bezopasnosti.*

27. 'Voennoe sotrudnichestvo Uzbekistana i Kitaia', *China Embassy in Uzbekistan*, no date, http://chinaembassy.uz/rus/dtxw/voennoe-sotrudnichestvo-uzbekistana-i-kitaya.htm

28. 'Kitai i Kazakhstan dostigli vysokogo urovnia vzaimoponimaniia—ministr oborony Kazakhstana', *Trends Kazakhstan*, 25 December 2009, http://ru.trend.az/news/politics/foreign/1607560.html; 'Podgotovka kazakhstanskikh voennosluzhashchikh v voenno-uchebnykh zavedeniiakh Kitaia', *Atyrau*, 26 January 2009,
http://atyrauobl.kz/podgotovka-kazaxstanskix-voennosluzhashhix-v-voenno-uchebnyx-zavedeniyax-kitaya/5950

29. H. Zhao (2006), 'The Shanghai Cooperation Organization at 5: Achievements and Challenges Ahead', *The China and Eurasia Forum Quarterly*, 4(3), pp. 105–23.

30. 'Nazarbayev Calls on Countries to Adopt Universal Declaration on Nuclear-free World', Interfax, 26 August 2010, http://www.interfax.com/newsinf.asp?id=185218; 'Kazakhstan calls on OSCE States to Adopt Declaration on Nuclear-free World,' RIA Novosti, 1 December 2010, en.rian.ru/world/20101201/161573340.html

31. V. Paramonov, and A. Strokov (2007), *Ekonomicheskoe prisutstvie Rossii i Kitaia v Tsentral'noi Azii*, Swindon: Defence Academy of the United Kingdom, Conflict Studies Research Center, Central Asian Series, 12 July.

32. On developments in Uzbek foreign policy in 2007–2008, see J. Nichol, 'Uzbekistan: Recent Developments and U.S. Interests', *Congressional Research Service*, 27 August 2008.

33. M. Laumulin (2006), *The Shanghai Cooperation Organization as Geopolitical Bluff?: A View from Astana.* Paris: IFRI, Series *Russie. NEI. Vision* no. 36.

34. S. Peyrouse (2011), 'Russia-Central Asia: Advances and Shortcomings of the Military Partnership', in S. Blank (ed.), *Central Asian Security Trends: Views from Europe and Russia.* Carlisle: Strategic Studies Institute, U.S. Army War College, pp. 1–34.

35. R.N. McDermott (2008), 'United States and NATO Military Cooperation with Kazakhstan: The Need for a New Approach', *The Journal of Slavic Military Studies*, 21(4), pp. 615–41.

36. On this point, see E. Madiev, 'Perspektivy internatsionalizatii kitaiskogo iuna v ramkakh ShOS,' *Kazakhstan v global'nykh protsessakh*, 2, 2010, pp. 124–9.

37. G. Gleason (2006), 'The Uzbek Expulsion of U.S. Forces and Realignment in Central Asia', *Problems of Post-Communism*, 53(2), pp. 49–60.

38. In a cable released by Wikileaks, the United States is allegedly able to prove that China offered the Kyrgyz authorities three billion dollars to close down their base at Manas. See D. Trilling (2010), 'China Gives U.S. Base Advice', Eurasianet.org, 29 November, http://www.eurasianet.org/node/62454

39. T. Ambrosio (2008), 'Catching the Shanghai Spirit: how the Shanghai Cooperation Organization Promotes Authoritarian Norms in Central Asia', *Europe-Asia Studies*, 60(8), pp. 1321–44.

40. S. Peyrouse (2006), 'Le tournant ouzbek de 2005. Éléments d'interprétation de l'insurrection d'Andijan', *La Revue internationale et stratégique*, 64, pp. 78–87; N. Megoran (2008), 'Framing Andijon, Narrating the Nation: Islam Karimov's Account of the events of 13 May 2005', *Central Asian Survey*, 27(1), pp. 15–31.

41. M. Katz (2008), 'Russia and the Shanghai Cooperation Organization: Moscow's Lonely Road from Bishkek to Dushanbe', *Asian Perspective*, 32(3), pp. 183–7; S. Peyrouse (2009), 'Facing the Challenge of Separatism: The EU, Central Asia and the Uyghur Issue', *EUCAM Brief Paper*, no. 4, January, http://www.eucentralasia.eu/fileadmin/user_upload/PDF/Policy_Briefs/Policy-Brief-4.Peyrouse.pdf

42. A. Iwashita (2004), 'The Shanghai Cooperation Organization and Its Implications for Eurasian Security: A New Dimension of "Partnership" after the post-Cold War Period', *Slavic Eurasia's Integration into the World Economy and Community*, Hokkaido: Slavic Research Center, Hokkaido University, pp. 259–81.

43. K.L. Syroezhkin (2006), *Problemy sovremennogo Kitaia i bezopasnost' v Tsentral'noi Azii*. Almaty: KISI.

44. A.J.K. Bailes, P. Dunay, P. Guang, and M. Troitskiy (2007), 'The Shanghai Cooperation Organization', *SIPRI Policy Paper* no. 17, May.

45. See the Declaration of the Tenth Meeting of the Council of the Heads of the Member States of the Shanghai Cooperation Organisation, 11 June 2010, http://www.sectsco.org/EN/show.asp?id=225

46. See their respective viewpoints in R. Zeb (2006), 'Pakistan and the Shanghai Cooperation Organization', *The China and Eurasia Forum Quarterly*, 4(4), pp. 51–60; 'India Keen to Become Member of SCO', *The Times of India*, 1 June 2010, http://timesofindia.indiatimes.com/india/India-keen-to-become-member-of-SCO/articleshow/5995619.cms

47. See the Iranian viewpoint in A.U. Noi (2006), 'Iran and the Shanghai Cooperation Organisation: Is it possible for Iran to become full member of the SCO under pressure of Nuclear Issue?', *Perceptions*, Autumn-Winter, pp. 79–104.

48. A.A. Pikayev (2008), 'Enlarging the Shanghai Cooperation Organization. Is Iran a Viable Member?', *PONARS Eurasia Policy Memo*, no. 15, August.

49. Interviews conducted at the main Chinese think tanks and research centers working on the former Soviet Union in Shanghai, Beijing, Lanzhou and Xi'an, September-December 2008.

50. V. Paramonov, and A. Strokov (2006), *Russian-Chinese Relations: Past, Present, Future,* Swindon: Defence Academy of the United Kingdom, Russian Series, September; B. Lo (2006), 'China and Russia. Common interests, Contrasting Perceptions', *CLSA Asian Geopolitics.* London: Chatham House, May.

51. Lo, 'China and Russia. Common interests, Contrasting Perceptions,' p. 4.

52. M. Laruelle, 'Russia Facing China and India in Central Asia: Cooperation, Competition, and Hesitations,' in Laruelle, Huchet, Peyrouse, and Balci (eds), *China and India in Central Asia. A new "Great Game"?*, pp. 9–24.

53. B. Lo (2008), *Axis of Convenience. Moscow, Beijing, and the New Geopolitics.* Washington DC, London: Brookings Institution Press and Chatham House.

54. A. Frost (2009), 'The Collective Security Treaty Organization, the Shanghai Cooperation Organization, and Russia's Strategic Goals in Central Asia', *The China and Eurasia Forum Quarterly*, 7(3), pp. 83–102.

55. A. Cooley (2009), 'The Stagnation of the SCO. Competing Agendas and Divergent Interests in Central Asia', *PONARS Memo* no. 85, September.

56. Also called the three extremisms (*sange jiduanzhuyi*). This ideological drive is sometimes called the 'Shanghai spirit.' See, for example, M. Oresman (2003), 'Catching the Shanghai Spirit', *Journal of Social Sciences* (Shanghai), no. 12, December, republished on http://www.foreignpolicy.com/articles/2004/05/01/catching_the_shanghai_spirit

7

India and Central Asia
Potential Implications for Power Rivalries in Eurasia

K. WARIKOO

Stretching from the Caspian Sea in the west to the western frontiers of China in the east, Central Asia has played an important role in the history and politics of Eurasia. In its past history, the Silk Route system provided a trans-continental bridge facilitating multilateral exchanges between Central Asia, Russia, China, West Asia, and the Indian subcontinent. During the nineteenth and early twentieth centuries, Central Asia was a zone of triangular contest between Britain, Russia, and China, which has been romanticized as the 'Great Game'. The disintegration of former USSR and the subsequent emergence of independent Central Asian Republics (CARs), all having predominantly Muslim population, changed the balance of power in this region. Due to its geographical proximity to China, Russia, West Asia, and South Asia, this region has emerged as a distinct geopolitical entity stimulating global attention and interest. Neighbouring countries like Russia, China, Iran, Turkey, Pakistan, and India have been pursuing competing, often overlapping, strategic, economic, and cultural interests in the region. They have been in the forefront of building new linkages with the independent CARs. On their part, the CARs have moved into a multilateral network of international relations by becoming members of United Nations (UN), Commonwealth of Independent States (CIS), Economic Cooperation Organization (ECO), Organisation of Islamic

Cooperation (OIC), Organization for Security and Co-operation in Europe (OSCE), etc. These Republics, keen to be self-reliant and independent, perceive the involvement of such international institutions in Central Asia as a guarantee for their independence. The political regimes in Central Asia have played their cards well, balancing their security interests by establishing bilateral and multilateral relations with Russia, China, USA, European Union, SCO, SCTO, OSCE, OIC, etc.

Central Asian Republics have passed through a stage of transformation into a new political, social, and economic order. Though post-Soviet Central Asia witnessed the rise of Islamic militancy, trans-border terrorism, inter-ethnic tensions, and ethno-religious resurgence, the conflicts in Afghanistan and Tajikistan helped in blunting the appeal of Islamic fundamentalism and its politics in Central Asia. However, inter-state border problems and economic difficulties remain potential sources of internal destabilization. Though there are problems of borders and disputes over water sharing, no Balkanization of the region or secession of any part has taken place. However, concerns have been expressed over the progress of democratization and sustainable economic development. Apprehensions of any breakdown of the sovereign statehood of the CARs have been proved wrong, with the consolidation of their national identity overcoming the difficulties of transition. These countries successfully completed their transition to sovereign independent statehood. The emphasis of the CARs throughout the period of their independent statehood has been on making bilateral relationships viable and effective.

Central Asia's geo-strategic importance is due to its rich energy reserves, existence of gas, and oil pipelines connecting China, Russia, Europe, Caucasus, and the Trans-Caspian region. Whereas the geo-strategic significance of Central Asia and big power interests in the region make it an area of great importance, there is need to engage in genuine partnership in the region in a spirit of non-hegemonic intentions. Cross-border energy projects have two major problems—investments and vulnerability to supply interruptions. The challenges like sovereignty of the nations, political barriers, security of supplies, lack of a holistic approach to energy security, paucity of infrastructure, etc., need to be met in order to develop the security aspect of energy cooperation and gradually bring it into the socio-economic dynamics in Central and South Asia. Apart from dialogues, knowledge-sharing mechanism, and bilateral transport linkages, a comprehensive framework is required to facilitate energy transit and trade by providing a level playing field to all countries concerned. Afghanistan becomes important as it provides a land bridge between Central Asia in the north and South Asia in the south. And the CARs have always been keen to extend their oil, gas, and transportation linkages with South Asia to the south, through Afghanistan, in order to reduce their dependence on the existing linkages with Russia. This will become possible only after Afghanistan becomes peaceful and stable.

The Afghan crisis has influenced all the CARs. Rise of the Taliban to power variously affected these countries, which sought to build secular democratic states. Though they followed different approaches to the Afghan conflict, there has been unanimity among the CARs over the threats posed by Islamist extremism of Taliban, terrorism, and drug trafficking. Security of Tajik-Afghan border remained the crucial issue. Tajikistan witnessed bloody civil war and conflict during the early and mid-1990s which fragmented the society and polity besides causing severe economic damage to the country. In the late 1990s, the country moved forward towards reconciliation between opposition and the government. Afghan conflict accompanied with trans-border terrorism, and arms and drug trafficking caused instability in the region. The crisis deepened during the Taliban period when Osama bin Laden and Al-Qaeda turned Afghanistan into the hub of terrorism and narcotic trafficking, adversely affecting security in the entire region. However, in the post-September 11 period, when Taliban were defeated and a new broad-based government was formed, the CARs felt relieved. Though the ouster of Taliban relaxed the security concerns of Central Asian countries bringing new hopes of building secular and democratic polity in Afghanistan, the CARs are now getting wary about the western moves of withdrawing their troops from Afghanistan and are deeply concerned about the security of the region.

India and Central Asian Republics

India and Central Asia have shared a geo-cultural affinity and a long tradition of historical contacts that dates back to antiquity. Notwithstanding the physical barriers of the high Himalayan and Hindu Kush mountain ranges, there existed close socio-economic and cultural ties between the people of

India and Central Asia. These linkages were cemented by the ideological force of Zoroastrianism, Buddhism, Islam, and Sufism; by the influx of Aryans, Sakas, Kushanas, Turks, Mughals, etc.; and by high mobility of statesmen, scholars, spiritualists, artists, craftsmen, literati, traders, etc. The movement of people, trade and ideas and the reciprocal cultural influences enriched the horizons of human development and left a deep imprint on the political, economic, and social life in the entire region.

Indian art, culture, and philosophy made a profound impact on the pre-Islamic Central Asia. The archaeological findings in northern India and Central Asia reveal remarkable parallels in stone and bone tools, pot forms, and other artefacts, which suggest a rare intensity of communication across the Himalayas since pre-historic times. Several important places on the Silk Route system such as Khotan, Kashgar, Balkh, Bamiyan, etc., developed into important centres of Buddhism, when parts of Central Asia and north-western India were integrated into a single kingdom under the Kushanas.

The establishment of Islam in Central Asia and its spread to India in medieval times lent a new dimension to the existing ties in the region. Influx of Muslim artisans, traders, Syeds, and mercenaries from Central Asia reshaped the geopolitical history of India. The Mughal rule that lasted for over 300 years changed the societal composition in India and led to the growth of an Indo-Islamic culture.

The incorporation of Central Asia and India in the Russian and British empires respectively and the subsequent Anglo-Russian rivalry in the region restricted the contacts between India and Central Asia. Tsarist Russia sought to use its strategic position in Central Asia to apply pressure on India which was perceived to be a sensitive nerve of the British Empire, which when touched, would put a brake on the British interference with Russian affairs in Europe. This Russian policy of strategic diversion was countered by the British by adopting a sustained forward policy in the region. After the October Revolution (1917), the British sought to halt the progress of Bolshevism in Central Asia. In their vain attempt to create and buttress 'tiny independent states in the Caucasus, Trans-Caspia, Central Asia, Persia, and Afghanistan, near the borders of India—hostile to Bolshevik Russia and under the tutelage of Britain'[1], the British used Kashmir and its frontier territories as a forward base to attain their strategic objectives in Central Asia. The British visualized India's north and north-west frontier as frontier listening posts and staging grounds for monitoring the developments in Central Asia and Xinjiang, and also for extending the British influence there, to stall the Russians. Curzon believed in the concept of India as a South and Central Asian power. India maintained a Consulate General in Kashgar till early 1950s. That Nehru had envisioned the need for India's maintaining physical contact with Central Asia, which becomes clear from his letter to Joseph Korbel, head of UNCIP Mission in 1948, urging him not to let Gilgit and northern areas, the frontier areas of Kashmir, having common borders with Xinjiang be part of Pakistani arrangements in Pak-occupied Kashmir so that the continuity of overland trade and traffic between India and Central Asia could be ensured through these high mountain passes/territory. Obviously, the idea behind this move was not followed up even by Nehru himself later on.

After India gained independence in 1947, her relations with Central Asia were renewed in the overall spirit of Indo-Soviet relations. When Central Asia had ceased to be an area of interest for the world, India was in constant touch with the people and developments there. During the Soviet period, India enjoyed an edge over its near and distant neighbours, in reaching out to Central Asia, due to friendly Indo-Soviet relations. Central Asia was accessible to Indian leaders/visitors, which was not the case with others. So much so, direct Indo-Central Asian contacts developed in diverse fields like trade, education and culture, science, technology, and films in the heyday of friendly Indo-Soviet ties, thereby creating a greater mutual understanding among the two sides. Indian Airlines used to operate bi-weekly flights to Tashkent.

The movement of trade, ideas, and reciprocal cultural influences have left a deep imprint on the social life and cultural traditions of this region. Popular usage of Indian spices, tea, medicinal herbs, etc., and quest for Indian films and songs in Central Asia, even today, reflects the age-old Indian connection. A common cultural pattern embracing various forms of expression like astronomy, philosophy, language, literature, folklore, architecture, arts and crafts, calligraphy, textiles, and food and dress habits developed in the process of socio-economic interaction between India and Central Asia. It is this consciousness of historical and cultural association dating back to antiquity and permeating the psyche of the people of the two regions, which provides a firm basis for constructive Indo-Central Asian cooperation in diverse sectors of socio-economic development.

On the diplomatic front, India established state relations with all the CARs soon after their independence, and opened diplomatic missions. Exchange of high-level political, diplomatic, business, and cultural delegations has been taking place between India and CARs regularly. India provided line of credit for the CARs. India views Central Asia as its extended neighbourhood and an area of vital strategic importance. There is convergence of views and interests between the CARs and India, on fundamental issues such as (a) need to maintain social harmony and equilibrium by promoting inter-ethnic harmony and peaceful co-existence; (b) commitment to secularism and democracy and opposition to religious fundamentalism; (c) recognition of threat to regional security and stability from trans-border terrorism, arms and drug trafficking, religious extremism, and ethnic-religious secessionism; (d) commitment to the principles of territorial integrity of nation states and inviolability of state borders; and (e) promoting economic, scientific, and cultural cooperation. This mutual political understanding needs to be reinforced through synergy of thought and action between various Indian government agencies, universities, and institutions so that the historical and cultural linkages between India and Central Asia are strengthened and developed into a fund of goodwill, love, and harmony at the grassroots level.

Strengthening Cultural Ties

Soon after their independence, the CARs have been experiencing the resurgence of indigenous culture and traditions. The CARs are attaching great importance to the rediscovery of their past and are consolidating their national identity on the basis of their indigenous ethno-cultural heritage. This offers ample opportunity to India to reinvigorate the age-old historic-cultural ties with Central Asia.

The Government of India has taken several steps like establishing full-fledged Indian Cultural Centres in Tashkent, Almaty/Astana, and Dushanbe besides setting up India Chairs/Study Centres in Osh, Tashkent, etc. India has also been facilitating the visit and study of few hundred students from various CARs at various Indian universities and institutes by providing scholarships under its ITEC and ICCR programmes. Time has come to review the efficacy of these cultural centres and cultural exchange programmes. Experience shows that for fulfilling the targets and stated objectives in theory, little impact has been created on the ground so that Indian political and strategic objectives in Central Asia could be attained.

It is high time that all the antiquities, frescoes, manuscripts, inscriptions, artefacts, etc., which are lying scattered in various parts of Central Asia either at the sites or in local museums are documented. Indian specialists/ archaeologists need to work urgently in close collaboration with their Central Asian counterparts, to undertake the hitherto neglected task of identification, location, documentation, and dissemination of such a rich and common historic-cultural legacy. Similarly, there is need for preparing a cumulative catalogue of the artefacts, manuscripts, etc., which were excavated by the Western archaeologists such as Aurel Stein, Albert Grundwel, Albert Von le Coq, Paul Pelliot, Sven Hedin, L. Warner, Count Otani, and also by the Soviet archaeologists in various parts of Central Asia, which are presently scattered in different museums throughout the world. Steps also need to be taken to identify and preserve the literary, historical, and artistic works. Old classics in Kharosthi, Turkic, Persian, Uyghur, Mongolian, etc., that have been found in various parts of Central Asia, can be microfilmed and published possibly with English translations. International Institute of Central Asian Studies, Indira Gandhi National Centre for the Arts (IGNCA), Samarkand, and UNESCO should co-opt various experts in the field and initiate a concrete programme of identification, documentation, video-filming, and preservation of these antiquities, which can otherwise be lost into oblivion.

The Archaeological Survey of India needs to step in to help in excavating, conserving, and restoring such ancient sites which are presently lying in a dilapidated condition, so that the testimony of historical and cultural relationship between India and Central Asia does not get destroyed through the vagaries of nature, time, and neglect. These sites and monuments, now in ruins, can easily be restored and developed into important cultural centres after doing the requisite renovations and providing all the facilities of a modern museum.

The process of academic and cultural exchanges between Indian and Central Asian centres of learning, universities, institutes, etc., needs to be streamlined and institutionalized, so that Indian specialists on Central Asia are able to collaborate with their counterparts in their areas of study/specialization. This can be made possible through liberal support to various Area Studies Centres on Central Asia by the UGC and various government agencies. Another vital area of cultural cooperation is joint production of films, television serials, publication of books, exchange of print and visual materials, and regular exchange of artistes.

Enhancing Trade Relations

Though India's trade with Central Asia goes back to the Silk Route days, Central Asian Republics form a minuscule proportion of Indian export-import trade. After the collapse of USSR and emergence of independent Central Asian Republics, the situation changed drastically. There was a sharp decline in the Indo-Russian/CIS trade. During the year 1990–1, Indian exports to USSR were of the order of US$ 2935.04 million, whereas imports from USSR amounted to US$ 1422.14 million. In 1992–3, Indian exports to CIS dropped to US$ 584.62 million, whereas Indian imports were worth US$ 258.17 million only. Indian trade with CIS started growing from 1996–7 onwards. Indian exports to CIS reached US$ 915 million as against imports from CIS worth US$ 841.01 million during 2002–3. Though trade between India and Central Asian Republics has started picking up from the year 2004–5 onwards, it is far behind the actual potential. Total volume of this trade for the period 1996–7 to 2009–10 has only been US$ 2981 million. (For details see tables at the end of this essay.) As such, India's potential in the traditional sector is yet to be harnessed.

The main obstacles in the trilateral trade are:

1. Lack of direct overland access
2. Macroeconomic instability in Central Asia
3. Inadequate banking facilities
4. Strict visa regimes and language barriers
5. Lack of trade dynamism and entrepreneurship among Indian businessmen.
6. Failure of India to secure air connections, remove customs/tariffs bottlenecks to motivate Indian enterprises for joint ventures in CARs.

India can substantially raise its level of exports of tea, pharmaceuticals, and consumer goods to CARs. India also needs to focus on trade and investment opportunities in the service sector including banking, insurance, healthcare, IT software, tourism, and education (in English medium). Indian concept of alternative medicine has become very popular in CARs. India needs to become a construction sector player in the exploitation and distribution of the Central Asian energy resources. Indian firms need to join international consortia for oil and gas exploration in Central Asia and the Caspian, thus securing energy security for India. India has sound technology of refineries at par with established international standards. So, India can help in modernizing refineries in CARs. There is scope for India's involvement in modernizing refineries, laying pipelines, investment in retail outlets/infrastructure, and marketing of petroleum products.

There is enough scope for cooperation with Kazakhstan in uranium processing, nuclear reactors, space stations, refining and processing of oil, laying of pipelines; with Tajikistan on setting up of joint ventures for exploration and processing of silver, aluminium, and uranium; with Kyrgyzstan on joint ventures in various sectors like IT, pharmaceuticals; with Uzbekistan in joint ventures on textiles, food/fruit processing, oil and gas processing/refining, pharmaceuticals, production of transport planes, etc. India would do well in foraying into management and marketing of petroleum products rather than exploitation. Swap deals is another option. India and Iran can enter into such swap deals. There is need for evolving new mechanisms regarding the energy relationship between India and Iran which has become all the more necessary due to US sanctions on Iran forcing India to seek alternative modes of payment to Iran for its oil imports. It becomes imperative to evolve a trilateral cooperative fuel swap arrangement between Iran, India, and CARs, under which Iran could export its energy to India from its terminals in return for an equal amount of oil tapped by Indian firms in Central Asia which can be delivered by them across the border to Iran.

India and Kazakhstan

Kazakhstan looks itself as a bridge between Europe and Asia with its focus on establishing multilateral economic and relations with all countries within the CIS, with Russia, USA, European Union, China, etc. With its borders touching Russia in the north, Kyrgyzstan, Uzbekistan, and Turkmenistan in the south, and China in the east, Kazakhstan enjoys a central position in Eurasia which also contributes to its unique strategic importance in the region. According to President Nazarbayev of Kazakhstan who broached the idea of Eurasianism, Kazakhstan being at the centre of Eurasia, would be a connecting link between Russia, China, and the Muslim world.

Kazakhstan has been making efforts to expand friendly relations with all countries, especially in close and extended neighbourhoods. India is the first country outside the CIS, which was visited by the President of Kazakhstan, Nursultan Nazarbayev, in the year 1992. Trade between India and Kazakhstan does not match the existing vast potential in this sector. According to statistics, bilateral trade was around US$ 313.85 million in 2009–10 as compared to just 16.96 million US dollars in 1996–7. Since 2002, Kazakh-India Joint Working Group on Combating International Terrorism has been working on the joint action against terrorism, extremism, drugs trafficking, illegal trade of arms, and organized crime. Kazakhstan-India Inter-governmental Commission on Trade, Economic, Scientific, Technological, Industrial, and Cultural Cooperation has been playing a sheet-anchor role in cooperation between the two republics in the fields such as trade, economy, energy, information technology, science and technology, etc. President Nazarbayev paid a state visit to India on 23–26 January 2011 and he was the Chief Guest at India's Republic Day celebrations on 26 January. During his visit, India and Kazakhstan adopted a joint declaration on strategic partnership. Kazakhstan has been supportive of India's permanent membership of the UN Security Council. However, given the past experience of China outbidding India to acquire the Petrokazakh deal in 2005, one hopes that the agreements between ONGC Videsh Ltd with 25 per cent stakes and Kazmunaigaz with 75 per cent for exploration of oil and gas in Satpayev oil block gets implemented. Another project between NPCIL and Kazatomprom, envisaging cooperation including supply of uranium to India is also in the agenda.

India and Uzbekistan

Being situated between the two giant Central Asian rivers—Syr Darya and Amu Darya, and bordering all the countries of Central Asia plus Afghanistan, but with no borders with Russia and China, Uzbekistan is well described as the heart of Central Asia. With a territory of about 4,48,000 sq. km and population of over 26 million, Uzbekistan is the most populous country in the region. Uzbekistan enjoys a unique geopolitical location in Central Asia. Being conscious of the richness of their natural resources, agriculture, and their ancient and rich historic-cultural heritage and unique geopolitical position, Uzbekistan and its people harbour the aspiration to be the regional power in Central Asia. President of Uzbekistan, Islam Karimov's priorities have been to ensure peace and security, stability, and sustainable development. As a means to consolidate the sovereignty of Uzbekistan, a policy of reducing its dependence on Russia, diversification of economic relations, and making new alliances outside the CIS has been adopted. Uzbekistan moved closer to the United States and Europe, besides being the member of NATO's Partnership for Peace programme. At the same time, indigenization of Uzbekistan's security and defence structures has been undertaken.

India and Uzbekistan have taken several tangible steps towards security cooperation. Sharing same views on Afghanistan, both countries have been cooperating on the issues of terrorism, drugs trafficking, and arms smuggling. Apart from the training of Uzbek military personnel in India, India has purchased a military transport aircraft built by the Chakalov Aircraft Factory at Tashkent. During the recent state visit of Uzbek President Islam Karimov to India on 17–18 May 2011, both countries declared that their relations had been elevated to a long term and strategic partnership, which would encompass active cooperation in a wide spectrum of areas including political, economic, counter-terrorism, education, health, science, technology, tourism, culture, etc. Both sides shared their views on the unstable situation in Afghanistan and the challenges emanating from the region.

However, Uzbekistan views Afghanistan and Pakistan as the transit corridor for access to South Asia, as an alternative to existing routes to Russia in the north. Uzbekistan, with the support of South Korea, has developed Novoi region as free economic zone and the main logistic hub for transit trade and freight flows. Korean Air has been managing Novoi airport since 2009. Now, Novoi is being provided to USA as air base. Meanwhile, Uzbekistan, Iran, and Afghanistan are developing trans-Afghanistan corridor. Iran has initiated work on building Kerman-Zahidan rail which will go directly to Pakistan. Iran has also constructed railway to Herat; thus connecting western Afghanistan. Uzbekistan is working to connect Kharaton and Mazar-e-Sharif in Northern Afghanistan, which is planned to be connected to Meshad-Zahidan and Pakistan.

Foreign and Transport ministers of Uzbekistan, Iran, and Turkmenistan met in Tehran in November 2010 and agreed to build a new transportation corridor between Persian Gulf and Central Asia through Iran. President Karimov had earlier visited Turkmenistan on 19–20 October 2010 and discussed with Turkmen President G. Berdemuhamedov about the issue of opening of a transport corridor of Uzbekistan-Turkmenistan-Iran-Oman-Qatar in the region. Soon after, Karimov visited Qatar on 23–24 November 2010. This initiative has the support of Persian Gulf states as well as Saudi Arabia. Thus, Indian efforts to reach Central Asia through Iran via Bander Abbas, Chah Bahar, and through Afghanistan via Delaram-Zaranj are being sidestepped.

Uzbeks see India's role as that of stopping Chinese penetration through China's growing presence in Central Asia, or even Russian influence. Whereas Uzbekistan's official position is to support 'one China' policy and oppose Uyghur separatism in Xinjiang, on the Kashmir issue, Uzbekistan's standard position has been to support dialogue as a way to resolve the Indo-Pak dispute.

There is scope for greater Indo-Uzbek cooperation in matters of counter-terrorism, intelligence sharing between defence and security establishments, Afghanistan, etc. Value of bilateral trade between India and Uzbekistan has increased from a mere US$ 10.74 million in 1996–7 to US$ 124.9 million in the year 2009. There is need for setting up joint ventures in textile, leather, sericulture, food and fruit processing, pharmaceuticals, machinery and instruments, IT, etc. Indian textile company Spintex, which has acquired three textile mills in Uzbekistan, is a success story. Recently, ONGC Videsh Ltd. and Uzbekneftegaz have signed an MOU on cooperation in oil and gas exploration, production, joint participation in oil producing assets in Uzbekistan and third countries.

During a visit to Uzbekistan in December 2004, the author visited Chakalov Aircraft Factory in Tashkent. Kucherov, the then Chairman of Tashkent Aircraft Production Corporation, was keen to upgrade his company's cooperation with India. He was keen to cooperate with HAL, Bengaluru. This factory was a joint stock company, 51 per cent share being owned by Uzbekistan. And at that time, 25.6 per cent share were offered to international investors. One doubts whether India has availed this opportunity. Since 1990s, India has been acquiring IL-76 military transport aircraft and later, since 2001, six refuelling planes were purchased by India.

Towards a Mutual Transit Corridor

India needs to explore viable and alternative oil and gas transit routes to Central Asia. Russia-China-Central Asia-India pipeline route is a distinct possibility. Similarly, India can secure direct land access to CARs, via Ladakh-Xinjiang-Kyrgyzstan-Kazakhstan, thereby becoming part of the great Eurasian land bridge, which is in the making. Thus, India will be physically there in Central Asia. Only one country, China, is involved as transit point between India and Central Asian Republics. India needs to have a long term and comprehensive strategy in Central Asia, with a set of objectives and commitment/motivation to achieve the same.

1. Pakistan-Afghanistan route has a question mark, as Pakistan holds the key to switch off the gas/oil supplies at their will, thus rendering the huge infrastructure set up in India for the purpose, as infructuous. The uncertain situation in Baluchistan and Afghanistan also act as inhibiting factors for successful operationalization of this route.

2. The trilateral agreement between Iran, India, and Turkmenistan signed in February 1997, providing for the movement of goods through Bandar Abbas-Mashed-Tajend Route, in theory resolved the problem of access for Indian goods in CARs. But in practice, this route is still beset with several problems. There are problems of loading, unloading, reloading, restrictive customs and tariffs, container availability, different railway gauges in Iranian and Turkmen territory, warehousing, etc. India has completed the construction of Zaranj-Delaram road in Afghanistan, braving multiple attacks by the Taliban, with the objective of linking it to Chah Bahar port in Iran, for securing access to Central Asia. But Indian plans for enlarging Chah Bahar five times and constructing a railway line to Bam on the Iran-Afghan border, continue to be discussed endlessly with Iran, without any progress on the ground.[2] Besides, the oldest venture of the Shipping Corporation of India (SCI) with the Islamic Republic of Iran Shipping Lines (IRISL), known as the Irano Hind Shipping Company, is targeted by the US sanctions. With the

result, seven Indian vessels are lying idle. There is also a lurking fear that the seven vessels may be confiscated on some pretext, as the US is targeting the IRISL. US Under Secretary of Terrorism and Financial Intelligence, Stuart Levey stated in December 2010, 'IRISL, which we designated in 2008, has renamed and even repainted ships, and changed the nominal ownership of vessels, all to hide their connection to the shipping company'.[3]

So, India needs to revive its overland link with the Silk Route, and be part of the process, rather be out of it. India has done well, fostering bilateral relations with individual CARs. But, India has not been part of any regional security, political, or economic arrangement. India needs to have a comprehensive proactive policy and not a reactive one dominated by the Pakistan factor. For this, India needs to have access, besides being part of regional institutional mechanisms. India remained indifferent and out of Tajikistan peace process although Russia wished it to be there, 6 + 2 arrangement for dealing with Afghanistan crisis, and has been out of SCO. Now, it is the best time to join SCO in a dignified way. Indian diplomacy should ensure that India is invited to be a member of SCO. The SCO has evolved as an effective regional institutional mechanism of multilateral cooperation between CARs, Russia, and China.

As regards the two pipeline projects—Iran-Pakistan-India (IPI) and Turkmenistan-Afghanistan-Pakistan-India (TAPI) —the United States has been openly backing the TAPI project. Whereas, in case of IPI pipeline, India has been insisting on the delivery of gas at the India-Pakistan border, it has agreed to buy gas at Turkmenistan-Afghanistan border in case of the TAPI project, obviously under the United States pressure. United States Deputy Secretary of State on South and Central Asian Affairs, while speaking at an energy conference in Turkmenistan in November 2010, described the TAPI route as 'a stabilizing corridor, linking neighbours together in economic growth and prosperity'. However, Pakistan—the beneficiary of US largesse—went ahead in signing an agreement on pipeline with Iran in March 2010. Whichever pipeline project—TAPI or IPI—is joined by India, it should take into account the security concerns and see that the natural gas is delivered at India's borders with guarantees of assured and unhindered supply. Of the 1680 km long TAPI pipeline, 735 km pass through the tough terrains of Herat, Lashkar Gah, and Kandahar. And the route has too many impediments including mines. Besides, Afghanistan has taken a strident position asking India to link the transit fee to the gas fee, instead of a fixed fee as has been agreed by Pakistan and Iran for the IPI pipeline.[4] One wonders if Indian engagement with Karzai government in Afghanistan including US$ 1.5 billion aid for reconstruction and humanitarian assistance is yielding any positive results or not. As such, both the security concerns and commercial issues of transit fees to be charged by Afghanistan and Pakistan, and the final price of gas are yet to be resolved. However, the United States of America is promoting TAPI not only as an alternative to the IPI, but also as a means to break Russian monopoly on the export of Central Asian gas to outside markets.

Pakistan has been consistent in its policy of blocking the overland Central Asia-Afghanistan-Pakistan corridor to India for import of energy resources and export of Indian goods. The experience shows that Pakistan has not granted India any transit access to send even its humanitarian assistance in the form of wheat and other commodities to Afghanistan. The Afghanistan-Pakistan Trade Transit Agreement, which was finalized on 19 July 2010 in the presence of US Secretary of State, Hillary Clinton, while allowing Afghan trucks to carry goods to the Wagah border for onward dispatch to India, does not allow these trucks to carry back Indian goods to Afghanistan. In return, Afghanistan has allowed Pakistani trucks to go through Afghanistan to Central Asia, Iran, and Turkey. Earlier, Afghan trucks were allowed to carry goods only to the Pak-Afghan border at Torkham. Pakistan's Information Minister, Qamar Zaman Kaira, clarified that 'according to the agreement approved by Pakistan's cabinet, Afghan goods will be allowed to transit through Pakistan in sealed containers having tracking devices'.[5] Though India has recently allowed duty-free market access to Afghanistan,[6] it has been denied transit access through Pakistan to Afghanistan and onwards to Central Asia. Pakistan has linked this transit passage and other bilateral trade issues with India to the final resolution of Kashmir.

The establishment of multipurpose Gwadar Port complex with direct express highways, pipelines, and other infrastructures linking Pakistan to Xinjiang province of China through an upgraded Karakoram Highway and onwards to Central Asia, poses a major challenge to India. Pakistan recently approved US$ 90 million for the restoration of Karakoram Highway.[7] Indian policy makers need to review India's policy towards the region and also to expedite the process of upgradation/construction of border roads and related infrastructure in order to ensure better connectivity with Indian frontier stations like Ladakh.

As such, the proposals to open up the traditional Leh-Demchok-Gartok-Lhasa and Leh-Demchok-Yarkand-Kashgar trade routes need to be considered actively on an urgent basis, so that India will be able to open up its direct channel of communication with China's frontier province of Xinjiang and through it with the CARs. The existing unresolved state of Sino-Indian border in Ladakh need not come in the way of pushing such proposals, as Nathu La pass in Sikkim has already been opened for trade purposes. Besides, Srinagar-Muzaffarabad road has been opened, notwithstanding Pakistan's intransigence and insistence on Kashmir being the core issue and dispute between India and Pakistan.

The United States has been promoting the concept of Greater Central Asia, which seeks to interlink and integrate Central and South Asia. The United States has already merged the South Asia and Central Asia Bureaus in the Department of State into one. Whereas the United States' goal remains to wear away CARs from the Russian and Chinese influence, it is practically strengthening infrastructural linkages between the CARs, Afghanistan, and Pakistan. The United States assisted in the construction of a bridge over the Pyanj river connecting Tajikistan and Afghanistan. Given its experience with Pakistan, India needs to tread with caution on the concept of Greater Central Asia, which assigns a crucial role to Afghanistan and Pakistan. Whereas Afghanistan has direct borders with Central Asia, Pakistan has ensured its direct access to Central Asia via Karakoram Highway and now the Gwadar Port.

The CARs, being cautious and wary of the dominating influence of the powerful neighbours like Russia and China, and the current regimes in Central Asia getting irritated at times by the United States manoeuvres and initiatives in the name of promoting democracy and human rights, look towards India as a friend and partner, which does not have any political or territorial ambitions in the region. India is also expected to play a balancing role in the big power games in Central Asia.

India's Trade with Kazakhstan (in US$ million)

Year	Exports	Imports	Total Trade
1996–7	4.39	12.57	16.96
1997–8	15.13	36.03	51.16
1998–9	38.00	12.43	50.43
1999–2000	27.19	13.45	40.64
2000–1	50.08	14.04	64.12
2001–2	45.70	7.39	53.09
2002–3	46.88	12.73	59.60
2003–4	74.81	9.26	84.07
2004–5	81.42	15.39	96.81
2005–6	90.86	26.30	117.16
2006–7	83.18	88.30	171.48
2007–8	111.99	76.78	188.77
2008–9	131.68	159.03	290.71
2009–10	136.54	154.91	291.45

India's Trade with Uzbekistan (in US$ million)

Year	Exports	Imports	Total Trade
1996–7	8.14	2.60	10.74
1997–8	17.59	2.71	20.30
1998–9	12.83	1.67	14.50
1999–2000	9.94	12.97	22.91
2000–1	9.39	10.58	19.97
2001–2	6.53	17.27	23.80
2002–3	5.08	20.54	25.62
2003–04	15.14	27.70	42.84
2004–5	21.35	31.46	52.81
2005–6	24.44	26.13	50.57
2006–7	29.69	33.91	63.60
2007–8	40.32	16.20	56.52
2008–9	45.53	70.74	116.27
2009–10	54.03	29.97	84.00

India's Trade with Tajikistan (in US$ million)

Year	Imports	Exports	Total Trade
1996–7	0.80	0.73	1.53
1997–8	–	1.12	1.12
1998–9	2.53	0.51	3.04
1999–2000	2.33	2.38	4.71
2000–1	0.54	3.55	4.09
2001–2	1.34	1.22	2.56
2002–3	0.08	8.65	8.73
2003–4	3.95	4.47	8.42
2004–5	4.09	6.59	10.68
2005–6	5.89	6.24	12.13
2006–7	7.95	7.46	15.41
2007–8	9.81	12.40	22.21
2008–9	17.47	16.71	34.18
2009–10	16.85	15.71	32.56

India's Trade with Kyrgyzstan (in US$ million)

Year	Exports	Imports	Total Trade
1996–7	0.98	–	0.98
1997–8	10.79	0.01	10.80
1998–9	8.70	0.10	8.80
1999–2000	13.80	1.82	15.62
2000–1	17.59	4.43	22.02
2001–2	10.97	0.56	11.52
2002–3	14.67	0.47	15.13
2003–4	38.20	0.54	38.74
2004–5	49.57	0.63	50.19
2005–6	28.09	1.47	29.57
2006–7	37.08	0.76	37.84
2007–8	31.52	0.91	32.43
2008–9	22.92	1.03	23.95
2009–10	26.84	0.64	27.48

India's Trade with Turkmenistan (in million US$)

Year	Exports	Imports	Total Trade
1996–7	1.38	0.27	1.65
1997–8	1.68	0.02	1.7
1998–9	1.93	0.11	2.04
1999–2000	5.64	0.38	6.02
2000–1	2.71	1.12	3.83
2001–2	4.35	1.95	6.30
2002–3	10.29	5.40	15.70
2003–4	19.21	9.34	28.55
2004–5	15.26	10.87	26.12
2005–6	18.83	12.35	31.18
2006–7	33.99	11.95	45.94
2007–8	36.09	8.55	44.64
2008–9	41.40	12.10	53.50
2009–10	36.15	10.00	46.15

Source: Export Import Data Bank, Department of Commerce, Government of India, Accessed at http://commerce.nic.in/eidb/default.asp

Notes and References

1. For further details, see K. Warikoo (1989), *Central Asia and Kashmir: A Study in the Context of Anglo-Russian Rivalry*, New Delhi, pp. 183–202.
2. See Sandeep Dikshit (2010), 'Cost of Indifference Being Paid in Afghanistan', *The Hindu*, 30 December.
3. See Jayanth Jacob (2011), 'Shipping JV with Iran may Sink', *Hindustan Times*, 12 February.
4. See Jayanth Jacob (2011), 'Kabul Rider on TAPI Gas Pipeline Shocks Delhi', *Hindustan Times*, 19 June.
5. See 'Pak Lets Af Trucks on Way to India Pass,' *The Times of India*, 8 October 2011, p. 17.
6. See *The Hindu*, 4 June 2011.
7. See *Hindustan Times*, 30 July 2011.

8

Central Asia as Potential Theatre of Non-traditional Conflict

AJAY PATNAIK

Traditional conception of security emphasizes on threats that are essentially related to external military threats, which undermine the security of the sovereign state and its territorial integrity. Post-Second World War period was the time of resurgent realism which centred on security around the nation-state and emphasised the use of force as a means to resolve conflict between states. Hans Morganthau considered that security of the state was best achieved by the maximization of military power. Throughout the Cold War period, security perspectives were based on state-centric approach of classical realism and neo-realism, which considered empowerment of military power as the cornerstone of national security.[1]

However, as experience shows, sources of insecurity are not only the mutual competition among states but also the failure of states to provide for peoples' security. According to traditional notions of security, sovereignty, and statehood are adequately secured by military defence of state interests and its territory. The security concept that evolved in the 1980s broadened the concept of security to include non-military security threats or non-traditional threats that originate from a variety of problems such as economic, social, environmental, political, and so on. It focuses on human security and is centred on the empowerment of the people in comparison with various problems, conflicts, and issues.

Richard H. Shultz defines non-traditional security as a complex myriad of threats—internal, regional, and transnational—wherein a large number of actors are involved, both governmental and non-governmental, where violence is generated not only by conventional physical force, but by economic, environmental, and social forces. He further categorizes the non-traditional threats as natural environment threats like epidemics, diseases, droughts, catastrophic flooding, and pollution further exacerbated by social unrest and violence/internal conflict/complex emergencies (dissident groups, civil war, rebel, or secessionist movements, organized crime refugee-related issues) and non-traditional regional and transnational threats, including cross-border insurgency, ethnic militias, foreign-based terrorism, international organized crime, and internal war spill over.[2]

According to Barry Buzan, a security analyst, there is a tri-pronged approach to security studies in the post-Cold War era. First school of thought is the Traditionalists, who retain the military focus of security. Second school of thought is the Wideners, who extend the range of security issues to include threats other than military ones. Third school of thought is the Critical Security Studies, who have a questioning attitude to the whole framework in which security is conceptualized. Buzan proposes a constructivist method for security, which synthesizes all the three schools of thought and offers a multisectoral approach, including in its ambit the environmental, economic, social and political as well as military sectors, and including cross-linkages between them.[3]

It seems that the new security concerns are not mutually exclusive but overlap and have linkages with traditional security issues. The act of addressing these non-traditional security issues has become apparent for the following reasons:[4]

1. Many of these issues are beyond the capacity of the individual states to tackle alone.
2. Increasing inter-dependence of security issues.
3. Increase in the environment of traditional non-state actors as security threats, for example, Al-Qaeda.

The Buzan theory is germane to Central Asian security in the past two decades. Central Asia, comprising of Uzbekistan, Kazakhstan, Tajikistan,

Turkmenistan, and Kyrgyzstan, have become the focus of attention of several regional and global powers. However, the importance of the region is mostly recognized from a strategic point of view. Huge amounts of natural resources such as oil, gas, minerals, etc., have attracted outside powers. At the same time, the challenge is not just to balance the interests of external powers, but the internal conflicts that can arise from many unresolved problems within the states. Terrorism, border dispute, ethnic conflicts, competition for energy, and pipeline along with poverty and environmental degradation create instability and affect security of the Central Asian states.

The threats to Central Asian security are both external and internal. Though military security is still relevant, challenges from non-traditional threats seem greater than traditional ones. Ethnic, religious, and linguistic issues are part of the social sphere which can create instability. Similarly, poverty, hunger, unemployment, and unequal distribution of wealth are related to economic insecurity. Environmental issues are going to pose the biggest challenge to the regional states in the near future. The desiccation of the Aral Sea is endangering the health and lives of hundreds of thousands of people cutting across republics. Water-related confrontations are very much likely, given the problem of water in the region. The cross-linkage between traditional and non-traditional issues that Buzan talks about can be relevant to the Central Asian context as well. Many issues like water, environment, terrorism, and interethnic relations can also become catalysts for conflict between states. This paper highlights how some of the non-traditional security threats can impact relations between states and how states in the region try to avoid such possibilities.

Water and Environment

Central Asian countries possess considerable energy resources. However, they are distributed unequally. While Kazakhstan, Uzbekistan, and Turkmenistan possess world's significant reserves of fossil fuel—oil and gas—Kyrgyzstan and Tajikistan have limited access to these resources, but possess considerable water and hydropower resources. Naturally, aspiration of each of these countries is to direct the natural resources, first of all, for the benefit of their own country.

There is a serious mismatch between the supply of water among upstream and downstream countries. Lower stream countries, especially

Uzbekistan and Turkmenistan, are more dependent on water resources of the upper stream countries like Kyrgyzstan and Tajikistan where water is in abundance. The two main basins of Syr Darya and Amu Darya rivers are shared by several states, but the lower stream especially the more populous states like Uzbekistan and Kazakhstan are in a disadvantageous position as compared to less populous upper stream countries—Kyrgyzstan and Tajikistan. Despite the fact that Syr Darya is divided among four countries, beginning from Kyrgyzstan, passing through Uzbekistan, Tajikistan, and finally running in to Kazakhstan, its water is not evenly distributed. Uzbekistan, the most populous country in Central Asia, does not control the important stretch of the Syr Darya with the Karakum reservoir that passes through Khodjent region of Tajikistan and gives later only 9 per cent of the total usable water for regulation in the Syr Darya basin.[5]

According to Uzbekistan, hydroelectric projects both in Tajikistan and Kyrgyzstan are being planned unmindful of Uzbek apprehensions that damming up of rivers that feed great Amu Darya and Syr Darya waterways, will starve it of the irrigation facilities on which its agriculture depends. The launching of hydroelectric power stations entails filling up of reservoirs over several years. Therefore, if these upper stream countries went ahead with such power projects, Uzbekistan would face a huge water shortage problem during the period of the filling up of the reservoir—a situation that could be disastrous for agriculture of the country.

However, from Tajikistan's perspective, the reality is different. According to Tajik scholar Abdurahim Juraev, 'If nature has deprived Tajikistan of plain lands, it has simultaneously lavished the country with its infinite wealth—water. However, till now Tajikistan has chosen for itself the role of being a source of water, not its destination.' Potential of water power in Tajikistan are unique; it occupies one of the leading places in the world, but uses only 5 per cent of this potential. As a result, hydropower resources are distributed unevenly in the territory of the republic.[6] Nearly 93 per cent of the total area of Tajikistan is occupied by mountains. This creates possibilities as well as restrictions in the process of economic and social development. Nowadays, energy independence for Tajikistan has become an especially critical issue. Considering all of these, sharp deficiency in the availability of electric power, increasing tariffs for electricity and gas, and the increasing tendency to import from abroad, have created special difficulties for maintenance of basic conditions of life for a number of years.[7]

Water sharing, thus, could be a cause of actual or potential conflicts involving the Central Asian states. For instance, Tajikistan's plans for expanding upstream hydropower capacity by completing a number of dams along Amu Darya, unfinished from Soviet days, have roused concern in Uzbekistan. Similarly, Kyrgyzstan's Kambarata I and II have generated fears of conflict with neighbours. Uzbekistan has done what it can to block construction of the biggest hydroelectric project in Tajikistan—the Rogun project. Uzbekistan has called upon the international community to conduct an independent study of the Rogun project, noting that much has changed in the region since the Soviets first conceived the plan in 1976.

The Tajiks accuse the Uzbek government of curtailing the overland transit of goods to their landlocked country although the Uzbeks insist that the delays in railroad shipments have nothing to do with the dam issue. The Uzbeks have also partially suspended electricity supplies from Turkmenistan to Tajikistan and cut off their own exports of urgently needed natural gas to the Tajiks. Some experts contend that these reprisals will hit Tajik industry hard and plunge its entire population into darkness. Others say that such fears are exaggerated.[8] Not only states in the region, but even Russia has been dragged into dispute in the water conflicts since major projects in Tajikistan and Kyrgyzstan were planned with expectations of huge Russian investments. When Russia showed reluctance, the regional partners were not pleased. From a geopolitical point of view, the above two Central Asian states are closer to Russian allies as compared to Uzbekistan. Russia's reluctance to assist the projects might affect its strategic influence.

Russian President Dmitry Medvedev, during his visit to Uzbekistan in January 2009, after meeting his Uzbek counterpart Islam Karimov on 23 January declared that Russian investment for building hydro-electric power stations in Kyrgyzstan and Tajikistan would be undertaken only if schemes took in to account the interests of other states of the region.[9] Such projects, involving rivers that cross state borders, had to be agreed by all affected countries, not just direct beneficiaries who are required to adhere to environmental and other international standards. This indicated a major shift in the earlier Russian position that favoured hydro-electric projects both in Tajikistan and Kyrgyzstan. Earlier, Russia's position of supporting the projects coincided with Uzbekistan's pro-US policies. Since 2005, after the United States' base in Uzbekistan was closed, the relations between Moscow and Tashkent looked up. Thus, water issue is also likely to have cross-linkages like inter-state relations and geopolitical moves of external powers.

Poverty and Deprivation

Transition from a centrally planned economy to a market-oriented one has so far been both complex and painful. The social sector remains in bad shape and can create socio-political unrest until urgent steps are taken. Unemployment, both official and disguised, is at a high level. In Kazakhstan, for instance, the registered unemployment rate rose from 0.4 per cent in 1992 to 4.2 per cent in 1996 and despite some improvement was still at a high of 3.9 per cent in 1999. Real wages plummeted, and barring Uzbekistan where it was more in 1997 as compared to the beginning of 1993 and Kyrgyzstan where it was roughly the same, other states registered significant drops (in Tajikistan it was 95 per cent less).[10] The official rate of unemployment in Kyrgyzstan was 18 per cent in 2004. In rural areas, long-term unemployment exceeded 70 per cent, especially among the youth. The unemployment rate in Uzbekistan in 2002 was 35 per cent. There were about 80,000 unemployed in Kazakhstan, 74,000 in Kyrgyzstan, and about 47,000 in Tajikistan in early 2007.[11]

The fall in employment and real wage, combined with declining spending in social sector and the removal of subsidies brought down real wages, increased unemployment and under-employment that affected the general living standard of the masses. Kazakhstan largely removed subsidies for food, housing, transport, and other items in October 1994; and it was soon followed by Kyrgyzstan. Subsidies were replaced by targeted cash payments. Beginning with 1993, a wide range of subsidies were withdrawn in Uzbekistan and central heating and public transport subsidies were abolished in 1996, though price control, almost for all foodstuffs, and subsidy for some services including municipal services, remain in effect. Turkmenistan did away with most food subsidies by 1996, and the relatively small subsidies for bread and public transport that remain are largely funded by state enterprises through cross-subsidization. Substantial subsidies, however, remain for gas, electricity, and water. Tajikistan replaced its general bread subsidy with targeted cash compensation to families in 1996. Subsidies for electricity and irrigation have been reduced; though substantial subsidies continued for transport, housing, and utilities.[12]

In Kazakhstan, government spending on social-assistance programmes had decreased from 10 per cent of GDP and almost four-fifths of government expenditure decreased in 1997 to 5.4 per cent of the GDP or a quarter of the government expenditure, of which over four-fifths went to pensions. In January 2002, the government introduced the state-targeted social assistance programme, which provides means-tested assistance to individuals and families living below poverty line in each Oblast (province). The government also announced a substantial increase in funding for social-assistance programmes over 2002–7, which is aimed to eliminate income poverty.

Since 2002 reforms, Kazakhstan's social protection system's main components are the social assistance programme and other allowances, housing benefits, and the pension system. The targeted social assistance has been successful in reaching the poorest people; and according to World Bank's 2002 poverty assessment, it halved the poverty headcount from what it would have been without the programme. But there are concerns that the amount allocated are too little to address severe poverty. The average value of the transfer to recipient families in 2002 was 4330 Tenge per head, which is 8 per cent of the official poverty line. Funding for the programme is by Oblast administration, and oblasts with higher local revenue have more to spend on assistance than the poorer oblasts, which exacerbates the funding problem.

Expenditure on education and health dropped substantially during the 1990s. Expenditure on education from public budget was equal to 3–4 per cent of GDP in every year from 1994 to 2003. Before GDP started to grow after 1999, there was a sharp drop in total expenditure. Drop in preschool places, like elsewhere in Central Asia, was quite pronounced fact. Private education institutions have emerged, especially to offer vocational training and tertiary education. These developments at the preschool and higher level, according to Pomfret, increased inequality of access. Expenditure on the health sector has been around 2 per cent of the GDP, but the private health sector has expanded. In short, during the 1990s, despite social trauma of the transition from Central Planning, the government's stance on social issues was quite weak.[13] With commonly used US$ 2.15 per day poverty line, both Kazakhstan and Turkmenistan had poverty headcounts of less than 10 per cent. But Kyrgyzstan and Tajikistan had a very high share of the population living below the poverty line. Forty-nine per cent of the population in the Kyrgyz republic and two-thirds of Tajikistan's population lived below the poverty line.[14]

The Central Asian governments find it difficult to balance both public expenditure needs and government revenue. For example, minimum wages and pension in the public sector declined by 40 per cent in 2000–1. During the same period, Tajikistan faced food shortages due to droughts. The government of Uzbekistan had to increase charges on bread, gasoline, and public transport, pushing up consumer prices further.[15] Surveys in Kyrgyzstan in 1993 and 1996 showed strong evidence of decline in social protection offered by the state and of the increased cost of raising children as benefits such as kindergarten or school meals, etc., previously provided by the state or the workplace have disappeared. Households with many adults or pensioners were also more poorly placed in 1996 than in 1993, indicating that the value of the generous Soviet-era pension was being eroded. In Kazakhstan, privatization transferred valuable public assets to a small group. Although private health and education provision is emerging, many people are excluded from these services by poverty. Reduced human capital, according to Pomfret, will harm future growth prospects and the emergence of an alienated underclass will challenge social stability.

The Rich-Poor Divide

The way privatization was launched, there appeared a small class of 'new rich' and a large class of so called 'new poor'. This, according to Ilkhamov, had to do with factors resulting both from the disintegration of Soviet political and economic network and from the difficulties associated with the subsequent transition to a market economy. The 'new poor' are mostly rural inhabitants who have endured the worse of the socio-economic shock caused by the changes of the last several years. The conditions that gave rise to this social group are fraught with the danger of social explosion.[16]

The consequences of a deep crisis in agriculture in Uzbekistan, underlines Ilkhamov, are impoverishment of rural population, widening gap between town and village, and an increasingly large flow of the unemployed labour force from rural areas to large cities. During 1992–2000, the average number of migrants from rural to urban areas was about 90,000 a year. Between 1995–2000, half-a-million people thus migrated; majority of whom were ill-educated, unskilled, and can only be in low-paid labour-intensive jobs. Exposure to the social contrasts of big cities and the visible social and cultural chasm between rich and poor evoke feelings of social alienation among rural migrants, which may inevitably lead them to 'new' radical movements.[17]

A family budget survey conducted by Uzbek State Committee of Statistics showed that between 1989–99, social stratification increased and so did the level of impoverishment of the population. A significant portion of the population, who retrospectively considers themselves in the Soviet past as middle class, now finds themselves among the poor, most of them can be regarded as the so called new poor, argues Ilkhamov. In order to survive in worsened living conditions, they are compelled to sell their property and cattle in the rural areas.[18]

In Kyrgyzstan, the reforms, however, resulted in a rapidly widening gap between rich and poor and greater distress for many.[19] An FAO Study of four Ali Okmots (local administrative units) in the beginning of 2004 (Kara Alma, Kyzl Ungur, Arslanbob, and Kaba) showed that the share of the extremely poor and poor was 49, 37, 44, and 42 per cent respectively. Very poor are those with less than 400 Soms monthly income and poor include those with 401–600 Soms monthly income group. In 2001, around 50 per cent were classified by official estimates as poor and 13 per cent as extremely poor. In Jalalabad Province, the share of the population classified as poor was as high as 55 per cent, with per capita annual income of 3854 Soms or monthly income of about 320 Soms, which was only 37.4 per cent of the national average.[20]

Even the local jobs in some Central Asian states get very low salaries. The jobs, offered by the local administration, do not attract many registered unemployed. As a result, many people prefer to stay unemployed and rely on odd jobs. This was accepted by one head of the Regional Department of Labour Exchange in Andijan province of Uzbekistan in 2002.[21]

Timothy Edmunds has drawn attention to the fact that although the focus of nation-builders has been the relationship with the Slavic population, the actual division is between power and powerlessness. A small group enjoys too much power, while the rest of the population cutting across ethnic groups belong to the category that has been deprived of since independence. The largest segment of the powerless constitutes almost the rural Kazakhs. While concluding that inter-ethnic problems are not that much serious, Edmunds underlined that the asymmetric distribution of power and resources might give rise to parochialism unless attended to seriously.[22] One example of such a crisis is that of Kyrgyzstan, where squatters outside the cities have become a major problem for the government. A ring of settlers' buildings, nearly equal to the area of the city itself, surrounds capital Bishkek. These include recent arrivals to the city that have no jobs, are more disoriented and prone to nationalist influences, and it is they who provide support to overtly nationalist parties.[23]

Intra-regional Divide

An interesting study by the Ferghana Valley Working Group of the Centre for Preventive Action indicates the intra-regional problems that have cropped up in all the three countries that share the Ferghana valley. Given high population density and rural-agricultural nature of the valley region, especially in Kyrgyz and Uzbek parts, these intra-regional problems could be difficult to handle, unless addressed properly.[24] While the state is withdrawing more and more from social sector, the concentration of political power in the Centre has created tensions. In some cases, globalization has created financial centres away from the resource rich areas and thereby creates regional friction.

In Kyrgyzstan, according to the above report, the decision to end agricultural subsidies in 1998 exacerbated regional differences. The north was already getting most of the foreign investment. Given the already low income levels in south Kyrgyzstan and the ethnic split between the Uzbeks and the Kyrgyz, the government's policy of decentralizing service delivery—shifting responsibility for the social safety net, education, and healthcare from the national to the local and regional levels—is causing considerable friction.

In Uzbekistan, though a number of large foreign companies invested in Ferghana valley, like Daewoo in Andhijan; Coca-Cola in Namangan;

Turkish companies in silk production, cotton processing, sewing machines, and textiles; Mitsui and US oil companies in the oil sectors; many small- and medium-sized enterprises were facing difficulties due to currency controls and new tax regulations favouring large-scale enterprises. The study found out that most of the 7000 small businesses were closed down in Namangan.

The Tajik province of Leninabad is still playing the lead role in attracting foreign investment and the regional elite blames the civil war and the Kulyabi dominated government for limiting the potentiality of the province to attract foreign investment.[25] For Tajik part of the valley, economic development and investment are hampered by government's lack of interest. Official statistics indicate that as little as 7 per cent of state investment went to the north, implying the magnitude of north's exclusion. In these circumstances, economic problems through falling living standards and rising unemployment are likely to be doubly destabilizing. These factors are very likely to provoke more resentment against the central government.[26]

Discussing in the context of Kazakhstan, Marvin argues that privatization and liberalization has negatively impacted the position of the regional elite in north and east, with ownership of enterprises, utilities, and natural resources passing into the hands of individuals and groups outside the regions, especially to those based in the national capital and abroad. In Uzbekistan, he writes, centralized control over lucrative sectors of agriculture, notably cotton, was expanded in the name of promoting an autarkic form of national economic development.

Growing dominance of the southern groups in Kazakhstan created concern in the northern, eastern, and western regions and prompted the emergence of a number of predominantly Kazakh political movements with a strong regional flavour, although central authorities subsequently undermined them. Though the balance of power had begun to swing in favour of the central authorities by the end of 1990s, the regional elite continues to exist as a distinct group with interests that frequently contradicts those of the centre.[27] The regional shift, argues Pomfret, has been visible in Kazakhstan. The coal mining provinces of Karaganda and Pavlodar had 16.6 per cent of the national population and 29.3 per cent of the GDP in 1993, with per capita product about double the national level; but by 1998 they were producing only 19.1 per cent of the GDP, their population share had fallen to 14.8 per cent and per capita product only 25–30 per cent above the national level. Meanwhile, the population share of Almaty and its surrounding province increased from 16.7 to 18 per cent and share of GDP from 14.2 to 21.4 per cent. Per capita income in Almaty jumped from 40 per cent above the national average in 1994 to more than double the national average in 1998. There are large changes over such a brief period. The petroleum producing regions Atyrau and Mangistau only increased their combined share of GDP from 9 to 9.5 per cent, implying that although Kazakhstan's growth was fuelled by the hydrocarbon sector, the real beneficiaries were in the commercial capital rather than near the oil field. This pattern is continuing in the post-1999 oil boom period. There are 50 to 60 'sick towns' that depend on a single large enterprise in the Soviet period.[28]

Labour Migration

The failure of the local labour market in some Central Asian states to provide jobs has resulted in large scale migration. The decline of real wages in Kyrgyzstan and Tajikistan, the growing unemployment, especially among the youth in these two states and Uzbekistan, and the restrictions on trade and commerce in Uzbekistan, have pushed younger workers to migrate to Russia and other CIS states. Tajikistan, the poorest country in the region, has been a major supplier of seasonal labour to Russia. According to official sources including Russia's Federal Migration Service and Interior Ministry, there were about 6,00,000–8,00,000 Tajik migrant labourers in Russia in 2004 of which 90 per cent were illegal workers.[29] The number of Tajik emigrants to Russia ranges from 5 per cent to possibly as high as 18 per cent of the population, of which a significant majority works illegally.[30]

The largest number of migrants comes from Tajikistan's mountainous regions. But estimates show that between 17–30 per cent of the working-age population of any given Tajik district is labour migrant in another country.[31] According to official statistics, 30,000 Kyrgyz migrants work in Russia, but unofficial sources in both Russia and Kyrgyzstan put the number around 2,00,000–5,00,000, which means that about 5–10 per cent of the total Kyrgyzstan population work in Russia. Uzbekistan has between 6,00,000 and 1.5 million migrants or 3–6 per cent of the country's population, working not only in Russia, but also in Kazakhstan.[32]

There have been movements of workers within Central Asia, especially to Kazakhstan from neighbouring countries due to its oil-driven economic growth. Even poorer areas in Central Asia attract impoverished people from neighbouring countries, who leave their homes in search of work even for a pittance. South Kyrgyzstan, which itself is underdeveloped and is reeling under difficult socio-economic conditions, is a destination for illegal labour migration from Uzbekistan and Tajikistan. The use of migrant labourers has the potential to spark unrest in south Kyrgyzstan by pushing wages further down, adding to local unemployment and social tension. This region was already a scene of inter-ethnic riot between Kyrgyz and Uzbek groups in 1989–90.[33]

Surviving on extremely harsh conditions, cheated by local agents, faced with intimidation and psychological pressure from local nationalist groups as well as from law enforcement authorities in Russia, the migrants enjoy no social and human rights since most of them are illegal in official parlance. The local labourers in Russia face the prospect of wage loss under pressure from cheaper labour sources coming from Central Asia. There is example of a conflict between Tomsk Rubber Footwear Plant which imported labour on a large scale in 2002 and the Tomsk Regional Employment and Migration Departments.[34] They have been detained without legal aid, deported, attacked, and even killed by local racist elements. Migrant workers have been targets of vilification campaign due to the presence of some elements among them who take to narcotic trafficking and other crimes. Popular disdain for religious terrorism makes the Central Asians targets of suspicion in Russia.[35]

The states of Central Asia cannot ignore the implications that economic stagnation and crises have on the society. In situations of prolonged crises, the divisions within society come to the surface and further complicate the situation. In multi-ethnic Central Asia, where some ethnic minorities are spatially concentrated and belong to groups that have their titular states, globalization carries the danger of deepening historical and existing fault-lines unless calibrated carefully. Ignoring social problems in the name of macroeconomic reforms and letting reforms rapidly widen the gap between rich and poor and greater distress for many is bound to push ever increasing number of marginalized into the arms of radical movements and generate conflicts in Central Asia.

Inter-ethnic Divide and Religious Extremism

Each Central Asian state has a number of ethnic minorities in its territory, whose number is around 20–30 per cent in all states. Even if many Russians have left the region, there are other ethnic minorities in each republic. Ferghana valley, which has been a populated and urbanized region for many centuries, hosts a number of ethnic groups who share this space. Since the valley is shared by three countries, there are a large number of overlapping minorities in each republic, who live in compact areas giving rise to irredentist demands. In 1989–90, the Central Asian region witnessed a number of inter-ethnic riots. Since the Soviet Union was then in existence, these riots did not give rise to inter-state disputes. The post-Soviet situation in Central Asia, however, has not deteriorated to the extent that led to inter-state conflicts as in the case of Armenia-Azerbaijan and Georgia-Russia in the Caucasus. Yet, the riots that were seen in Southern Kyrgyzstan in 2010 leading to killing and exit of minority Uzbeks to neighbouring Uzbekistan could have flared up inter-state conflict, but it did not lead to a conflict that it would not happen in future.

The relation between Tajiks and Uzbeks are equally problematic. Some of the historical cities in Uzbekistan like Samarkand and Bukhara are said to have a large number of Tajiks, who not only accuse Uzbekistan of underreporting the number of Tajiks but also of assimilating them into Uzbek identity. Kazakhstan has of course a large number of Russians in north and east of the country, bordering Russia. The fear that this minority might be instrumental in seceding this part of Kazakhstan to merge with Russia has seen many efforts by Kazakhstan to change the situation, redrawing the administrative boundaries to limit the demographic preponderance of the Russians, shifting the capital to Russian populated Astana, and denying dual citizenship to Russians. These steps have from time to time aroused anger in Russia and there were apprehensions of Russian interference on behalf of its diaspora.

Another major threat confronting Central Asian states is related to religious extremism and terrorism. There were attempts in 1999 on the President's life and a series of bombings in Uzbekistan. Militants even took over administrative buildings and freed other militants from jail in Andizhan in 2005, resulting in a number of deaths from state retaliatory action. In

1999–2000, militants occupied villages in Batken district of Kyrgyzstan. In Tajikistan, Islamic extremists even captured power by force for a brief while in 1992 and the resulting civil war of five years had led to nearly 1,00,000 deaths and internally displaced even a larger number of people.

The forces representing such groups are non-state actors and the states in their own way are dealing with this danger. However, from time to time, this threat also endangers relations between states. Relation between Uzbekistan and Tajikistan has been affected by terrorist threats although both states suffer from such dangers. Uzbekistan frequently closes its borders with Tajikistan, which the former accuses of not doing enough to stop the movement of terrorists through its territory from Afghanistan. As a result, movement of people and goods through the border suffers. Even the borders are mined to prevent infiltration, which also threaten ordinary people living near the border.

Threat of terrorism has pushed many of the regional states closer to Russia, which now has a strong military presence in Tajik-Afghan border. Same is the situation in Kyrgyzstan, where Russia has an airbase. The security dependence on Russia pushes these states away from the West, creating a geopolitical imbalance. There are now strict controls over flow of labour to Russia and Kazakhstan from other Central Asian countries. Though economic and demographic necessity requires movement of labour, the fear of extremists and terrorists sneaking in has created strict border and immigration controls, resulting in tension between sender and recipient countries.

Inter-state Cooperation

As has been stated already, there has been no instance of inter-state conflict in post-Soviet Central Asia. Though there are tensions and disputed borders, the states have been restrained in their response to some of the issues that could have created inter-state conflicts. There are also instances of cooperation that arouse hope that in future the states can find common solutions to problems like water-sharing and inter-ethnic disharmony. One such example is the village of Check on the boundary separating Uzbekistan and Kyrgyzstan that runs through this village—two-thirds of the settlement lies in the Nooken district of Kyrgyzstan and the remaining one-third in Pahta-Abad district of Uzbekistan. Uzbekistan has reinforced the right bank in its part of the border but the entire village of 4500 people is prone to floods because the river Tentek does not have embankments in upstream Kyrgyz territory. The floods in 2004 and 2005 washed away the Kyrgyz part of the river bank submerging about 100–10 hectares of land downstream. Bank overflow upstream in the Kyrgyz side of the border affects the downstream Uzbek fields and settlements. During the spring floods in Kyrgyzstan, even the Uzbek side had to declare an emergency and gear up for damage-control.

In 2004, Uzbekistan even offered US\$ 2,00,000 to Kyrgyzstan for reinforcing the right bank of the Tentek. But lack of funds for the whole project, again, prevented this work from being done. In an effort to bypass bureaucratic red-tape, local Kyrgyz, and Uzbek authorities and the community are now trying to manage the border-rivers by supporting local water user groups. And there are early signs that the idea works.[36]

Similarly, when militants captured villages in Kyrgyzstan in 1999 and 2000, it was Uzbekistan which came to the rescue and sent aircrafts to bomb the militants out of mountains in Batken. Similarly, when 2010 riots broke out against the Uzbek minority in Osh in southern Kyrgyzstan many were killed and over 70,000 fled to the Uzbek side of the border. Yet, the Uzbek government did not react in a manner that would have exacerbated tension with Kyrgyzstan. It did not take advantage of the weakness of the Kyrgyz government when it was engaged in power struggle with anti-government protesters; nor did it intervene on behalf of the Uzbek diaspora, though it has territorial claims over the Kyrgyz side of the Ferghana valley. The fact that such a serious inter-ethnic dispute and political crisis in Kyrgyzstan did not lead to inter-state conflict which shows that in Central Asia there is very little possibility of non-traditional threats transforming into inter-state traditional security problems. Since all the states are aware that being members of CIS, they cannot change Soviet era boundaries by force and would have substantial minorities in their borders; they have tried to accommodate minorities in the state building process.

Central Asian states have moved a long way since the days of inter-ethnic riots in the 1989–90 and nationalist euphoria following independence. Kazakhstan has allowed Russian to be used for official purposes. Russian is used on a par with the Kazakh language in state organizations and organs of local self-government. In Kyrgyzstan, all languages, including Russian, are guaranteed free development and use. In the revised edition of Uzbekistan's language law, adopted in December 1995, knowledge of Uzbek was no longer made a compulsory requirement for employment in the state sector and some other professions that were meant to serve the population. The new law permits the use of not only the state language but also other languages in management and administration as well as in preparing different kinds of documentation where the majority of the staff of the corresponding enterprise or institution uses any of those particular non-titular languages.[37]

In Tajikistan, a government resolution, 'On the programme of the government of Tajikistan on development of the state language and of other languages in the territory of the republic of Tajikistan' was adopted on 21 October 1997, which had two parts—one on the state language and the other on non-Tajik languages. Part two concentrated on special arrangements aimed at maintaining and harmonizing the development of all other languages, including courses in those languages at educational institutions, TV and Radio broadcasts, etc.

The states are also doing their best to keep on checking nationalist movements and organizations that can negatively impact inter-ethnic and inter-state relations in the region. In Kazakhstan, constitutional provision prohibiting groups that promote 'social, racial, national, religious, class or tribal discord' has been invoked to ban Kazakh nationalist organizations like Zheltoqsan and Alash as well as separatist Russian and Cossack organizations like Ednistvo and Union of Cossacks. Similarly, blatantly chauvinist Kazakh nationalist newspapers like Kazakhstanskaya Pravda and Orda have been banned. The state has ensured that such nationalist elements from different groups do not find their way into the legislature.[38]

In Tajikistan, the role of such nationalist organizations like Rastokhez diminished after independence, since they failed to broaden their popular support base. The presence of non-Tajiks who account for nearly 35 per cent of the republic's population is another factor for the limited appeal of the nationalist parties. Even during the euphoric days following the fall of Communism, the Tajik opposition could muster only 39 per cent votes in the presidential elections of November 1991. In Uzbekistan, groups such as

Birlik and Erk have similarly become marginalized in the political arena.[39] A major platform for fighting terrorist and extremist forces and avoiding inter-state conflicts is the SCO, which has an Anti-terrorist Centre in Tashkent. Hopefully, this cooperation mechanism would be helpful in meeting the challenges of other non-traditional threats that could destabilise the states internally and lead to regional instability.

Conclusion

Today non-traditional threats pose serious danger to the security and stability of states in Central Asia more than threats from traditional sources like a hostile external power or a group of powers. The territorial integrity and sovereignty is assured by the involvement of major powers like Russia, the United States, and China in maintaining regional stability. The border with China is settled and the Western forces are in Afghanistan which has a friendly government that is putting pressure on Central Asian militants. Yet, the non-traditional threats can transform into traditional security challenges under certain circumstances. However, the experience of the last 20 years has shown that Central Asian states have not let such issues lead to conflict among states and at times even cooperated to resolve such issues.

Notes and References

1. A.P.S. Chouhan and Jyoti M. Pathania (2011), 'Non-traditional security: A Conceptual Analysis', in Ajay Patnaik and Anuradha Chenoy (eds), *Non-traditional Threats to Central Asian Security*, KW Publishers: New Delhi.
2. Richard H. Shutlz. Paper presented by him at the International Security Studies Program. The Fletcher School of Law & Diplomacy, cited in A.P.S. Chouhan and Jyoti M. Pathania, op. cit.
3. Barry Buzan (1983), *People, States & Fear: The National Security Problem in International Relations*, Chapel Hill, University of North Carolina Press, p. 253. For more details, see Chouhan and Pathania, op. cit.
4. Chouhan and Pathania, op. cit.
5. Anita Sengupta (2009), 'Central Asia: Water as an Apple of Discord', *World Focus*, 30(8), August.
6. Abdurahim Juraev (2011), 'Tajikistan on Way to Energy Independence', in Ajay Patnaik and Anuradha Chenoy (eds), *Non-traditional Threats to Central Asian Security*, KW Publishers: New Delhi.
7. Ibid.

8. Muhammad Tahir (2011), 'As Central Asia Dries Up, States Spar Over Shrinking Resources', *RFE/RL*, 24 July.

9. Asyl Osmonalieva (2009), 'The Stans Debate Russia's Energy Politics', 16 March, p. 2, www.mindsandcommunities.org.

10. *Economic Reforms in Kazakhstan, Kyrgyz Republic, Tajikistan, Turkmenistan, and Uzbekistan*, IMF Occasional Paper 183, Washington DC, 1999; *United Nations Statistical Year Book for Asia and the Pacific 2002*, pp. 262–3.

11. *Country Profile: Kyrgyzstan*, Library of Congress, Federal Research Division, January 2007; *Interstate Statistical Committee*, CIS, 2007; *UNDP Country Report 2002*.

12. Ibid.

13. Richard Pomfret (2006), *The Central Asian Economies Since Independence*, Princeton and Oxford: Princeton University Press, pp. 57–9.

14. Even if World Bank's dollar-a-day to measure the poverty rate is accepted, Kyrgyzstan had nearly 19 per cent below the poverty line. Pomfret, op. cit., pp. 114–15.

15. *Economic Reforms in Kazakhstan, Kyrgyz Republic, Tajikistan, Turkmenistan, and Uzbekistan*, op. cit.; *United Nations Statistical Year Book for Asia and the Pacific*, op. cit., pp. 96–7.

16. Alisher Ilkhamov (2000), 'Divided Economy: Kolkhoz System vs Peasant subsistence Economy in Uzbekistan', *Central Asia Monitor*, No. 4.

17. Ibid.

18. Ibid., p. 11.

19. *Calming the Ferghana Valley*, Preventive Action Reports, vol. 4, The Century Foundation Press, New York, 1999, p. 75.

20. *Poverty in Kyrgyzstan*, http://www.fao.org/docrep/j2603e/j2603e05.htm

21. Zakirjan Ibragimov, 'Ferghana Valley's unemployed feed a thirsty Russian Labour', Business & Economics, http://www.eurasianet.org/departments/business/articles/eav 100302.shtml

22. Timothy Edmunds (2000), 'Power and Powerlessness in Kazakhstani Society: Ethnic Problems in Perspective', *Central Asian Survey*, 19(2), p. 470.

23. Irina Kostyukova (1994), 'The Towns of Kyrgyzstan change their Faces: Rural-urban migrants in Bishkek', *Central Asian Survey*, 13(3), p. 433.

24. *Calming the Ferghana Valley*, op. cit.

25. *Calming the Ferghana Valley*, op. cit., pp. 79–85.

26. Ibid., p. 124.

27. Neil Marvin (2002), 'Patterns of Centre-regional Relations in Central Asia: The Cases of Kazakhstan, the Kyrgyz Republic and Uzbekistan', in James Hughes and Gwendolyn Sasse (eds) *Ethnicity and Territory in the Former Soviet Union: Regions in Conflict*, Frank Cass: London, Portland, OR, pp. 176–7.

28. Pomfret, op. cit., pp. 15–18.

29. 'Tajikistan-Labour Migration from Tajikistan Drops as Economy Improves', BBCMonitoringService, 16.04.2004, http://tcc.iom.int/iom/artikel.php?menu_

id=45&artikel_id=224&history_back=true; *Radio Free Europe/Radio Liberty (RFE/RL) Newsline,* 8(185), Part I, 29 September 2004; *RFE/RL Newsline,* 8(202), Part I, 25 October 2004; *RFE/RL Newsline,* 8(206), Part I, 1 November 2004; 'Kyrgyzstan: New protocol with Russia offers protection for labour migrants', *IRIN,* Ankara, 6October2003,http://tcc.iom.int/iom/artikel. php?menu_id=45&artikel_id=67&history_back=true

30. *Central Asia HDR 2005,* Chapter 6, 'The Social Development Challenge', UNDP Regional Bureau of Europe and Commonwealth of Independent States, p. 141.

31. Remittances to Tajikistan from abroad in 2006 was between US$ 400 million to US$ 1 billion, or between 20–50 per cent of Tajikistan's total GDP. Aaron Erlich, 'Tajikistan: From Refugee sender to Labour Exporter', *Migration Policy Institute,* 2006.

32. *Central Asia HDR 2005,* ibid., pp. 140–1.

33. http://www.irinnews.org/report.asp?ReportID=36527&SelectRegion=CENTR AL_ASIA; 'Many faces of migration in Eurasia', *RFE/RL Central Asia Report,* 4 (40), 15 June 2004.

34. The migrants worked for an average monthly salary of 3200 rubles (US$ 100) to 4500 rubles (US$ 150), much lower than the demand made by local Russian workers. Zakirjan Ibragimov, 'Ferghana Valley's unemployed feed a thirsty Russian Labour', http://www.eurasianet.org/departments/business/articles/eav 100302.shtml.

35. Official data from Russia's penitentiary system showed that in 2006 there were 4700 imprisoned Tajiks. Aaron Erlich, 'Tajikistan: From Refugee sender to Labour Exporter', op. cit.

36. Asian Development Bank, *Country Water Action: Kyrgyz Republic and Uzbekistan,* 'Border Residents Manage "Mad" River' http://www.adb.org/water/ actions/KGZ/mad-river.asp, based on the article of Asia Water Wire journalist, Egamberdy Kabulov, December 2005.

37. Vladimir Mesamed (1998), 'Linguistic Situation and Language Policy in the Republic of Uzbekistan', *Orient,* 38, 1997, p. 151; Graham Smith et al. (eds), *Nation-building in the post-Soviet borderlands,* Cambridge, pp. 200–1.

38. Ian Bremmer and Cory Welt (1996), 'The Trouble with Democracy in Kazakhstan', *Central Asian Survey,* 15(2), pp., 188–9.

39. *RFE/RL NEWSLINE,* 8 (154), Part I, 13 August 2004.

9

River Water Politics in Central Asia

P.L. Dash

Much water has flowed under the bridges of Central Asia since the Soviet disunion. What was state property in Soviet yesteryears has become national wealth of different independent countries. Trying and vying with each other to ascertain their control over various water bodies of the region, the independent states are facing intricate challenges hard for them to surmount and difficult for analysts to understand. It is sometimes incredible to fathom the depth of mutual animus. In Soviet times, there was no question of any constituent republic quarrelling over sharing water of rivers or a sea. State control over natural resources, particularly those of water resources, has not changed much. Yet, post-Soviet Central Asia is perhaps the only region whose water bodies are mired in interstate and intrastate disputes with no signs of any solution in the foreseeable future. This makes researchers and analysts to devote special attention to river water politics in different states of Central Asia, sharing of water bodies located in the region, and evolving a pattern of interstate cooperation on equitable sharing of riverine resources. The problem is larger than any one of us has so far imagined. This essay aims at analysing the extant predicament on the water front in Central Asia by taking major and minor rivers as complex variables for assessment and highlighting the depth and breadth of the issue vis-à-vis the absence of definite state policies to assuage the gravity of the situation.

Background

Water is an essential ingredient of life. From time immemorial, man has been attracted to settle on the shores of water bodies. Civilizations have prospered and perished on these shores. However, disregarding this human proclivity has landed Central Asia in a piquant dilemma. In the Soviet time, water resources were mismanaged, canals were dug and rivers were diverted, dams were erected, and hydroelectric stations built. Efforts were made to divert Siberian rivers to Central Asia; an infeasible project found abandoned, when it was observed that no such fantasies would ever work. But Central Asia had to develop and for this reason various misconceived steps were taken. But harnessing of Central Asian rivers continued. Reservoirs were built to generate electricity, industries were set up, and river water was harnessed to agricultural fields; spray irrigation was introduced in vast cotton fields and all efforts were made to fix water quota for each republic in order to ensure optimum use of water in three more populous downstream countries of Uzbekistan and Turkmenistan in the Amu Darya basin and Kazakhstan on Syr Darya basin, disregarding that the rivers that originated in upstream countries of Tajikistan and Kyrgyzstan. Uzbekistan, Turkmenistan, and Kazakhstan are rich, more influential, more populous, bigger in size, and endowed with hydrocarbon resources compared to Kyrgyzstan and Tajikistan, which are less developed, smaller in size, mostly mountainous, relatively poor in resources, and their pastoral populations, historically peripatetic, live in hills. However, it is these two countries that possess the source of two major rivers and have plenty of fresh water tributaries flowing down to join the main river flow of Amu Darya and Syr Darya.

In Soviet years, these two countries did not object to excessive use of water by downstream countries; now they do. In those years, they kept quiet when the anomalous water quota was fixed by Moscow because they were getting other compensations; now they protest because compensations have dried up. The unified policy for water use was for the collective benefit of all, while now the situation is different, when each one is to fend for itself. Three interrelated points were then completely forgotten. The first was that the origin of the rivers is in the upstream countries of

Kyrgyzstan and Tajikistan, who might protest and one day demand money for water use or compensation for the damage they suffer due to excessive draw of water downstream. The compensation system was earlier prevalent in the former Soviet Union, when downstream countries of Uzbekistan, Kazakhstan, and Turkmenistan provided upstream countries with coal, gas, and oil in lieu of the damage they suffered due to excessive usage of water by themselves for agriculture and industry.[1] The second was Moscow's mediation always on all issues of development which is no more available to independent countries and third was the lackadaisical attitude in all five states, who conveniently forgot the sixth and most important user of the rivers—the Aral Sea, which these two Central Asian rivers fed with fresh water. Excess use of river water in its entire course deprived the Aral Sea of its source of water supply as a result of which the Aral Sea desiccated itself and shrank from 67,000 to 17,000 sq. km—far too away from the coastline. Between the coastline and the sea, now there is a salty sand bed, and with desert storms blowing, it is a pointer to a potential health hazard for the surrounding and contiguous regions. In a nutshell, problems are many and solutions are far too few.

7 + 2 + 1

The core of the river water dispute is between the countries of the region located in the Aral Basin. There are seven countries—Kazakhstan, Kyrgyzstan, Tajikistan, Turkmenistan, Iran, Afghanistan, and Uzbekistan—and all of them are stakeholders to the catastrophic ecological disaster sweeping the region. All of them save Iran and are a contributing factor to the crisis. Iran and Afghanistan have not yet overtly claimed a water share from the Aral Basin rivers; thereby leaving the Central Asian five to fend for themselves and decide what they consider proper. Numerous powwows in the last two decades among the countries of Amu Darya and Syr Darya delta have yielded little result that would augur a positive outcome. The net consolation is that despite differences, countries are negotiating and a multilateral process is on to resolve water sharing problem.

Other than these seven countries, the two other stakeholders are the two major rivers themselves—Amu Darya and Syr Darya. These are exotic rivers, crisscrossing mountains and valleys, deserts and oases, and big cities and numerous village households. All of them suffer if the river suffers and all of them, therefore, have a responsibility to ensure that the rivers are their common wealth; they are a gift of God and ought to be preserved to benefit them all. The atheists and non-believers in the Soviet era broke this sanctity by often diverting the river water in the name of development in various ways. This was over harnessing the God's gift and the result is intractable intrastate conflicts with nagging environmental fallout.

Amu Darya that originates in the snowfields and glaciers of Pamir mountains in Tajikistan and Kyrgyzstan flow a distance of approximately 2400 km from across the mountains through the Karakum desert right up to the Aral. On its journey, it passes, crosses, touches, divides borders, leaves, and re-enters the territory of five countries—Kyrgyzstan, Uzbekistan, Afghanistan, Tajikistan, and Turkmenistan. Amu Darya receives its water flow from the numerous tributaries running from the Pamir to form its main flow. It does not increase its flow by receiving water from the countries it passes through. Eighty per cent of Amu Darya's flow is contributed by Tajikistan followed by 8 per cent by Afghanistan, 6 per cent by Uzbekistan, 3 per cent by Kyrgyzstan, and 3 per cent by Turkmenistan and Iran together; most of which flow from Iran.[2] Amu Darya divides the state borders of three sets of countries: Uzbekistan and Afghanistan, Tajikistan and Afghanistan, and Turkmenistan and Uzbekistan.

Syr Darya originates from the glaciers and snow peaks of the Tien Shan mountains in north of the Pamir, meanders a journey of 2500 km, cutting across four countries from Kyrgyzstan to Uzbekistan to Tajikistan to once again Uzbekistan until it finally enters Kazakhstan from where it travels to the Aral Sea. Mostly fed by snowmelts of the glaciers, Syr Darya receives 74 per cent of its flow from the mountainous areas of Kyrgyzstan followed by 12 per cent by Kazakhstan, 11 per cent by Uzbekistan, and 3 per cent by Tajikistan.[3]

The single most exotic stakeholder of this entire Central Asian river system is the Aral Sea. Its desiccation is unfortunate; but an unavoidable reality experienced as much by the river flows drying up at the mouth as by the countries of the region controlling them. The hugeness of the problem elicited international intervention and the United Nations was involved to initiate a 'Save Aral' project to deal with the crisis that has partially succeeded—partially because the ecosystem of the river flow has been irredeemably damaged. It, therefore, requires as huge an effort as the enormity of the environmental disaster.

Thus, we have a clear situation in the Aral Sea basin where there are seven countries; five of them primary and two are secondary users of the basin water, two rivers and one sea. Collective efforts of all of them could alone salvage the situation, while a negative and hostile approach by any one of them may further jeopardize the whole process. The possibility of mutual hostility lurks large because there is enough evidence of controlled and uneven river flow distribution—in the region, unequal contribution—to the river flow by different countries, water-rich and water-poor countries existing as neighbours, who often posture menacingly at each other, carelessness about the ecological consequences of water policy in each given country, location of dams and reservoirs in potentially polemical places that invite boundary disputes, and a host of other local and regional feelings of possessiveness of the rivers on the basis of 'mine and theirs' are all triggers of potential hidden conflicts.

The asymmetry is direct and visibly confrontational. The disputes are primarily between two sets of countries—upstream states where the rivers originate and downstream countries where the mighty flow of the rivers journey through, between the arid plains covering 80 per cent of the basin area and the mountainous regions with 20 per cent territory, between countries who contribute less to the river flow and consume excessively, between those who pollute the rivers and degrade the environment and those who contribute clean water to the flow and demand ecological safety, between highly and sparsely populated regions, between developed and underdeveloped areas. Since water is necessary for all and its abuse in the past has put all the stakeholders in a fix, the demand of the day is to promulgate a national water policy in each country, formulate collectively regional water policies in consonance with the interest of the region and coordinate action to ensure regional environmental safely. The geography of the basin countries must not be forgotten simply because it cannot be changed. Despite all differences, a formula must be hewn out from the extant predicament, where Tajikistan and Kyrgyzstan to a greater extent and Afghanistan and Iran to a lesser extent occupy just 20 per cent of the basin area and contribute 90 per cent of the water flow of Amu Darya and Syr Darya.[4]

Other Rivers, Other Problems

While the focus is invariably on acuteness in the Aral basin on the western front, the eastern flanks are equally vulnerable to the absence of sustainable water management policies. All Central Asian rivers are transnational and trans-boundary, originating in one country and flowing to or through one or many countries to fall in a lake or a sea. It is this predicament that catapults Central Asia to a potential conflict zone in terms of water sharing. The water sharing question crops up at three different levels: first within each country there are several small rivers that travel only a few kilometres. They are not perennial rivers and seasonally dry up. They pose minor problems. When such small glacial rivers become perennial, they maintain the continuum and mingle in the main flow of the river. This second category of rivers poses interregional water sharing problems. They are conflict triggers at the grassroots level due to their flow entering the boundaries of another state. When they merge with the mainstream of the river they transcendentally affect the whole issue and become part of the river water sharing problem because dams are normally built on these rivers. The third types are big rivers flowing from one country and passing through another or more countries. They constitute the crux of the problem. Several such rivers fall into the two Central Asian lakes—Issyk-Kul in Kyrgyzstan and Balkhash in Kazakhstan. However, the absence of any detailed study on cross country tributaries of big Central Asian rivers makes it difficult to focus on grassroots issues.

Some of the trans-boundary rivers, straddling the Central Asian space, are Talas and Chu between Kazakhstan and Kyrgyzstan; Ili between China and Kazakhstan; Tarim between Tajikistan, Kyrgyzstan, and China; Irtysh between China, Kazakhstan, and Russia; Tobol, Ural, and Ishym between Kazakhstan and Russia.[5] For the past two decades, these Central Asian rivers, particularly those sharing with China have become the subject of intense debate in bilateral relations between China on the one hand and other Central Asian countries on the other. China's emphasis on developing its north-western flanks of Xinjiang and harnessing river waters to meet the growing demands of development has triggered a dispute between Kazakhstan and China, the former accusing the latter to have released effluents to the Ili and Irtysh rivers that pollute the river flow, choke it at many a point, and severely affect ecology and environment in Kazakhstan. The uncompromising attitude of both sides worsens the process of negotiation and solution to water sharing issues evades both countries.[6] Each of these cross country rivers listed above are potential conflict zones. All things related to rivers—dams, reservoirs, lakes, water sanctuaries for birds, hydroelectric stations, and estuaries—are under scanner; particularly those located on the borders between two or more countries. It is often difficult to gauge who is involved in the dispute, who is the responsible party for water pollution and who damages the eco-balance of the region and who should take remedial measures to save the river systems from further decay. The Stalin era policy of divide and rule holds no longer good for the common property of state as practised in the Soviet era has evaporated; the attitude of political leaders to treat rivers and other related water bodies have hardened over the past two decades, making rhetoric more pronounced than searching practical solution. However, what awaits all countries of the region is a tangible framework and concrete water management policy by each individual state that would take common interest of the region into account and sustain and maintain the ecological balance of the river system so as to protect exotic values of all Central Asian rivers. Instead available to us, there are evidences of bitter bickering concerning all states involved in conflicts as to how to share river waters and riverine resources.

Reservoirs and Uzbekistan

There are several reservoirs in Central Asia, both big and small, located along the flow of the many rivers. A region aplenty with fresh water and famous for its hydro resources is beset with disputes concerning the reservoirs. A state-wise analysis of reservoirs would be in fitness of this essay. The reservoirs are built along the river flow. There are many reasons for disputes over reservoirs. A reservoir on the upstream of a river flow minimizes its flow downstream. Absence of water sharing arrangement is a potential dispute trigger. Inadequate arrangement for sharing hydroelectricity generated on the dams becomes often a core dispute among states. However, the crux of the problem stems from the collapse of the Soviet era unified water and resource management mechanism that has not yet been properly divided among the states of the region. Therefore, discords have arisen over one country not releasing adequate amount of electricity in winter to another country, thereby depriving a neighbour of heating facilities in bitter cold or releasing excess water by an upstream country in an unwanted season, thereby flooding large areas of a neighbouring state. These have happened quite frequently in the past two decades. These disputes have cropped up primarily because of the demographic asymmetry of the region. Alone in one country—Uzbekistan—half of the region's 56 million people live. The water demand of this country for fresh potable water for daily consumption is naturally far higher than all other four countries of the region put together. It is precisely why Uzbekistan has maximum number of reservoirs and lakes.

The biggest of them is Chardara reservoir on Syr Darya, where the river exits from Uzbekistan and enters Kazakhstan near Chardara city. Built during 1965–8, the reservoir was commissioned in 1968 with a full capacity of 5.7 cu. km. Its water surface area is 900 sq. km—70 km in length and spanning over 20 km at its widest point. The reservoir is an embodiment of 'divide and rule policy' of the Soviet era. Located along the north-eastern rim of Uzbekistan, bordering on southern Kazakhstan, the reservoir cut across the borders: located in Kazakhstan, but visibly surrounded on all sides save the north by Uzbek territories.[7] Sharing the reservoir's water and electricity generated at Farkhad and Karyakum hydroelectric stations as well as marine resources would remain a potential apple of discord between the two downstream countries forever.

Uzbek experts say that Uzbekistan has altogether a total of 55 reservoirs with a capacity of 19.8 cu. km of water, whereas only two reservoirs—Nurek and Karyakum—in Tajikistan store 15 cu. km.[8] Uzbekistan has territorial and water quota pretensions to all its neighbours because the two major rivers of the region—Amu Darya and Syr Darya—almost completely bypass Uzbekistan. Many reservoirs do so too. The irony is compounded further by Uzbekistan contributing only 8 per cent of the river flows, while consuming 80 per cent of the available water of the Central Asian river basin. It is this predicament of Uzbekistan, the most populous country of the region that pits it against all its neighbours. Ironically, Uzbekistan has borders with all other Central Asian countries, including Afghanistan, but does not have borders with any big power such as China and Russia.

While it is impossible to analyse the implications of all 55 reservoirs on the Uzbek territory in a small article, it is worthwhile remembering some prominent ones that interested students could verify from the available maps. Charvak reservoir in the north of capital Tashkent is an important point to note. It supplies potable water to Tashkent. Three more famous reservoirs are Kattakargan near a city of the same name, Chimkargan reservoir on Kashkadarya and south Surkhan reservoir on Sukhandarya. Uzbekistan remains one of the leading cotton growers in Central Asia and all these reservoirs cater to the need of cotton cultivation as well as other crops grown in the country. Besides Uzbekistan is endowed with a few lakes, mostly saline and shallow, the biggest of them being Aydarkul lake. In Karakalpakstan, there is a cluster of lakes on eastern and western flanks of Amu Darya before the river falls into the Aral Sea. However, the water bodies of Uzbekistan are as exotic an issue as disputes surrounding them are too complicated to fathom. It is the irony of fate that the most populous country of the region is bypassed by major rivers.

Turkmenistan

The Turkmen republic is an arid, semi-desert country bordering Uzbekistan in the east and north, Kazakhstan's Mangistau oblast in the north-west, Caspian Sea in the west and Iran and Afghanistan in the south. The country is fortunate enough to have Amu Darya passing entirely through its eastern flank from the moment it enters from the Afghan Uzbek borders to Afghan Turkmen borders right up to Gaz Achak in Lebap Velayat in Turkmenistan, where the river re-enters Uzbekistan. The country is thinly populated with just 6 million people living scattered all across its territory, but mostly on the river valleys of Amu Darya in the east. In the Soviet years, efforts were made and materialized in building the Karakum canal joining Amu Darya with Murgab and further stretching the canal to Uzyn Su. This was a major diversion of the Amu Darya river flow that deprived its mouth of fresh water as a result of which the river dried up at mouth and desiccation of Aral had begun. While harnessing of Amu Darya water never stopped, Turkmenistan has built four reservoirs at various locales to meet its water and hydroelectricity needs. Although the country has plenty of gas reserves and does not require hydro power, its four reservoirs generate and supply electricity to the periphery where they are located. Gas supply in the country is gratis.

South of Mary, the ancient Merv on the Silk Road, there is Khauz Khan reservoir that supplies fresh water to the city. Besides, it has two reservoirs at Tedzhen and Tashkapri on Karabil upland on Murgab. All these reservoirs cater to the fresh water needs of the country. The country has also a lake at Karamet Nyaz, an artificial lake built west of Kerki, soon after the Amu Darya water was diverted toward Karakum canal. This is also a fresh water reservoir. Along with two other reservoirs—Lolota and Sarryazin—built on Murgab itself, they cater to the needs of local population and irrigate nearby fields.

Turkmen scientists have been working on how to increase the fresh ground water reserve for their country by conserving rain water and preserving catchment ground water sources. Soon after independence, Turkmenistan built a bypass canal from the Tuyamuyun reservoir that led to severe water shortage in Khorezm province of Uzbekistan, triggering serious differences between the two. The quota of Amu Darya water distribution system between Turkmenistan and Uzbekistan has been fixed for many years on 40-40 basis with 20 per cent under international control. However, the population distribution is far too anomalous on both sides. No part of the Amu Darya is more glaring of this anomaly than the part that flows just along the dividing line of borders between Uzbekistan and Turkmenistan. Along this stretch, nearly 14 million people live on the Uzbek side in the valley while only 4 million dwell on the left flank of the river on the Turkmen side. Yet, the water quota is same for both.[9]

The water needs of 14 million Uzbeks cannot be equated with the requirements of 4 million Turkmen. The situation calls for consensual rectification and rescheduling of the water quota for each of these users. The situation stands aggravated with near zero contribution by Turkmenistan and its insistence on maintaining the status quo of consumption despite difficulties faced by other end users of the river flow. Unless urgent measures are taken, the extant dispute may snowball into a water war between the two. There is another thorny problem between Uzbekistan and Turkmenistan that concerns the Sarykamish lake. Uzbek-Turkmen borders in Karakalpakstan divide the lake into two parts, larger part being in Turkmenistan and two different lakes of the same water body located on Karakalpakstan. The problem here is not only about how to determine mutual borders but also about fishing rights, exploitation of marine resources, sharing of navigational zones of this salty lake that calls for mutual co-operation. Sarykamish is a huge water body and bickering over it without any consensus would severely affect bilateral ties between Turkmenistan and Uzbekistan in an irreversible way. Turkmenistan's policy of 'positive neutrality' clashes with the dictatorial democracy of Uzbekistan. Both look at national interest avidly, thus providing little space of accommodation on thorny issues, more so water problems that tell severely on Turkmen national interest. Being a semi-desert country, Turkmenistan is extremely sensitive to interstate water issues, and as Uzbekistan feels, tends to seek a solution in its favour disregarding needs of other neighbours; hence the impasse.

Kyrgyzstan

Kyrgyzstan is a mountainous country. Located between the Altai and Kyrgyz mountain ranges, this Central Asian country is privy to have possessed the source of the two major Central Asian rivers—Amu Darya and Syr Darya. Innumerable tributaries trek their meandering journey through mountain passes of Kyrgyzstan and they crisscross as if they compete with time and space to cascade from heights and mingle with the eternal flow of crystal clear water of glacial rivers. Several population points stud their pathways, away from the mainstream of civilizations; yet, these small tributaries remain least studied aspect of Central Asian river water system. In the area we find three types of rivers: few of them are very small in length, turbulent in flow, and abruptly end in a small water body. Second, there are hundreds of tributaries flowing along the mountainous terrains with distinct names and mingling in the main flow of either Amu Darya or Syr Darya; thus, they lose their identity. There are yet numerous other rivers with clear distinction of their own, but Amu Darya and Syr Darya remain the mainstay of river water system in Central Asia and influence the water management policy of all five countries. Kyrgyzstan has enormous hydroelectric potential varying between 140–60 billion kWh.

Kyrgyzstan has four major reservoirs—Toktogul on the Naryn river, Andhizan on Karadarya river, Kirov reservoir on Talas, and Chu reservoir on Chu near Orto Tokey. All these are famous water bodies with hydroelectric stations on them that supplied electricity in the unified grid system of the Soviet era. With independence, Kyrgyzstan is the water and electricity surplus country in the region. It has also three lakes: Issyk-Kul, Song Kel, and Chatyr Kel; all with tremendous potential of fresh water and marine sanctuary. An upstream country, it holds the key to water supply to the downstream states. And being less developed, less populated and poor, it is often held on bargain by downstream, populous, and prosperous neighbours—an aspect in relationship that has been sharpened in post-Soviet years. Equally significant is the fact that independence has provided Kyrgyzstan with an opportunity to value its national wealth while dealing with unwilling and uncompromising neighbours, and water is one of them.

The Andhizan reservoir is located in the eastern most point of the Ferghana valley on the borders of Kyrgyzstan and Uzbekistan; therefore, a potential conflict trigger because of its very location. All around Ferghana, there are numerous tributaries in the formative zone of Syr Darya, which are flowing from the mountains of Kyrgyzstan to the valleys in Uzbekistan. Given the ethnic conflagration between Uzbekistan and Kyrgyzstan, particularly the pogrom of Osh in 2010, when ethnic Uzbeks were massacred by irate Kyrgyz, the sharing of river waters always remains an apple of discord between the two. Near Osh flows the south Ferghana canal that runs from Andhizan reservoir to the city of Ferghana, carrying water and crossing ethnic borders many a time. Ferghana is the most populous valley in Central Asia and the valley's borders are too intricately drawn to be too easily shared by three mostly hostile neighbours—Uzbekistan, Kyrgyzstan, and Tajikistan. Andhizan is located on one side of the Ferghana valley which is completely on the Kyrgyz territory, bypassing Uzbekistan only by a touch of the border, while Andhizan city is deep inside the Ferghana valley. On the opposite end of the Ferghana, there is Kairakkum .reservoir, located on the territory of Tajikistan, but touching Uzbek border right at the start of it. Such border intricacies are conflictive zones for independent countries to fight. The Soviet supranational umbrella is no more available to protect the common interest of the region.

Tajikistan

Tajikistan is another upstream, water rich country of Central Asia. Its hydroelectric potential is pegged at some 500–50 billion kWh. Together with Kyrgyzstan, it accounts for nearly 85 per cent of the water in Central Asia.[10] There are many tributaries originating from the glacial mountain heights that flow to form mighty Amu Darya. Mountainous and sparsely populated, rivers from Tajik territory such as Vakhsh, Kafirnigan, Zarafsan, and Kyzyl su flow to the Pyandzh. Wakhan Darya, originating from the Wakhan corridor of Afghanistan also flow to the Pyandzh that subsequently becomes Amu Darya from the Uzbek city of Termez and beyond all the way to southern Aral Sea. Tajikistan is a solid contributor to the water system of the Amu Darya basin. It also contributes to Syr Darya in the north. Its rivers are sometimes so wide on the mid-flow at many stretches that they look like natural reservoirs. Look at the Bekabad reservoir on Syr Darya; you feel exactly like that.

Tajikistan has a number of reservoirs, the largest of then being Kairakkum on the Syr Darya flow. The reservoir's east end touches Uzbekistan on the Ferghana valley. The east-west flow of Syr Darya on the Tajik territory has a brief stretch riddled with two reservoirs: on the east end Kairakkum and on the west end Bekabad—both located on Tajik territory but touching Uzbek borders and lying between very densely populated cities of Kokand and Khozhand. Naturally, the river and the reservoirs are responsible for water supply to the region for all purposes. Had the Syr Darya route been different from what it is on Uzbek side of the Ferghana valley, interethnic hostility and discord over river waters could have been altogether different. Major rivers, nay major reservoirs nearly bypass Uzbekistan—a potential reason for the country to enter into negotiations with neighbours for meeting its water needs.

Aside from Kairakkum and Bekabad, the Nurek reservoir on the Vakhsh is another one. For many years Nurek has served Tajikistan well in irrigation and hydropower generation. However, Vakhsh has remained mired in controversy over building another hydroelectric station called Rogun. The proposal to build Rogun dam began in 1959 in the Soviet era, the technical planning was completed in 1965, and construction began eleven years later in 1976. In 1993, on the thick of Tajik civil war, floods washed away the half-built dam. The Soviet Union was no more and Tajikistan alone was in no position to build Rogun. The dam entered into a triangular conflict zone; with neighbour Uzbekistan on its apprehensions that building the dam would affect irrigation in Uzbek cotton fields and with Russia for off and on agreements to build Rogun. At the centre of controversy and deeply in the quagmire of a bleeding civil war with Islamists claiming control over Kurgan Tyube, where Vakhsh flows, Tajikistan floated shares to raise capital for Rogun construction. The target was set at US$ 1.4 billion, but poor response gave the country just US$ 44 million. Agreements with Russia were renewed, but the stalemate continued over who would control how much and what of the dam. Meanwhile, Tajikistan called the project a 'plant of Destiny', while Uzbek president, Islom Karimov called it a 'stupid project' in October 2010. At the Prime Ministerial level, both countries have been negotiating to hammer out a solution to the Rogun issue. If built, Rogun will be the world's highest dam, 335 metres above the canyon floor with six hydroelectric stations generating electricity to the tune of 3600 MW.

Tajikistan shares a long border with Afghanistan and river Pyandzh divides the state border between the two countries. Mountain rivers from both countries contribute to the Amu Darya flow before Pyandzh becomes Amu Darya and travels to neighbouring Uzbekistan and beyond to Turkmenistan, both border countries with Afghanistan divided by the westward flow of Amu Darya. So far, Afghanistan has not staked its claim to river water sharing with any of its three northern neighbours or else it could have added a different chapter to river water conflict in the region. The other neighbour China, however, has claimed territorial possession of some land in Tajikistan and Kyrgyzstan much to the native chagrin. In 1996, Kyrgyzstan signed the first border agreement with China ceding 30,000 hectares of land which was approved by the Jogorku Kenesh or Parliament in 1998. When the second agreement was signed in 1999 without consulting the parliament and ceding 90,000 hectares of Uzengi Kuush region, there were countrywide protests as much against Akaev as against Chinese pressure tactics. No mapping of the border has been published since.[11]

Kyrgyz members of Parliament refused to ratify the treaty, stating that copies of the treaty had not been shown to them and that the ceded area is of farming significance to Kyrgyzstan. China, on the other hand, threatened that in the event of Kyrgyzstan not ceding the demanded territory, it would ask Chinese farmers just to cross borders and settle there.[12] It is alleged that the territory acquired by China from Kyrgyzstan in Naryn oblast and from

Tajikistan in Gorno Badakhshan has the sources of potential Central Asian rivers. Tajikistan was, however, happy that China settled down for less territory than it had earlier demanded. China is privy to holding the source of all mighty rivers of India, Pakistan, and Bangladesh and on other sides of the Himalayas trying to acquire river sources on high mountains in Central Asia in order to gain a strategic foothold there. China's pressure tactic and obdurate diplomacy have these small Central Asian countries worried and besmirched their relations. They are forced to cede China their territories despite disapproval of their domestic constituencies. Former Kyrgyz president Askar Akaev had faced a stormy parliament. The Kyrgyz-Tajik land deals with China is a glaring chapter in coercive diplomacy that China has pursued in recent years to browbeat its small neighbours and keep them under control. Water rich Tajikistan has also a number of lakes Sarez on Bartang, Yashil Kul on Gunt, and a huge shallow water body called Karaat. All of these lakes are located on the eastern flank of the country not very far from the territory acquired by China, and most importantly origins of the rivers of which these lakes are a part, are now under Chinese control.

Kazakhstan

An overarching country in the centre of Asian heartland, Kazakhstan, is a huge country studded with many lakes, rivers, and water bodies. The country's water dispute is primarily with China and secondarily with other Central Asian neighbours. Kazakhstan is a recipient, downstream country whose contribution to Central Asian river flow is insignificant. A total of 23 trans-border rivers flow on the territories of China and Kazakhstan and the absence of a transparent policy for sharing their aquatic resources beclouds their bilateral relations. For many years, the two countries have been looking for an amicable solution to optimal usage of water of the Ili and Irtysh rivers, but a solution is evading them for stringent Chinese attitude. As an upstream country, China ought to understand that Ili feeds 70 per cent of the water in Balkhash lake. The lake is peculiar in its structure; half saline and half sweet and home to species of fish and birds found nowhere else. The area around the Balkhash including Almaty, the Soviet era capital of Kazakhstan, is relatively densely populated. Ili, originating in Karat mountain range of Chinese Xinjiang, enters into Kazakhstan little beyond Yining, travels in the north-west direction and falls into the sweet water part of Balkhash. On its flow, there is a huge Soviet era reservoir called Kapchagay that caters to the irrigation and industrial requirements of Kazakhstan aside from supplying potable water and generating electricity. On the Kazakh side of the river, there are several tributaries feeding the flow of Ili. However, excessive harnessing of Ili in upland China endangers the downstream flow and destroys ecological balance of the region.

Kazakhstan has all rivers flowing northward except the Ural. The southward flowing rivers are small, mountainous streams mingling with bigger rivers. Among major rivers of Kazakhstan, there is Ural in the west of the country that comes from Russia, the Syr Darya in the middle of the country that comes from Kyrgyzstan and Uzbekistan and flows into the Aral, Ili in the east originates in China and falls in the Balkhash and Irtysh mingles with Ob in Russia goes northward to Obskaya Guba. River water is a primary source of sustenance for agriculture, industry, and human life. Kazakhstan is fortunate to have enough fresh water to meet her needs, but excessive use of river water by upstream countries pits it against neighbours in a war of words unpalatable in bilateral relations.

Kazakhstan has four more trans-boundary rivers—Tobol, Talas, Ishim, and Shu. All of them originate in a neighbouring country and enter Kazakhstan at various points. Take for example, river Irtysh. Average water stock of this river for many years is around 30 cu. km of which one third enters Kazakhstan from China.[13] The river flow is highly regulated, both upstream and midstream by Bukhtarmin and Shulbin dams respectively. As excessive exploitation of the river flow at various points decreases its capacity, release of industrial effluents pollute it, thereby making the river water unfit for human consumption around the river zone and raising alarm for restoration of the earlier purity of Irtysh, while the Satpaev canal dug out of Irtysh suffers from degrading pollution.

The Ili Balkhash basin is no different. There is a widespread concern about the quality of potable water in the region. Chemical pollutants not only spoil pristine river flow, but contaminate ground water too. A study of samples from Uyghur region of Almaty oblast has revealed that the level of metal contamination of ground water in Ili Balkhash basin is so high that it is even considered unsuitable for irrigation. Kazakhstan has been accusing China of erecting water storage facilities along Ili, Sumbe, Narynkol, and elsewhere that severely affect the purity of water flow downstream.

Drawing a high and unspecified amount of water from the flow and releasing chemical effluents to the river as well as increasing acreage of land under cultivation, both in the Chinese and Kazakh segments add to the river basin getting untenably polluted. Ever since bilateral Sino-Kazakh dialogues on border and water disputes began in 1999, both sides have met several times; but a tangible solution is nowhere in sight. In conclusion, one could say that all Central Asian countries in general and each of them in particular are too besotted with water problem. Only a common approach, selfless and pragmatic assessment, would help them share what is God's gift. Any one country trying to project national interest on a chauvinistic platform would forever jeopardize the prospect of a tangible solution.

Notes and References

1. Nurbek Atakanov (2010), 'Water-Energy Problems in Central Asia, Russia and the Muslim World', 219(9), pp. 91–3.
2. Phillip Micklin (2002), 'Water in the Aral Sea Basin of Central Asia: Cause of Conflict or Cooperation? Eurasian Geography and Economics', 43(7), p. 508.
3. Ibid.
4. D. Mamatkanov (1996), 'Vodnyie Risursy Gornoi Territorii Basseyna', *Vestnik Arala*, 1(Spring), pp. 5–7.
5. Oleg Sedorov (2003), 'Vodniye Resursi Tsentralnoi Azii kak Istochnik Regionalnykh Konfliktov', *Tsentralnaya Aziya I Kavkaz*, 5(29), p. 184.
6. A. Kenshimov (2006), 'Sotrudnechestvo Mezhdu Respublikoi Kazakhstan a Kitaiskoi Narodnoi Respubliki v Oblasti Vodnykh Otnoshenii, Kazakhstan I Kitai, Strategicheskoe Partnyorstvo v Tselyakh Razvitiya, materialy Mezhdunarodnoi Konferentsii', *Almaty*, pp. 115–23.
7. See the Atlas: Russia and the post-Soviet states, Arguments and facts Publishers, Moscow, 1993, p. 31.
8. D. Azizov, http//www.hydroworld.com/index/display/newsdisplay/129545192 html.
9. P.L. Dash (2003), 'Central Asian Republics: Discord Over Reverine Resources', *Economic and Political Weekly*, XXXVIII(6), February 8–14, p. 523.
10. Nurbek Atakanov, op. cit., p. 91.
11. Marlène Laruelle and Sebastien Peyrouse (2009), *China as a Neighbor: Central Asian Perspective and Strategies*, Central Asia and Caucasus Institute and Johns Hopkins University, Washington, p. 82.
12. Arkadii Dubnov (2001), 'Kirgizskie Palki I Kitaiskie Kolesa', (Kyrgyz Spokes in Chinese Wheels), *Vremya*, 22 June.
13. A. Kenshimov, op. cit., p. 116.

10

Compelling Compulsions of Ethno-Cultural Identity and Integration Process in Central Asia*

Laura Yerekesheva

In the contemporary Central Asian discourse, the integration subject is quite a new and challenging one. Its evolvement as a specific analytical paradigm was made possible as a result of the collapse of the Soviet Union and all the consequences associated with this event. The two decades of independence and integration's attempts allow us defining its main crucial stages that are closely linked with the nation-building and identity issues. It could be said that integration became one of the substantial parts of the more broad structural changes facing all the former Soviet and now new independent states of the region. The economic reforms, political liberalization, evolving new ideological paradigm based on finding cultural and religious identities anew—all this became a substantial part of the structural changes that people of the former peripheries had to undergo. The time factor too was a rather constrained one becoming very condensed and pressed, thus reflecting to a certain extent and repeating in its own way the ongoing broader simultaneous process of globalization and atomization. The specificity of this 'dual force' was in that by 1990s it didn't merely pass by, but instead started embracing by itself the whole world, regions, and

* 'This essay is based on the lecture, given at Nehru Centre, Mumbai (India) on 18 December 2010.

countries penetrating into the local soil what paved a way to new patterns of identities being formed in an entirely new environment, intermingled, and interdependent world.

Under this new evolving structural paradigm, the answer to the chaos of rapid changes became vivid in the process of social coherence, solidarity, and steadiness, be it at an individual or various collective levels. This is how identity issues became exposed on individual, national, and cultural plains. In the socio-economic domain, this issue of identity was, interalia, manifested through the ideas of integration as an effective mechanism of social coherence within certain geo-economic and geo-political spaces. From this view-point, integration could be seen as a representative form of a specific collective identity of certain geo-economic and geo-political entities, taking place under the processes of global (globalization) and partial (atomization) coherence and distinction. Both generality and particularity are the main facets of this process which is manifested at all levels. Hence integration, as other types of identities, has dual functions: general integral on the one hand and specific, based on certain cultural patterns, on the other. It could mean that integration within different cultural milieus, though similar in a general context, however, will always vary bearing this or that unique cultural stamp. All this implies the following: (1) integration and identity issues are always interconnected; (2) integration is a two-way traffic reflecting both general and specific patterns of development of this or that geo-economic and geo-political space; (3) integration is a form of both social coherence and distinction at the same time. All these features of integration were glaringly exposed in Central Asia after 1991, the time when signs of globalization on the one hand, and convulsions echoing the break of the former Soviet colossus, on the other, coincided and made a double effect on the developmental patterns of the countries of the region. This article addresses the issues of cultural identity and structural frameworks and how they affect post-Soviet integration processes taking place in Central Asian region.

Identity, Culture, and Transformation

As it was mentioned above, integration could be seen as a representative form of a specific collective identity of certain geo-economic and geo-political entities, what implies the identity formation being one of the crucial factors, acquiring special importance at a time of transformations. Logically speaking, any transformation in any sphere, which could also be described as adjusting the past into the future through the present mechanisms inevitably highlights the issue of identity. In order to overcome the chaos, to find out the new path, first of all, the seekers have to find themselves. Who are we, from where are we going and what is our destination, what are we looking and aspiring for, and what are we going to change or modernize? In this regard, the restoration of one's own history and cultural patterns, search for cultural codes, particularly embedded in religions, that could be able to shed light on understanding modern processes, acquire importance. Integration here becomes a significant tool for social coherence, solidarity, and even survival thus adding new facets to collective consciousness leading to identity formation.

Collective identity formation in turbulent periods of history experiences its logic, projecting the issues of the past and future in its own orbit. In case of colonial societies, the colonial and post-colonial consciousness amplifies this significantly. To justify colonial societies' own self-sufficiency and cultural dignity, various interpretations of the glorious past and even brighter future are highlighted. The myths of cultural 'golden age' of the past as well as of the future occur, the religious and ethnic sentiments are fully exploited, the nationalism receives firm roots for its manifestation— this is the answer of the former colonies to the double pressure of change. Religious identity, in particular, gets a very strong hold over the unfolding drama of transformations and modernity. But once this step of radical manifestations is over, another search begins for a sustainable development to preserve, maintain, and further implement this newly found identity.

Identity formation's ebbs and flows are, as was mentioned earlier, interlinked with integration issues. In this regard, it could be said that being a form of collective identity, integration too inevitably experiences its same algorithm, surges, and fluctuations. It may explain why at certain spans of time the ideas of integration become fully mainstreamed or vice versa, absolutely neglected. The case of Central Asian space proves this very well. Recent history, following the break of the Soviet Union, suggests that one of the crucial obstacles on the way to integration was to overcome the colonial and new post-colonial mentality and paradigm also known as a 'big brother' syndrome. Actually, the colonial mentality is a reciprocal process, in a sense that not only the former colonies, but a former metropolis too has to get rid of a colonial mentality—superiority or inferiority. Russia too as a former metropolis and sovereign, as a former 'big brother', had to undergo its own transformations, at least on political and decision-making levels, not speaking about the grass-root consciousness. The early history of independence of both Central Asian countries and Russia has shown the process when the break of the former 'patron-client' formula caused the opposite reaction—search for another pattern of relations with new actors and political players outside the region. It is suffice to say here that the newly experienced identity of being independent and 'grown up' enough to lead own life, or of being 'free enough' from a burden of leading others, immediately resulted in the break-up of almost all major links and virtually in absence of any real integration processes.

From a methodological perspective, while speaking about integration as a form of collective identity, one inevitably comes to the notion of culture; since each collective identity is basically culture-based one. The culture here is understood in a broad sense as embracing all spheres of spiritual and material life of people—religious, scientific, economic, political, agricultural, educational, military, etc., within the course of their immediate or prolonged time and space, interaction among themselves: on inter-personal, collective, and societal levels, with the surrounding world, and with the already existing patterns of culture. In this sense, then, every aspect of men's activity will clearly bear a broad cultural dimension. Hence, integration may be viewed as a representation of culture-based collective identity. It means that the forms and paces of integration should always be correlated with the existing cultural patterns of the entities seeking it. In practice, it could mean that real integration as a process of social and, in a broad sense, cultural cohesion and solidarity is always subject to *shared* cultural patterns, that is, values, mores, traditions, history, models of development, etc. This leads us to the importance of shared history in integration processes on Central Asian and Eurasian spaces.

Shared History and Integration: A Backgrounder

Due to historical, geographical, economic, and other factors, there were always in the region uncountable migration flows of the people, an intermixture of various tribes and ethnic groups. The Eurasian steppes were seen mainly as a broad nomadic arena scattered by the oasis spots that had connected various cultures based on different ways of living; and that was a case of nomads and settled people, resulting in a special type of economy.[1] The history has shown that the dispersedly scattered tribes and groups of the same ethnic origin were involved in the orbit of the neighbouring cultures. That was the reason the region from the very beginning became a highly mosaic picture and gave birth to the specific mixed cultural type reflected most vividly in 'the leading zones of the sedentarization'[2] where the dichotomy 'we-other' failed to dominate the minds. The display of such interaction or certain impressionism that mixed the lines, perceptions, and ways of living was expressed in the multi-linguistic coexistence in the region (Turkic-Chagatay, Persian, Arabic); in the elements of ornament, decor, and art;[3] and with the spread of Islam, in the religion as well, which aimed at unifying this diversity.

It is worth briefly noticing that the Central Asian region—here understood as five former Soviet republics, starting from the 1730s—became a part of imperial Russian empire and then Soviet state. The modernization and early forms of integration for colonies started from the individual, social systems, and as such was connected with the scientific progress and industrialization which metropolis began to slowly develop in the peripheries of the empire. The building of the infrastructural projects such as railways, roads, post offices; the prolonged introduction of new Russian language-based education; 'bringing up' of the local elites ready to join the empire civil service as well as other ways of modernization—all this was met by the colonial peripheries albeit not initially wholeheartedly.

The other was the situation as the culture and cultural symbolism were concerned. In different cultural backgrounds this was expressed variously. In the context of a dispersed nomadic milieu which became the first to be incorporated in the Russian colonial orbit since 1731, the mutual adaptation of both centre and periphery was gradual, prolonged and rather tolerant. At that point of time during the reign of Anna Ioannovna and Catherine the Great, the Russian empire itself had to overcome its own traditionality and just began to put on the ideas of enlightenment and modernization. The specificity of religious beliefs of the nomads—rather syncretic, diluted, all-embracing had also played its role.

With the final inclusion of other parts of Central Asia in 1860s—the last resistant state was the Bukhara Emirate—both metropolis and new Asiatic colonies faced the challenge of finding the way of coexistence. This problem had drawn special attention in Bukhara, Samarkand, and Khoqand—the historically traditional centres of Islamic knowledge where the *Ulema* had to give a theologically-justified answer as far as their new colonial status was concerned. At the turn of the nineteenth to twentieth centuries it was in these places where the debates took place on the issue whether to apply to Turkestan, which became politically a dependent territory. The status of *dar al-Islam* (the land of Islam) or *dar al-Harb* (the land of war) was heatedly debated. This theological thesis acquired a considerable importance since based on it the particular actions towards recognition or rejection of Russian empire could be implemented. For example, the argumentation of theologian and thinker Taib (in 1905) as well as of one of the first reformers in Ferghana valley—Ibrat (in 1917)—was that it was necessary to recognize Russian governance due to the latter's undisputable technical and military supremacy (Komatsu 2007, pp. 6–9).

By the end of the nineteenth century, the further linking up among colonial centre and peripheries took place. Issues of modernization, particularly new knowledge, education, progress had acquired new dimension. The logical output of these problems became the *jadid* movement aimed at modernizing the social life, introducing schools of new types based on advanced new methods of education, the so called *novometodnye shkoly*. The jadids found themselves in the avant-garde of the process of adapting the traditional cultural systems to the new ways of development. At the same time, the ideas, favouring an urgent religious reformation of Islam became too prominent in the region. It is worth mentioning here that the outcomes of the World War I (1918) and the formation of a new type of international order had triggered the process when the religious identity issues became intertwined with the ethnic and more broadly—national identity. This was fully inevitable in view of the ideas of change that were in the air all over the Orient revolutions of the first decades of the twentieth century in Turkey, Iran, and China as well the national movement in British India. In this regard, pan-Islamism and pan-Turkism could be regarded as the glaring manifestation of the increasing role of religious and ethnic identities on the one hand, and as early integration attempts based on specific collective identity on the other. They were a specific answer of colonies to the challenges of colonial structural framework in which they seek a breakthrough. In other words, if we think of empire as of a certain integration of multiple cultures, then the anti-colonial struggle is always an identity-based one and hence, with the elements of some integration too.

The bright examples of this were an early twentieth century ideas on extending a wide cultural autonomy to Turkestan, articulated in 1907 by Turkestan *jadid* Makhmoudkhoja Bekhbudi. These ideas could be regarded as a certain specific starting point of the 'Islamic autonomous movement in Turkestan' (Komatsu 2007, p. 20). The creation of a cultural autonomy was perceived as a protection of ethnic identity, traditional culture, and its values identified first of all with Islam. Through this prism, the other ideas of Makhmoudkhoja Bekhbudi could be analysed as well, including the radical idea to forbid the migration of non-Muslims to Turkestan without the consent given to them by the local population. The religious part could be seen in the idea of creating own Spiritual Governing Body of Muslims in Turkestan, that could not be dependent on Russian authorities.[4]

Soviet Style Integration

With the inclusion of all Central Asian republics into the USSR in 1922, the idea of integration acquired a new 'socialist' form and had undergone major changes in terms of space and time. The radical Soviet modernization dissolved all barriers between the republics on the one hand, and created deep interdependent links between them and the centre on the other. Being itself a multiple-cultures-based integration project in an atheist environment, the Soviet Union too heavily exploited an identity factor to bind and mix together various parts of the union. In specific conditions of atheist propaganda, this identity factor was one based on ideology. Communist ideology as a new constructed identity aimed at social coherence became a driving force for Soviet style integration, the substitute for religious or ethnic identities. As such the Soviet style integration became another bright example of the interconnected links between identity and integration. At the same time, the Soviet experience, the collapse of the country in particular, also showed that improper usage of identity factor such as an absolute dominance of a constructed ideology over the religious and ethnic, so-called 'primordial' identities could have a devastating effect on the concept of integration itself.

However, it may be stressed here that the experience of establishing and maintaining tight links within the single Soviet entity could not be neglected at all and has added to the formation of a new spirit of share, as far as economic, financial, educational, transport, logistic, and other networks are concerned. Still, even in pure economic realm, the high dominance of ideology paved the way to a lopsided specificity of economic integration, when the distribution of resources, industrial structures, raw materials processing, and service sectors were generally kept apart from the raw materials production. Under this scheme, all Central Asian Republics (CARs) that is, Kazakhstan, Kyrgyzstan, Tajikistan, Turkmenistan, Uzbekistan became raw materials-oriented republics; mainly in the sphere of natural resources, that is, production of oil, gas, cotton, wheat, mining, and animal-breeding; while the processing, upgrading, and technological production based on these raw materials had been developed in other republics of the Soviet Union, particularly, in Belorussia (agricultural equipment), Ukraine, and Russian Federation.

Hence, it could be easily understood that the whole industrial or agricultural chain of production became scattered and zigzagged. On the one hand, it inevitably embraced various republics binding all of them together; and on the other hand, ideological factor defined the development of a lop-sided economies of each republic. Political and ideological tasks of strengthening the country against the possible disintegration became one of the main reasons why interdependence became a main principle of development in all republics. Moreover, one could also mention another crucial factor—the 'big brother' syndrome, that is, the dominance of certain ethnic groups, mainly Russian and Slavic, over the others, including Central Asians.

From this vantage point, the main aim of former Soviet authorities was to maintain the existing status-quo of dominance, both economic and ethnic, to the detriment of developing the strong peripheries which otherwise might become industrially or culturally independent. All mentioned in above instances explain why the CARs, being rich in natural and mineral resources, fertile land, and relatively educated human resources, lacked the strong full-cycle independent industries. Certain exception could be made with regard to Kazakhstan and Uzbekistan. In both of these former Soviet republics, there were several industrial plants and factories, particularly metallurgical in Karaganda, aviation in Tashkent, agricultural vehicles equipment in Pavlodar, and so on. However, the above mentioned factors led to the principle of narrow specialization when the equipment details necessary for making these factories workable were produced in other republics. For example, the technical equipment for agricultural vehicles has been produced in Belarus and parts of aviation production in Ukraine.

It could be said that Soviet Union had its own specific integration agenda, but this integration was specifically designed to answer not only economic, but also ideological tasks of the former USSR. Moreover, one could stress that ideological dominance was even more crucial in that hierarchy. Ironically, the socialist/communist ideas initially based on the domination of the material base of productive forces over all others, including ideological, became themselves the subject of controversy, when ideology dictated the economic purposefulness. It is not surprising that with the slightest changes in and relaxation of ideological mechanism during *perestroika* in second half of 1980s, the purely economic forces alone could not sustain the huge, extant Soviet mechanism due to the fact that they were to a certain extent artificially designed and were based on the predominant ideological lines. This explains particularly the fact why the Soviet economy has finally collapsed, not only because of the pure absence of liberal market (although this factor was rather crucial), but also due to the imperfect design and implementation of the already existing economic links. Ideological misinterpretation and practical lopsided emphasis on the socialist idea of equality became an obstacle for a true egalitarian integration within the then Soviet Union.

Mapping Integration in Contemporary Eurasian Space

Many of today's issues high on the agenda in the countries of the region are inherited from the past. In this regard, the most vivid legacy of the ideological dimension of integration processes or identity-integration links was the disintegration of the economies of Eurasia and Central Asia.

In early 1990s, after the collapse of the Soviet Union, the structural concept of Soviet style integration came to an end paving the way for the splash of identities. The identity-based disintegration process was too strong to talk about further integration. As a result, the idea of integration was not popular in most post-Soviet countries; rather it was perceived as a nearly futuristic dream of some of its propagators, mainly Kazakhstan President Nursultan Nazarbayev. In 1994, in an address at the Moscow State University, he particularly mentioned the need for integration in the post-Soviet space, as a life or death matter.

After the collapse of the Soviet Union, the interdependence and inter-complementary character of all economies were regarded as an obstacle towards the independent development of every newly sovereign state. Each of them tried to assert its own independent pattern of economic models, predominantly based on the liberal ideas of the 'invisible hand of the market' with the combination of the strong authoritative power of the state, usually a presidential form. It is suffice here to say that the transitional period from a socialist model towards the newly adopted one was an extremely painful process characterized by lack of production, poverty, huge disproportions in distribution of resources, and as a result, social insecurity and an increased gap between the rich and poor. At the time of asserting new economic models, constructing or reconstructing their own identity and foundations for a new ideology, all Central Asian states started elaborating their own independent policies. In pursuing this aim, the integration imperative became a kind of an obscure and a vague idea, which, as it was perceived by that time, had little to do with the 'truly' independent development. There were some voices in favour of restoring the economic links; however, they were considered as attempts of Russia to reconfigure and revive the old Soviet structural frameworks or as in case of Kazakhstan's President Nazarbayev, as a mere utopia.

The creation of the Commonwealth of Independent States (CIS) became a bright sample of this approach. Although this was the first integration initiative implemented after the collapse of the Soviet Union, it has been set up following the inertia and for the most part continued to be unworkable. At the beginning of 1990s, strong religious and ethnic based identity sentiments lent a feeling that the time for real integration has not yet come. It is thus explicable that the 1994 idea of Nazarbayev in favour of real integration has been taken politely, but without any great enthusiasm. All countries of the former USSR, including in Central Asian region, had yet to undergo the process of transformation in almost all spheres of life and to experience the religious and ethnic identities as old-new replacements for a previous ideological paradigm. That was a time of distinction and disintegration.

By the beginning of the twenty-first century, when the ideas of globalization and regionalization asserted themselves profoundly, the countries of the former Soviet Union were far behind this process. It took them nearly a decade to develop their own style integration, although one might notice that the real integration is still far from its developed forms. At the turn of the millennium, the role of Asian continents and countries on world affairs has been increasing. Huge Eurasian geostrategic space too is subject to crucial transformations which imply that each country and region should skilfully adjust itself to the ongoing changes. In this regard, each state, Kazakhstan in particular, is obliged to elaborate the corresponding macro-strategies while dealing with the internal and external policymaking, mainly at various levels—global, Eurasian, regional, bilateral, and so on. All of them are interconnected with each other and could not be separated.

On a cursory look at the so called 'integration map' in the Eurasian space, at the very first glance, one could find a rather significant number of various intergovernmental organizations aimed at integration in different spheres—CIS established in 1991; Eurasian Economic Community set up in 2000, and within it, the Customs Union forged in 2010; Collective Security Treaty Organization established in 1992, Shanghai Cooperation Organisation (SCO) established in 1996 and institutionalized in 2001; and Central Asian Cooperation Organization founded in 2006. All of them have undergone a long way either institutionally or operationally. Some of them were even able to totally change the direction of their development. For example, that was the case of the EurAsEC, which initially was conceived as the Customs Union in 1996. Theoretically speaking, Customs Union is one of the three steps towards real workable integration and a basis for a union between states. The initial idea was to let the newly independent states get the impulse for the growth of their production and economy. However, the time has showed the impossibility to embed this kind of integration from 'above', as a simple intention of the leaders. The real integration should undergo several steps from beneath, ranging from the creation of the free trade regime; exchange of services, goods, and their access to internal markets; formation of unified customs tariffs and unified system of measures of non-tariff regulation; introduction of unified currency regulation and control; and so on.

Once there are elaboration and further implementation of joint programmes of socio-economic development, creation of equal opportunities for business, common transport, and energy markets; equal opportunities for access to the markets of all countries-participants of foreign investments; equal rights for citizens to the education and medical help, rapprochement, and harmonization of national laws; creation of common legal space and so on are introduced and implemented; only then one could speak about workable integration. All this shows that real integration mechanisms taking place nowadays yet have to be further advanced, and that takes time.

The example of EurAsEC perfectly shows the way the whole ideas of integration took place. For example, after claims to establish Customs Union (in 1994) which, as has been mentioned now, was completely unworkable at that time; the idea was to transform this mechanism from above by changing the direction. It means that the first initial mechanisms as they were implemented in European Union as early as in 1950s, started taking place. Instead of Customs Union, it was declared to organize a free trade regime, exchange of services, goods, and their access to internal markets. Thus, on 10 October 2000, the EurAsEC community began to evolve, comprising five countries of Belarus, Kazakhstan, Kyrgyzstan, Russia, and Tajikistan. Later on, observer status was given to Moldova and Ukraine in 2002 and Armenia in 2003. Uzbekistan became a member of EurAsEC in 2006 only to leave it few years later.

It is worth noticing that EurAsEC tries to follow the European pattern in terms of its structural composition as well. It has Interstate Council as a supreme body comprising of leaders of the states and governments, Integration Committee, Inter-Parliamentary Assembly, and Common Legal Court. In 2009, the decision was made that starting from June 2010, the new structure, Customs Union, would be operational among three member countries—Belarus, Kazakhstan, and Russia. It could mean that the earlier idea of Customs Union as it was expressed in 1994 became realized only 16 years later. The meeting held on 9 December 2010 in Moscow of the supreme body of the Customs Union saw the adoption of the Declaration on Formation of Common Economic Space and the signing of 17 international treaties which indicated that the beginning of the full-scaled common economic space among three countries would start effectively from 1 January 2012. The Declaration stated that through the Customs Union and Common Economic Space, EurAsEC heads towards creation of the Eurasian Economic Union.

The instance of EurAsEC is very representative. It shows us how the structural shared legacy bequeathed from the Soviet period were combined with the attempts to somehow get in the last wagon of the outgoing train of globalization, to be embedded in this process and not to stay behind. To what extent this integration will be successful is still an open question, since there are many constraints within the political elites as the political ambitions and negotiating process. However, the structural framework is set up which provides substantial basis for its inevitable implementation in the future.

Following the thesis expressed above on integration and identity interlinks, the case of EurAsEC provides us with this example too. The construction and enhancement of a new Eurasian identity comes forward as a new paradigm and justification of creating joint integrative space. It is worth mentioning that this idea of common Eurasian space (*evraziistvo*) is highly articulated both in Kazakhstan and Russia as a significant cornerstone of internal and foreign policies. For Kazakhstan, it acquires such a place that even it could be regarded as a kind of national idea. Well acknowledging the possibilities as well as constraints, the geographical location brings Kazakhstan to maximally exploit its geography and turn the obstacles into the opportunities. The idea of evraziistvo is vivid everywhere, in cultural symbolism, the state being at the heart of Eurasia, economy, and politics. In 2006, President Nazarbayev initiated the creation of the Eurasian Economic Union, favoured the creation in Astana of the Eurasian Centre of the Water aimed at dealing with all problems of water resources in the region. There is a Eurasian Bank of Development set up jointly by Kazakhstan and Russia which invests in the economies of not only both countries, but of other ones. The new national university in capital Astana was given a name Eurasian National University after L. Gumilev, one of the propagators of the idea of evraziistva.

In the Central Asian region, the issues of integration are urgent on the agenda. In spite of the shared history and culture, economic, humanitarian, and cultural integration need to be elaborated further. Thus, the crucial obstacles lie not only in the field of pure economic performance, but cultural identity too. Along with the opportunities provided by the shared cultural roots, there are still tasks to overcome the narrow national mentality in understanding and conceptualizing the common cultural field, which has a big potential to become the ground of integration. The current situation in the field of integration on Central Asian and Eurasian spaces shows high interdependence and links between integration and identity.

Notes and References

1. A.M. Khazanov (2002), *The Nomads and the Outside World*. Almaty: Daik-Press, pp. 68–9.
2. A. Sengupta (2002), *Frontiers into Borders. The Transformation of Identities in Central Asia*. New Delhi and London: Hope India Publications/Greenwich Millennium, p. 2.
3. Ibrayeva, in particular, shows the resemblance between the motives of the Kazakh and Iranian ornaments. Using the sample of such elements as the horns of sheep, flowers, tree and astral symbols she stresses their spreading on the vast territory of not only Kazakhstan, but of Great Central Asia inhabited by the Turks, Mongols, Iranians. Korenyako, in his own turn, analyses the unified so-called animal style in Central Asia. (See Ibrayeva 1994, pp. 11 and 15; Korenyako 2002, pp. 5–21.)
4. H. Komatsu (2007), 'Dar al-Islam under Russian Rule as Understood by Turkestani Muslim Intellectuals/Empire, Islam and Politics in Central Eurasia' (Slavic Eurasian Studies, No. 14), Uyama Tomohiko (ed.). Sapporo: Slavic, pp. 6–9.
5. K. Ibrayeva (1994), *The Kazakh Ornament*. Almaty: Oner (Kazakhskii ornament).
6. V. Korenyako (2002), *The Art of the People of Central Asia and the Animal Style*. Moscow: Vostochnaya Literatura (Iskusstvo narodov Tsentralnoi Azii i zverinyi stil).

11

The Performative State
Nation Building and Nationalist Discourse in Uzbekistan

ANITA SENGUPTA

Each of us realize that today Uzbekistan is an integral part of the world community and global financial and economic market.

—Islam Karimov, 2009

In an increasingly globalized world, nation-state building is no longer an activity confined to the domestic arena. Situating the state within the global space and its 'image' in the international community becomes in many ways as crucial as the projection of homogeneity within the state. The relationship between politics and cultural symbols/'images', therefore, acquires and represents multiple possibilities. This relationship became particularly relevant for states that emerged in the wake of the disintegration of the Soviet Union in Central Asia. These were essentially states that had not seen the development of an independent movement prior to the implosion at the centre, and were states where an 'externally imposed collapse led to internally invented signs of certainty'.[1] Their emergence raised questions about the legitimacy of the state/nation not just from within the state but also from the global arena. How the 'new' states legitimized their existence as separate entities and redefined themselves a new form, both internally and externally, therefore, assumes importance. In the course of this redefinition, competing images were articulated and new discourses were generated. Nation building and nationalist rhetoric, therefore, was intended as much for the international public as the domestic audience whether it was the projection of Kazakhstan as the 'Heart of Eurasia' or Kyrgyzstan as the 'Island of Democracy'. Though not as well articulated, the image that the Uzbek state presented was that of an 'ancient state at the crossroads of civilization'.

This article is an attempt at examining the shaping of a 'post-Soviet' future through the performative role played by the state in the arena of culture, historical memory, images, and rhetoric. It seeks to do this by specifically taking into account the Uzbek case where the projection of aspects like a common ancestry and history play a significant part in creating the image of an ancient state with a homogeneous people. Here, the performative role of the state in face of the reality of a multiplicity of histories and identities in the region is evident. In fact, in a number of cases, it results in rhetoric or policy that takes note of this multifarious heritage and recognizes its significance in the wake of a homogenizing global tendency. However, imperatives of state building within the global arena are also evident in the irony of a state that proclaims its existence as an ancient state, retrieves its Turkish identity yet speaks of its promises and potentialities in the language of the newborn. Therefore, one finds in this phase of transition, the juxtaposition of a cultural rediscovery of the past and a projection of the state as a developmental state.

The article highlights the fact that while parts of the nationalist discourse was intended for a domestic audience, part of it was aimed at the international arena with the aim of capturing global attention. Public diplomacy and the creation and promotion of 'national' images were attempts to raise the prestige of the country and primarily aimed at the international business community and the global political leadership. The images and rhetoric that accompany Independence Day celebrations, for instance, not only articulate the existence of a cohesive state, for the domestic audience but a prosperous one attractive for both international tourism as well as investment. Similarly, the rhetoric of 'nation under threat' is not just a projection for unity within the state but also a call for international recognition of the fact that Uzbekistan is both a victim and part of a global 'fight against terrorism'. This article begins with the process of formation of the Uzbek state and the assertion of an 'Uzbek' identity both in terms of definitions as well as history. In the process, it notes numerous contradictions that are implicit in both and which, in many cases, the state itself recognizes. It concludes by looking at how the rhetoric that accompanies the reassertion of this identity is both a celebration of the state and a statement for the international community.

Identities and Definitions

In 1924, the people of a region who had defined themselves in local terms through history were transformed into Uzbeks, Tajiks, Kazakhs, Kyrgyz, and Turkmen—names that would define their identities subsequently. The rationalization of this division was made on the basis of language with the prediction that each of these nations would now develop themselves and their national cultures and identities within frontiers determined by these lines. The making of 'modern nation-states' in the Central Asian region was, therefore, based on the identification of distinct national groups. However, in the Central Asian region as in many other regions, this created numerous problems. In a number of cases like the Central Asian one, the state not only defined the boundary within which identity was to be circumscribed, but also defined the basis for the definition. The rationality on which this basis was determined defined the principal characteristic of groups and subsequently assumed a significance of its own. As nations were constructed within the boundaries of the state, the projection of a numerical majority defined in terms of rationally delimited criteria became crucial. In the ensuing number game, titular nationalities were often seen to gain in numbers, at least in official demographic records, at the expense of other groups. However, the determination of 'national' majorities and minorities is often a complex process where multiple factors play a part. In regions like Central Asia, where identities had historically been multiple and fluid, they created significant complexities that re-emerged in later years. It is not surprising, therefore, that it has been 20 years since the emergence of independent states in the region, and questions of 'nation building' still remain crucial.

Traditionally, there were two routes to the emergence of nations—nations could be created out of the transformation of an ethnic group in a multi-ethnic state into a self-conscious political entity or by the amalgamation of diverse groups and the formation of an inter-ethnic, composite, or homogeneous national culture through the agency of the modern state.

Although the two processes of nation formation have different starting points and raise quite different kinds of analytical and theoretical questions, the end result historically has often been the same and the two processes have much in common. The 'state to nation' model gives a strong role to the state in the construction of the new civic nations and political communities. Although the 'state to nation' route was historically territorial, it has always included within itself the cultural elements. The political nation, therefore, always incorporated both civic and ethnic factors, based usually upon the ethnic core that created the state.

In the Central Asian, and specifically the Uzbek case, an interesting combination of the two processes went hand in hand. The Uzbek case of modern nation-state formation is usually identified as a 'state to nation' model where the formation of the Uzbek Soviet Socialist Republic subsequently led to the creation of an Uzbek nation and finally to the formation of an independent state. However, an internal process of cultural transformation had already begun in the region by the turn of the century that had looked towards the amalgamation of the various groups under a common identity and a change in the functioning of the political structures. The current phase of state building in the Central Asian region is thus more correctly identified as a simultaneous process of nation and state building in what is being termed as 'nationalizing states'.[2] This implies that there is recognition of the fact that the state is an 'unrealized' nation and attempts are made to remedy the fact through active involvement of the state in the process of encouraging the language and culture of the majority. In the Uzbek case, it was also realized that this process of nation building actually began in a previous era when attempts were made at the construction of an Uzbek identity. While the importance of 'nationalizing' is realized, there is also recognition of its constraints in a multi-ethnic society. And this is evident in the way in which the state dealt with cultural factors like language and religion.

Language was regarded by early Bolsheviks as the key to the rational reorganization of the region and its division into separate entities. As separate languages were created for separate groups of people, language attained a significance of its own. However, there was recognition of the fact that numerous dialects were spoken in the region that was constituted as Uzbekistan, and most people were multilingual. The determination of the literary form of the Uzbek language and the subsequent changeover to the Cyrillic script was, therefore, not immediate. The Uzbek Encyclopaedia itself recognized that the Uzbek language has a number of dialects.[3] The literary Uzbek is just one of them. Similarly, the persistence of diglossia was recognized as a reality by the political elite, after the formation of the sovereign Uzbek state. While the necessity of a common culture among citizens was recognized as important, a hegemonic language regime was not a crucial part of the political agenda. While the imperatives of 'nation-building' led the Uzbek state to undertake a policy of 'language-regime', the same imperatives forced the state to be more accommodative.

Similarly, Islam was regarded as a viable and crucial component of Uzbek culture though it was downplayed in the initial stages as the Soviet power sought to rationalize the creation of states on 'objectives' grounds. However, a blending of religion into Uzbek national consciousness in the second phase of the formation of the state was seen as crucial. In fact, in the post-Independence phase, the requirements of economic modernization and the pragmatic imperatives of management of social pluralities became crucial in the determination of the relation of the state with religion. A sharp divergence was recognized between the formal structures that were identified by the state as pertaining to the sphere of religion and the actual existence of a set of beliefs among the people. The continuing existence of sects associated with Sufism attested to the fact that the nature of religious organizations in the region was not monolithic. The mixed cultural heritage of the people meant the continued existence of a set of beliefs that were never really removed even in the Soviet era. While the reality was that of a society with multiple religious traditions, the imperatives of the post-Soviet era demanded the projection of a singular faith that would form the basis of the foundation of the new state. However, faced with global 'radical' challenges in the post-Independence period, the emphasis soon shifted to the many pre-Islamic traditions of the region. As such, the political rhetoric of revival emphasized on the multifarious traditions of faith, rather than emphasized on the structures of an 'Islam'. These and numerous other contradictions like these complicated the process of nation building.

The rationalization of identities on the basis of which 'nationalities' were determined bring to the forefront the necessity of examining the ethnographic origins of the population, the self-definition of the groups of people themselves, and also the complexities that emerge from the way that groups were defined by the 'others' within the same environment. A crucial part of the debate is thus based on 'definitions'. For instance, the definition of 'Tajikness' or 'Uzbekness', that is, which would constitute the Tajiks or the Uzbeks, formed a significant part of the debate. Here, the fact that self-definition in the region had never been determined in terms of 'nationalities' became crucial. One of the principal problems which arose, as a result, was incorrect identification of the 'ethnic' criteria. For instance, in a number of cases, Tajiks declared themselves as Uzbeks in their identity papers. Therefore, they were recorded as such in all official demographic records. A related problem was the spatial distribution of these groups of people. This problem was of course most relevant in terms of the inhabitants of what were claimed as Tajik-dominated areas of Samarkand, Khojent, and Bukhara.

In the post-Soviet period, when these groups of people who had been delimited in the 1920s and 1930s into distinct republics, declared sovereignty, these questions once again became significant. Sovereignty also brought to the forefront the necessity for redefinitions not just for the newly created nation-state but also for the groups within the state. The place of the new states in the world order and questions relating to foreign as well as the domestic policy orientation of the newly constituted states assumed importance. For these, in turn, they would determine the newer political affinities and definitions of group identity. Could Uzbekistan and Tajikistan be considered to be part of the Turkic/Iranian worlds or say the Islamic world? Were they at all a part of the Orient or are the ties with its old political centre, Moscow, still strong enough to warrant their place as part of the western world? And more importantly, how did the Uzbek/ Tajik states visualize the options implicit in these identities? The above-mentioned issues became crucial for the newly constituted states. On the other hand, the determination of whether identities, as defined by and within the state, retained their clarity for the individual became equally significant.

Identities assumed significance in post-Soviet Central Asia, since the nation building process is seen to have been accompanied by a reawakening of what is characterized as the 'ethnic' identity of groups who, it had hitherto been assumed, had been assimilated within the structures of the titular nations. This 'ethnic' identity has been visualized as largely primordial and defined in general terms to indicate cultural aspects of identity like language, religion, or 'clan'. In the Central Asian case, the pre-Soviet identity of the groups who were later constituted as 'nations' assumes importance. Here, the fact that most of these groups were themselves complex amalgams of different group identities needs to be taken note of. The Uzbeks, for instance, were referred to as the 'Ozbeks of the ninety-two tribes', pointing to a multiplicity of group identity even among groups who are today considered to be 'nationalist'.[4] Ethnographic descriptions of the groups of people, from the end of the nineteenth century to the beginning of the twentieth century, who were defined as 'Uzbek' after 1924 show that they were, in fact, constituted out of numerous divisions and sub-divisions. A study that has examined the Uzbek groups only in the Upper Kashkadarya, in the regions of Kitab, Shehr-i-Sabz, Yakkabag, Chirakchin, and Kamashin, shows that the Uzbeks were constituted of the Kengis, Saroi, Kungrad, Barlas, Mangit, Uz, Kurama, Kutich, and others. It then goes on to show subdivisions of each of these Uzbek groups. The Sarois, for example, who numbered 29,940 people according to the 1926 census, are further subdivided into Kypchak Saroi, Kyrgyz Saroi, Mazhar Saroi, Tagiz Saroi, Ach Saroi, Naiman Saroi, Sanchikli Saroi, Aktunli Saroi, Serov Saroi, Sak Saroi, Zhoman Saroi, Mangit Saroi, Kushtamgali Saroi, Burgali Saroi, Nyekuz Saroi, and Kungrad Saroi. Each of these is then further subdivided. The Kipchak Sarois, for instance, were subdivided into Kanzhyegali, Kaz Oyeokli, Kipkoyeoli, Karga-Oyeogli, Mirza, Zhagarak, Avakli, Umakai, Naiman, and Chorkuza. The Sarois are also to be found among other Central Asian groups like the Kyrgyz.[5] Similarly, all the other groups are also divided into numerous groupings.

Also the situation was further complicated by the fact that groups like the Uzbek Kengis were supposed, by some, to have come from the Kitais. Other groups like the Uzbek Katagan, who were to be found in Katagan, Tashkurgan, Zarmaz, Gulistan, and other regions, were separated from other Uzbek tribes but some were mixed with the Tajiks. The Katagans had resettled in Zerafshan and in Hissar and only a branch called the Mylos remained in the Upper Kashkadarya region. Till the revolution, they had contact with Katagans in Afghanistan. The study, of course, concludes that the process of settlement of these 'tribes' amidst the settled agricultural population helped in consolidating the future 'Uzbek' nation.[6] The non-territorial nature of identity has also been noted among all the 'nationalities' who now constitute titular nationalities in the region. Similarly, the bilingual nature of large parts of the population and the fact that intermarriage was normal has been discussed. This was common to nearly all the urban and lowland areas that now constitute Uzbekistan and Tajikistan.

Such descriptions bring to the forefront the complexity of a situation where the people of the now sovereign republics of Central Asia had been linked for centuries by community of language, extended contact, ethnic or cultural interaction, and similar historical development. They were spreading over extensive arid, semi arid, and mountain tracts and were constantly intermixing in a process where scattered groups of once larger tribes, for example, Kypchaks, Mangits, and Naimanswere often incorporated to form unstable short-lived political unions. Of equal importance was the intermingling of the Turkic speaking nomads with the ancient Iranian agricultural population that began from the epoch of the great Turkic Khanates and continued till modern times. Given this constant process of meeting and breaking away of groups, questions about the nature of identity and consciousness among them assume significance. More important is the resolution of whether 'national identity' and 'political consciousness', as we know of them today, traditionally existed in the region, and if so, in what form. The Soviet 'nationalities policy' was, therefore, not without its problems. Yet interestingly, in the post-Soviet phase, there was a concerted effort to identify with the Soviet era definitions. More importantly, there was no movement out of the definitional constructs of Soviet times. The designation *Uzbek*, for instance, is being used in the Soviet sense to mean *nation*, whereas previously it had been used to mean a *tribal* classification of a dominant dynastic tribal tier, the Shybanids.[7] In fact, an entire history was created to justify the construct.

Rediscovery and Assertion

In his book, *The Modern Uzbeks: A Cultural History from the Fourteenth Century to the Present*, Edward Allworth, cites the following lines from the Uzbek poet Abdu Razzaq Abduvashidaw's ballad 'The Dear Soil',

Every Nation has its own desire
its own song, its own epic
It has its own place—its own garden
so far preserved 'thousands of years.[8]

This tradition 'preserved for thousands of years' has now become the focus of writings in the Central Asian region. It is a literature that looks beyond the recent past of Central Asia into a past that is glorified as the 'nation of desire'. In the Uzbek case, there is an attempt at equating Turan, Transoxiana, and Turkistan with the ancient Uzbek civilizational past. This theme of an ancient past for the Uzbeks that President Karimov himself emphasizes finds echoes in a large number of writings, which have been published in post-Soviet Uzbekistan. These remain interesting in terms of examining how the story of the Uzbek's past is now being told. One representative example of such writing notes:

> Encyclopedias written in almost all languages hold to the lopsided idea that Uz-
> beks are descended from the Uzbek Khan of the Golden horde from 1313–42,
> and from the Shaybanids, who arrived in West Turkestan in the fifteenth century.
> (Uzbek Khan brought down the Timurid dynasty and established Uzbek rule in
> its place.) True, tribal Turks called Uzbeks did arrive with the Shaybanids, but
> they dwelled in the territory of Turk Stan during the Timurid era, in that of the
> Khwarezmshahs before that, during the Karakhanids and during the reigns of all
> the Turk khans, because, they, after all, were the original Turkish people of Turke-
> stan, right? Why is this not openly acknowledged?[9]

The construction of political space in post-Soviet Uzbekistan has involved certain recurrent themes and elements that have made their presence felt time and again. One of the themes that emerged in a large corpus of literature is *ethnogenesis*. *Oz ozingi anglap et* or getting to know oneself began in the last days of the Soviet Union through carefully worded writings that departed from the usual practice of writing historical pieces in the form of fiction.[10] This meant an objective confrontation with the past and was distinct from efforts that traced a mythical history of origins of the Uzbeks. The current rediscovery of the past is also represented as a major change from the historiographical practices of the Soviet past when the possibility of studying the past independently was curtailed.[11] These writings are also distinct in their attempt at implying an equation between the histories of the Turkish peoples living in the region with that of the Uzbeks. This equation remains problematic. However, it remains interesting as a representative example of the way in which the state constructs borders by using spatial strategies that homogenize identity and space.

A brief historical journey through the reading of a text that traces the development of the Uzbek state is an interesting comment on how the Uzbek space is being constructed today. The article was published in the journal *Obshestvenni Nayuki* v. *Uzbekistane* which is the journal of the Academy of Sciences of Uzbekistan. The article points out that till very recently, Uzbeks were mistakenly identified with the Shaybanids. There was no cognizance of the local Uzbek speaking population in the region. In actuality, it is pointed out, the people of the region consist of both the Turkish speaking people of the cities and villages of contemporary Uzbekistan bearing the name Sart and also the descendants of the Shaybanid Uzbeks who had lived here in the last four centuries and assimilated with the ancient indigenous ethnic layer of the region and spoke in 'one single old Uzbek language—the language of Ahmed Yassavi, Alisher Navoi and Babur.'[12] It has also been pointed out

That the most ancient layer of the Uzbek people in the past consisted of the Sogdianas, Bactrians and Khwarezmians as well as the cattle breeding tribes surrounding them—the Sakas—a part of which in the ancient time spoke in different dialects of ancient Turkish language. To this were added new ethnic components from the oasis of Tashkent, the Khidalites, Aftalites…. With the advent of the Karakhanids, an ethnogenetic process began, and single anthropological type typical of Uzbeks takes place. Single territorial position started forming…. Much later ethnic components are Shaybanids…. Usually the history of the people is more ancient than its name. Uzbeks inherited only name from Shaybanids. It was political to begin with and then became ethnic.[13]

They would also point to the fact that while the Greek invasions would be an important event in the history of Uzbekistan, subsequent centuries would see the likes of the empire of Chengiz Khan and the states formed by his sons, an empire which according to this viewpoint was definitely Turk and not Mongol in origin. The Timurid period is also being taken up for close analysis, as the golden age when 'Uzbek' culture, society, and art developed. Amir Timur and his contributions are being examined in depth and his legacy is now being appropriated by the state as exclusively Uzbek. Timur's contribution as having put an end to 'tribal disunity' in the region is lauded as a major achievement. The fact that he represented the feudal interests of the time is being interpreted as a minor failing of the ruling classes to which Timur was no exception.

It is equally significant that having established the fact that the Uzbeks have an ancestry longer than the one usually given to them, there is a tendency to equate the history of Uzbekistan with that of Turkestan, which in its turn is equated with the much larger unit of Turan.[14] This is being attempted not only in terms of historical lineage, but also in terms of its literature. It is generally said that written Uzbek literature began with the Yassavids in the eleventh century. It is now being pointed out that Uzbek literature or Turkish literature of Turkestan (including Kazakh, Kyrgyz, Uighur, Karakalpak, and Turkmen) started as written literature in the seventh century before Christ. The basis for this claim is a poem written in 626 BC dedicated to the death of Alp Er Tonga and which is still comprehensible to a modern Uzbek. Rather ambitiously, the *Shahnama*, where Alp Er Tonga is referred to as Afrasiab, is being held up as proof that the ancient Turks, 'the forefathers of today's Uzbeks ruled over two-thirds of the known world seven centuries before Christ'.[15] It is interesting to note that once again there is an attempt to equate the history of the Turks with that of the Uzbeks without addressing the question as to whether the modern Uzbeks and the Uzbek language today is to be completely equated with a general Turkish history and the Turkish language.

Another interesting aspect is the contemporary stress on linkages with the Persian language, with an onus on a cultural heritage that is so interlinked with that of the Tajiks that one can hardly be distinguished from the other. While this can be probably explained as prompted by the so called theorists of 'Greater Uzbekistan', that calls for a reunification of the now Tajik lands to Uzbekistan, the total eclipse of the Arabic linkages as also of the Arabic language is more difficult to explain. This recalls the Soviet tradition of ignoring the Arabic heritage for obvious linkages of the latter with the Islamic culture. However, while heroic traditions are being celebrated, there is recognition also among the scholars that much of this is a construction. The book published on the occasion of the celebration of the 2500 years of Bukhara states clearly that there is no accurate data on the age of this ancient city. It is '... based on *legends* taken from Narsakhi's *History of Bukhara*' and that 'the people of Bukhara *claim* that the city has been around for three millennia.'[16]

Where Uzbek historiography has departed from the standard accounts of the past years in the interpretation of such events as the 1898 uprising in the Ferghana valley, the autonomous government that was set up in Kokand in the immediate aftermath of the overthrow of the Tsar in 1917 and the issues of Russian military conquest and the popular resistance that this faced. This deals essentially with the first phase of transition, when the Soviet system was establishing itself (1920–4) and the various alternative forms were emerging. The role of what was known as the *Basmachi* movement is also being re-examined. Uzbek scholars now refer to them as the *kurbashis* and *mujahids*.[17] They are now designated as having been leaders of national movements and though they followed different political aspirations they had the aspiration to liberate their land from the *kyzylaskers* and restore the *Emir* to power. Nowadays, their sacrifice has been vindicated in the establishment of independent statehood.[18] Similarly, trends like *Jadidism* and the writings of various Jadid scholars have been taken up for study.[19] The change in the attitude towards the movement is apparent even in the course of comparison of writings on the subject between the early 1980s and the post-Independence days.

Speaking on the occasion of the 2500 years anniversary of Khiva, President Karimov stressed:

> The Roman historian Pompey Trog who had lived two thousand years ago wrote the following about the most ancient ancestors of Turkish people: Bactrians, Sogds and Khorezmians may well compete with Egyptians by the age of their origins and genesis. They do not spare themselves both in labour and severe fight. They are extremely strong physically. They never give up a thing that belongs to them. They only go for victory. It was in Khorezm valley where the very first stones of the Uzbek statehood were laid 2700 years ago. In this regard the history of our national statehood can be considered along with such ancient states as Egypt, China, India, Greece and Iran. The history of Khorezm is foundation of the Uzbek statehood, the confirmation of its antiquity and might.[20]

A significant part of the official discourse is based on the image of a paternalistic state that stresses stability and development through what is identified as the 'Uzbek Path'. This is based on 'folk traditions and customs' and emphasizes on social protection and redistribution. It was clearly stated that the new social and economic policy would also *promote the social program* in the country. This policy would take note of the *unique way of life* of the various cultures and civilizations in Uzbekistan and would consist of a variety of forms and methods.[21] The necessity of developing the basis of one's own model of development is recognized; a model which would be based on market relations but would also take into account the national historical heritage, foundations of life, traditions, and mentality of the people. President Karimov points to this when he says,

> We have selected an approach of rejecting egalitarianism in the system of social protection of the population and finding our own path corresponding to moral values, way of life and frame of mind of the nation which took shape throughout millennia in the East.[22]

There is clear recognition of the fact that there can be no universal model of economic development which can be followed. The Uzbek model would have to take note of concrete historical, socio-economic, national-psychological, and demographic aspects. This is being interpreted to mean an emphasis on stabilization.

This would mean that while on the one hand there would be an effort to move out of the administered economic structures of the Soviet system, it would not do without taking into account the requirements of society. This in turn would entail the continuation of certain policies like the continuation of consumer subsidies on imported goods. It is interesting that Karimov refers to the disappearance of the Berlin wall between 'orthodox definitions of capitalism and socialism'. This is a possible pointer to movement towards a mixed economic pattern as the model of development.[23] What is interesting is that in the course of this transition it is clearly recognized that while ensuring the macro-economic stabilization of the society for market-oriented reforms in order to ensure economic growth, the foremost task is crucial too for ensuring the *welfare of the society*.[24] There is also stress on the fact that social assistance reaches those for whom it is meant. Also the development is projected on the basis of the gains of the last seven decades, which has transformed Uzbekistan into a 'developed' society as far as social indicators are concerned. The emphasis here is on the transformation without *shock therapy*.[25]

This is particularly evident in the case of monetary policy where quick transformation was postponed in favour of *stabilization with parity*. In fact, in all this, a *gradualist* policy is evident that makes place for the old within the new structures. The *Uzbek model of development* then goes on to point out that 'privatization is not the ultimate goal'. It is the means for ensuring competition of economic motivation and more importantly, the fact that each man must 'improve his own position without hampering the position of others'.[26] The *Decrees and Resolutions* of the Republic of Uzbekistan further stress on the fact that the 'social orientation (of the policies) should be reflected in every act under consideration'. The problems of protection of family with children during the reorganization are addressed.[27] President Karimov identifies the final objective of the economic policy as the construction of a strong democratic law-governed state and secular society with a *stable socially oriented market economy* and open foreign policy.[28] This is also reflected on the fact that it is still the state that has primary responsibility in implementation of programmes relating to land reclamation, irrigation, raising soil fertility, etc. Since Uzbek economy is primarily dependent on the cultivation of cotton, it is important that the state has a definite agricultural policy.[29]

This would mean that while there would be complete *deideologization* of the economy, the state would still be required to play the role of the chief reformer during the complicated transitional period. President Karimov points out:

> ... economy should prevail over politics and constitute its own content, to be more precise, the economy and problems of its further development form the core of the current policy.[30]

The first step was directed towards the establishment of a legal foundation for a new economic system, formation and consolidation of statehood, and elimination of old stereotyped thinking. This change in policy is reflected in new research, for example, one that looks into the theoretical and practical aspects of the new state policy in agriculture.[31] The dissertation points to the limitations in the agricultural policy in the recent past and examines the new policies on property, questions of social protection, and democratization of management in the state.

Yet there is emphasis on the fact that

> We have made a simple choice—to consistently advance towards market economy stage-by-stage—evolutionary, not by great leaps or by revolutionary destruction.... Popular saying has it never destroy the old house before you build a new one, it is unforgivable to neglect what could be used in the interest of economic reform during transition to market relations and make this process more efficient and less painful.[32]

Celebration and Performance

Once identities are constructed, states seek to institutionalize these identities both at the domestic as well as at the international level. The creation of new narratives of the Uzbek state was not just an attempt at homogenization. It was also an attempt at international projection and advertisement of the potential of the country. In Uzbekistan, for instance, there has been a consistent effort at promoting the image of a 'cultural gem'. The image that is portrayed is that of a culturally rich state at the 'Crossroads of Civilization'. In the 1990s, a number of UNESCO-sponsored events celebrated the ancient cities of Bukhara, Khiva, and Samarkand. In fact, this trend continues with a projected conference this year in Samarkand on Uzbekistan as the crossroads of the ancient Silk Route. Uzbekistan has sought to accentuate its ancient traditions and modern cultures by organizing celebrations of its major public holidays and staging fashion shows of traditional clothing at embassies. Frequent cultural events at Uzbek embassies keep Uzbekistan's cultural brand on public display.

It has been generally argued that the Uzbek government essentially promotes two different national images, one for domestic consumption and another for international community.[33] Holiday celebrations like *Navruz* and Independence Day are carried out differently inside Uzbekistan and at Uzbek Embassies. Events organized for the international community emphasize on traditional artifacts and modern paintings depicting Uzbek culture. These events promote national ceramics and *suzani* (embroidery) accompanied by traditional cuisine. Images of the blue domes of Samarkand's historical sites, of the Ark in Bukhara, and the Fort at Khiva decorate all official leaflets, books, and websites about Uzbekistan. There is also focus on promoting tourist attractions and other historical places in Uzbek Embassies and their publications. Erica Marat argues that Uzbekistan's external emphasis is on its cultural richness built around the history of its ancient cities. It largely leaves out the Amir Timur heritage that is central to Uzbekistan's national identity and essentially supports President Karimov's state power.[34]

Large scale spectacles are organized on Uzbek Independence day and Navruz. Independence Day celebrations feature a wide variety of cultural elements that characterize the country as a civic nation, while Navruz focuses exclusively on an ethnic definition of the nation.[35] A typical Navruz address by the President would stress the 'ancient' nature of the holiday and the importance of customs 'pertaining to our people'. The people are called upon to carefully preserve the 'priceless traditions and values in tune with the spirit and philosophy of Navruz across centuries and pass them on to the current generations'.[36] These are generally orchestrated by the state through carefully selected symbols of the nation. These spectacles feature historical or mythical figures, fireworks, youth in national costumes performing group dances, musical dance performance by folk groups from ethnic minorities, and large scale depiction of national symbols. The performance by ethnic minorities serves to highlight Uzbekistan's ethnic diversity to the international audience and is also a declaration of civic nationalism for the domestic audience. These spectacles, however, are basically intended for a domestic audience and the dialogue and lyrics as also President Karimov's speech is always only in Uzbek.

Uzbekistan's holiday spectacles are elaborate explorations of heritage with focus on medieval history and ethnic heritage that aims to strengthen the population's identification with the territory. The particular symbol that featured has varied with cultural policy. State building concerns during the early to mid-1990s were addressing with a focus on the symbol of the empire builder Amir Timur. Concerns with religious extremism are being addressed with a focus on the founder of the Naqshbandi Sufi order Bahaouddin Naqshbandh. These celebrations are also planned at the highest level, with the Prime Minister at the head of the organizing committee. The twentieth anniversary of the independence of Uzbekistan will be organized according to a resolution signed by the President which approved the programme of the organization, practical, cultural, educational, and awareness raising activities related to the celebration as well as the structure of the creative group to prepare the holiday programme in Tashkent. The slogan for the year is 'You are great and sacred independent Motherland'. The desire of the government to showcase the achievements of Uzbekistan over the last two decades has meant that neighbourhoods in central Tashkent have been flattened and several large markets like Farkhad Bazaar and small shopping centres have been demolished for reconstruction efforts. The official news agency distributed a statement to the effect that the 'architectural outlook of the capital ahead of the twentieth anniversary of Uzbekistan has not only preserved its historical attractiveness but is acquiring new humanistic and aesthetic content'.[37]

While in certain cases, there is a gap between what is projected for the domestic audience and for the external one in others, like the projection of a 'nation under threat', the domestic and international intentions converge. The image of a scared Motherland and particularly a scared Motherland under threat is increasingly evident in political rhetoric. On the one hand, the rhetoric seeks to rally popular feelings of patriotism and on the other, seeks international legitimacy for state violence. Since the late 1990s, there has been a shift in President Karimov's sense of the geopolitical identity of Uzbekistan, from a self-confident polity at peace with itself and its neighbours to a besieged island of civilization in a sea of anarchy that threatened to submerge it.[38] Nick Megoran notes that the portrayal of 'a nation under threat' is reflected in presidential writings, media reports, and even in popular culture. One representative example is a part of the speech delivered by President Karimov on the occasion of the First Session of Oliy Majlis of the Republic of Uzbekistan.

> Today our region is attracting attention of different extremist forces and centers that strive to undertake the expansion of religious extremism and international terrorism, to divert the states of the region from the democratic and secular path of development with a due rule of law. The drugs and arms trafficking represent a credible threat not only on the region, but also on the entire world. The current developments in the region and in the world urge us to create a system of security that would be able to guarantee in real terms the non-violability of our borders, territorial integrity of the country, stability and sustainable development of Uzbekistan. It is important that people comprehend the inseparable link between ensuring the public order, their personal safety and increasing their own watchfulness and an active participation in what is happening around them. It is necessary to promote the involvement of the population in eliminating extremism in all its manifestations, securing peace and stability in our common home.[39]

It is evident that the rhetoric is aimed at both the domestic audience who are urged to maintain public order in order to allow the state to move towards a path ruled by democracy and also at the international audience who are informed that the inability of the state to do so would be due to the threat faced by the state as a result of external extremist forces. The first channel that inculcated a sense of danger was presidential writings themselves. The same geopolitical visions were conveyed through the national news media (*Halk Sozi*), which presented opposite images of a happy and prosperous Uzbekistan in contrast to consistent images of neighbouring states as spaces of chaos. There is also the suggestion that the chaos in the neighbourhood is threatening to engulf Uzbekistan. Megoran defines how the image of a 'nation under threat' is also reflected in popular music which is often an important site in struggles to control, utilize, and define space.

The Andijan incident proved to be somewhat of a watershed. In the aftermath of the incident, there was need to justify the state action to the people and also to an increasingly critical international audience. A booklet was published from Tashkent that summarized the statements and responses of President Karimov to the local and international press about the Andijan events of 12–13 May 2005. Entitled, *The Uzbek People Will Never Depend on Others*, the booklet seeks to provide an explanation of the government's actions during the incident and show that this incident had nothing in common with the 'revolutions' that had led to changes in governments in Georgia, Ukraine, and Kyrgyzstan. Examining President Karimov's account of the events of May 2005, Megoran argues that four key themes have been deployed in the narrative to delegitimize the government's opponents: terrorism and criminality; inauthentic Uzbekness and deviant masculinity/religiosity; and constitutional illegitimacy and the subversion of the scientific laws of the state.[40] The events were portrayed as orchestrated by a trained (and foreign-aided) group of terrorist/criminal elements who were attempting to destabilize the state.

> During the first years of our independence we thought we were free and we had something different: we became members of the UN so now we would move towards democracy and everything ahead would be perfect. We freed ourselves from the Soviet communist ideology. But what filled the vacuum left behind? Different radical religious groups, of whom some were not always peaceful, began to make their presence felt in the region. Everywhere they proposed building mosques and they did so until we started opening our eyes. Something similar has been happening to our neighbors; for instance Kazakhstan has at the moment 1500 mosques of which 500 are not officially registered. Sometimes these groups offered loans or sometimes they showed their readiness to build these mosques for free.
>
> I want to reiterate again, using the ideological vacuum left after the collapse of communism, Hisb-ut-Tahrir put down its deep roots in the countries of

Central Asia and in Uzbekistan, in particular in the Ferghana Valley. In the city of Tashkent you can find evidence of this sect.[41]

President Karimov's reactions following the events in Osh in April-May 2010 has been described as 'dispassionate and reasonable' by Kyrgyz state officials. Karimov argued that the tragedy was not the fault of either the Kyrgyz or the Uzbeks, but was organized by 'third parties' with the key objective of drawing Uzbekistan into the conflict. President Karimov's reactions elicited keen interest among the international audience. It demonstrated the maturity of state reaction in the face of provocation and reiterated the image of 'threat'. As far as the domestic audience was concerned there was little coverage of the events in Kyrgyzstan and practically no information on the events that led to a change of government. Similarly, border control policies of the Uzbek state have been identified as theatrical/performative.[42] It has also been argued that this has in fact resulted in depressed trade flows within the region. The boundary enforcement measures introduced at the Uzbek borders have been justified in terms of protecting the economic and political security of the state. Nick Megoran has described how the portrayal of Uzbekistan as a 'threatened state' is also reflected here. He has demonstrated how government framed the state border not merely as a legal line on the map but rather as a moral border where Uzbekistan was depicted as a realm of order, progress, stability, and wealth surrounded by disorder, backwardness, chaos, and poverty. However, such boundaries also tend to overlook economic considerations and fail to come to terms with everyday experiences of negotiating borders.

Conclusion

Prior to the formation of nation-states, the state was never seen as crucial for the determination of the identity of communities. It was at best seen as a guarantor of an arrangement under which all communities existed. This was transformed in an era of 'nations and nationalism' when it was asserted that identities were to be largely defined by the nation state. In fact, in a number of cases, the state not only defined the boundary within which identity was to be circumscribed but also the basis for the definition. The rationality on which this basis was determined defined the principal characteristic of groups and subsequently assumed a significance of its own. As nations were constructed within the boundaries of the state, the projection of a numerical majority defined in terms of rationally delimited criteria, became crucial. In this projection the state came to play an increasingly significant role not just in defining the 'nation-state' but also in legitimizing it within the international arena. It is this performative role of the Uzbek state that been the focus of this article. The article has underlined that the performance of the state was aimed at the creation of 'brand Uzbekistan'—a stable, prosperous state with a vibrant ancient culture.

Notes and References

1. Sally Cummings (2010), 'Inscapes, Landscapes and Greyscapes: The Politics of Signification in Central Asia', in Cummings (ed.), *Symbolism and Power in Central Asia: The Politics of the Spectacular*, London and New York: Routledge.
2. See for instance Annette Bohr (1998), 'The Central Asian States as Nationalizing Regimes', in Graham Smith et al. (eds), *Nation Building in the Post Soviet Borderlands: The Politics of National Identity*, Cambridge: Cambridge University Press.
3. *Uzbeskaya Soviyetskaya Respublika*. Taskent: Redakskaya Uzbeyekoi Sovietskoi Entsiklopedii, 1981.
4. Zeki Velidi Togan's (1890–1970) examination of the origin of the Uzbeks and the Tajiks from *Bugunku Turkili Turkistan ve Yakin Tarihi*, Cilt I Bati ve Kuzey Turkistan, Istanbul 1981.
5. K. Kuvakov (1972), 'O Nekotoriye Rodoplyemyennikh Gruppakh Uzbekov Byerkhei Kashkadarii', in Kh. Z. Ziyayar and B.V. Lunin (eds), *Ethnographichyeskoye Izucyeniye Bita i Kulturi Uzbeyekov* (Akademia Nayuk Uzbek SSR,) Tashkent: FAN.
6. Kuvakov, 'O Nekotoriye Rodoplyemyennikh Gruppakh Uzbekov Byerkhei Kashkadarii', p 19.
7. F.A. Brockhaus and I.A. Efron (1902), *Entsiklopedicheskiy Slovar*, 34 (St Petersburg), pp. 608–10.
8. Edward Allworth (1990), *The Modern Uzbeks-From the Fourteenth Century to the Present: A Cultural History*, Stanford, CA: Hoover Institute Press, 1p. 319.
9. Tahir Qahhar (1996), 'Uzbek Literature,' (translated from Uzbek by William Dirks) *World Literature Today*, (Summer), p. 611.
10. See for instance, Muhammad Ali (1994), 'Let Us Learn About Our Heritage', in H.B. Paksoy (ed.), *Central Asia Reader—The Rediscovery of History*, New York and London: M.E. Sharpe.
11. See for instance, Buriboy Akhmedov (1996), *Timur The Great, His Life, Social and Political Activities*, Tashkent: Abdullah Kadiri National Heritage Publishers.
12. A.A. Askarov (1997), '*Nekotoriye Voprosi Istorii Stanovlyeniye Uzbekoi Gosudartsvo*', *Obshestvenni Nayuki* v. *Uzbekistane*, 3–4.
13. Askarov, '*Nekotoriye Voprosi Istorii Stanovlyeniye Uzbekoi Gosudartsvo*'.
14. Akhmedov, *Timur The Great*.
15. Qahhar, 'Uzbek Literature', p. 612.

16. Alisher Azizkhodjaev (ed.), *Bukhara is an Oriental Gem*, Tashkent: Sharq, 1997.

17. R. Radjov, 'The Bukhara Kurbashi' (1997), in *Scientific and Cultural Heritage of Mankind To the Third Millennium, Theses of Reports of the International Symposium dedicated to the 2500th anniversary of Bukhara and Khiva*, Tashkent: Uzbekistan.

18. A large corpus of literature has now appeared on the Basmachi movement in the form of dissertations in the Historical Sciences. They point to the fact that the movement should now be viewed as an 'armed upsurge of the local population.' See for instance: Nazira Abdukadirovna Norjigitova, *Istoriographia Basmachi Dbyezhyeniya' v. Turkestane (Sovietski Period), Avtorefarat, Kandidat istorichiskikh nayuk, Akademiya Nayuk Respubliki Uzbekistan* (Tashkent 1995); Ruslan Akhmedovich Khakimov, *Zaruvyezhnaya Istoriographia; Istorii Basmachestvo v. Srednei Azii 1917-1932, Avtorefarat, Kandidat istorichiskikh nayuk, Akademiya Nayuk Respubliki Uzbekistan* (Tashkent 1992); H.G. Khidoyatov, *Basmachyeskoye Dvyezhyeniye v. Sovryemyennoi Sovyetologii, Avtorefarat, Kandidat istorichiskikh nayuk, Akademiya Nayuk Respubliki Uzbekistan*, Tashkent, 1993.

19. See for instance Avror Mykhtarovich Khudaikulov, *Prosvyetityelskaya Dyeyatyelnost Djadidov Turkestana, (kontsye XIX-nachale XX B.) Avtorefarat, Kandidat istorichiskikh nayuk, Akademiya Nayuk Respubliki Uzbekistan* (Tashkent, 1995). Olyeg Valeyentinovich Shapovalyenko, *Molodyezh Turkestana v Revolyutsionnom Dvyezhyenii Nachale XX Beka, Avtorefarat, kandidat istorichiskikh nayuk, Akadyemi Nayuk Uzbyekskoi SSR* (Tashkent, 1990).

20. Address by Islam Karimov (1997), President of the Republic of Uzbekistan on the Occasion of 2500 Years Anniversary of Khiva (October), pp. 2–3.

21. G. Karimova (1995), *Politico Aakonomichyeskoiye Reforme v Uzbekistane Realii I Perspektivi*. Tashkent: Uzbekistan.

22. Islam A. Karimov (1995), *Uzbekistan Along the Road of Deepening Economic Reform; Basic Principles of Political and Economic Development of Uzbekistan*, Tashkent: Uzbekistan, pp. 115–16.

23. Karimov, *Uzbekistan Along the Road of Deepening Economic Reform*.

24. *Respublika Uzbekistan: Ukazi i Postnovlyeniya, Vtoraya Kniga* (Tashkent: Uzbekistan, 1994.

25. Karimova, *Politico, Aakonomichiskiye Reforme*.

26. See 'Uzbek Model of Development', in Karimova (ed.), *Politico, Aakonomichiskiye Reforme*, p. 22.

27. Karimova, *Politico, Aakonomichiskiye Reforme*.

28. See for instance, Islam A. Karimov (1995), *Uzbekistan Along the Road of Deepening Economic Reform; Basic Principles of Political and Economic Development of Uzbekistan*,Tashkent: Uzbekistan; *Nash Putch Nezavecyemoi Gosudartsvyennosti i Progressa*, Tashkent: Uzbekistan, 1994.

29. See Karimov, *Uzbekistan Along the Road of Deepening Economic Reform*, pp. 52–66.

30. Karimov, *Uzbekistan Along the Road of Deepening Economic Reform*, p. 10.

31. Ibaydulla Aargashyev (1995), *Politika Gosudartsva Nezavisimovo Uzbekistana na Syele: Tyeoriya i Practika, Avtorefarat, Kandidat politichiskikh nayuk, Tashkentskii Gosudartsvyennei Institut Vostokovyedyeniya*, Tashkent.

32. Karimov, *Uzbekistan Along Road of Deepening Economic Reform*, pp. 11–12.

33. See for instance, Erica Marat (2010), 'Nation Brading in Central Asia: A New Campaign to Present Ideas about the State and Nation', in Sally Cummings (ed.) *Symbolism and Power in Central Asia, The Politics of the Spectacular*, London and New York; Routledge.

34. Marat, 'Nation Brading in Central Asia: A New Campaign to Present Ideas about the State and Nation'.

35. Lara L. Adams and Assel Rustemova (2010), 'Mass Spectacle and Styles of Governmentality in Kazakhstan and Uzbekistan', in Sally Cummings (ed.), *Symbolism and Power in Central Asia, The Politics of the Spectacular*, London and New York: Routledge.

36. See for instance *Greeting Address by President Islam Karimov at Grand Celebrations Occasioned to the Holiday of Navruz*, Press Service of the President of Uzbekistan, 21.3.2011.

37. Cited from, 'Uzbekistan: Tashkent Clears Out the Little People Ahead of Independence Day', *Eurasianet*, 6 July 2011.

38. Nick Megoran (2005), 'The Critical Geopolitics of Danger in Uzbekistan and Kyrgyzstan', *Environment and Planning D: Society and Spaces*, 28 (3).

39. Address by H.E. Mr Islam Karimov at the First Session of Oliy Majlis of the Republic of Uzbekistan.

40. Nick Megoran (2008), 'Framing Andijon, Narrating the Nation: Islam Karimov's Account of the Events of 13 May 2005', *Central Asian Survey*, 27(1), March.

41. Islam Karimov, *The Uzbek People Will Never Depend on Others* (Tashkent), p. 18.

42. See Nick Megoran, Gael Raballand, and Jerome Bouyjou (2005), 'Performances, Representation and the Economics of Border Control in Uzbekistan', *Geopolitics*, 10(4).

12

Tajikistan and Kyrgyzstan
Economic Challenges Facing Less Developed States in Central Asia

R.G. Gidadhubli

Tajikistan and Kyrgyz Republic are the less developed states of Central Asia. Several questions arise in understanding and analysing the issues concerning economic backwardness of Tajikistan and Kyrgyz Republic. What are the reasons for their backwardness? What are the resource potentialities and constraints of Tajikistan and Kyrgyzstan? What are the trends in economic development during the last two decades? What are the causes affecting their economic development? How far have these two sovereign and independent states managed to overcome the problem of backwardness during the last two decades? What are the prospects of economic development of Tajikistan and Kyrgyz republics during the next decade or so? An effort has been made in this essay to examine and analyse some of these issues.

Background

Before analysing various issues concerning the backwardness of Tajikistan and Kyrgyzstan, it may be worthwhile to understand the economic background of the region. Historically, Tajikistan and Kyrgyzstan being part of the former Soviet Central Asia were economically least developed republics. They were inhabited mainly by nomadic and semi-nomadic tribes. They were under the Tsarist Empire before they attained the status of republics as distinct nationalities during the Soviet era. Even as they were benefited by socio-economic developments during the seven-odd decades of Soviet rule, they were relatively less developed economically even among the Central Asian states such as Uzbekistan and Turkmenistan. They were the smallest republics in terms of territory in Soviet Central Asia. After the Soviet breakup, China has acquired about 30,000 sq. km of area from both these states, claiming them to be part of China in the past. Geographically, both are landlocked and predominantly of mountainous terrain. Tajikistan has about 90 per cent of its territory as mountain. Both countries have limited arable land. Both are landlocked countries surrounded by Uzbekistan, Kazakhstan, China, and Afghanistan as neighbours. While both are blessed with major rivers like Amu Darya and Syr Darya; hence possessing abundant water resources. As upstream states, they have immense scope for generating hydroelectricity. In terms of resource potentialities, both Tajikistan and Kyrgyzstan possess modest quantities of non-ferrous and precious mineral resources, including gold, silver, and antimony, which provide some opportunity for economic development. Moreover, Tajikistan has been endowed with significant quantity of bauxite resources which has helped it in industrial development and uranium that has made it the cynosure of all eyes worldwide. But both lack hydrocarbon resources which affect their economic development.

It needs to be noted that being part of the former Soviet Union, their socio-economic needs were met from the assistance provided by Moscow. Hence, in the social sphere, Tajikistan and Kyrgyzstan as other Central Asian states achieved progress in terms of high rate of literacy in education sphere, fairly low infant mortality and high life expectancy by virtues of fairly good health facilities provided by the state. Moreover, they had significant pool of technically skilled labour power educated and trained during Soviet era that provided both these states human resource potential for economic development. The fact that these states had overcome utter backwardness bequeathed from the past in a relatively short span of five-six decades during the Soviet period was widely appreciated even by Western and Eastern critics. Jawaharlal Nehru had strongly praised the economic development of Central Asia in general and Tajikistan and Kyrgyzstan in particular in his book 'Glimpses of World History'.

Economic Trends and Performance

The first decade of Independence witnessed a sharp decline in the economic development as evident from various economic indicators. According to UN Economic Survey reports, trend of real GDP indicated that sharp decline persisted during the first decade of independence. As compared to 1991 base year, real GDP of Tajikistan was 30 in 1996 and 57 for Kyrgyz republic, which meant 70 per cent decline in five years in the case of Tajikistan which was the lowest decline among the Central Asian states. This period was the worst since both the states also suffered annual hyper inflation rate ranging between 800–2000 per cent per annum till 1996. This was partly due to shortcomings in monetary policy such as excessive bank credit and lack of stabilization measures. Even by the year 2000, both these states had not touched the GDP level of 1991. In the case of level of employment, which is another economic indicator, both Tajikistan and Kyrgyzstan have suffered; since they suffered from high level of unemployment rate exceeding 40 per cent of labour force and about 55–60 per cent of the population was living below poverty line. Moreover, both the countries were deeply in economic debt.

While the fact of sharp economic decline was evident, there are some variations in the data from different sources. For instance, according to Tajikistan Country-Brief report, annual real GDP was declining between 1990 and 1996 at –7 per cent to –29 per cent per annum. As reported by the Tajik National Bank since 1997, Tajikistan's GDP average annual growth rate has been about 7 per cent reaching a peak of 10 per cent in 2004. The bank predicted continued average of 7 per cent annual GDP growth until 2009. As per official sources both these republics attained positive growth trend in GDP since 1997. Similarly, inflation rates have been steadily decreasing, and Tajikistan is slowly paying off its external debt. By the year 2000, both Tajikistan and Kyrgyz Republic attained positive trend in economic growth rates as other Central Asian states. Joormat Otorbaev of Kyrgyzstan has stated that economy was growing at 5 per cent to 6 per cent per annum during 2000–5. There was growth in construction sector as well as in the service sector.

Since 2005, both the states could not sustain growth momentum. The Kyrgyz economy suffered due to several causes. First, there was fall in the price of gold which was one of the major sources of hard currency earnings of the country. Second, oil and natural gas prices started increasing rapidly since 2004 up to 2009 which caused major hardship to the exchequer since the country is a major importer of oil and natural gas. Third, cardinal steps were not taken to ensure sustained economic growth. Hence, there was rising unemployment of 17–20 per cent since 2006, leading to large scale migration to Russia. In the case of Tajikistan, economic growth reached 10.6 per cent in 2004, but dropped below 8 per cent during the period 2005–8. Inflation rates were steadily decreasing and Tajikistan was slowly paying off its external debt. At the same time, the Tajik economic development was affected due to the effects of higher oil prices and then the international financial crisis. Over and above, there was lower remittances from Tajik workers abroad, which otherwise constitutes a major source of revenue to the exchequer. As a result by 2008, more than half of the population continued to live in below subsistence minimum. According to World Bank data, more than 47 per cent of its 7.5 million people live on less than US$ 2 a day.

According to official sources, since 2009, there was some positive improvement in growth performance of economy. In 2010, Tajik economic growth had picked up to some extent indicating modest increase of GDP to above 4.5 per cent. This was mainly due to higher global prices for aluminium and cotton. Agricultural sector growth was about 9 per cent and industrial output grew by over 10 per cent. The Tajik economy benefited from over 20 per cent increase in remittance inflows in 2010 as compared to 2009. On the basis of these optimistic growth performance, Asian Development Bank experts estimate sustained GDP growth of above 5 per cent in 2011.

Mining and industry sectors did experience initial setbacks. Tajikistan's aluminium plant built during the Soviet era continued to be one of the major industrial units in the country and it also contributed to economic revival as aluminium was a major export commodity. Industrial sector was otherwise not a major economic activity in both the states. Moreover, during the last two decades, both the states suffered due to lag in technology. Agriculture has been a major sector of the economy of both the states even as mining, Industrial activities are carried out on a modest scale. However, being mountainous states arable land is limited. In the case of Tajikistan, about 7 per cent of the land area is arable. This poses a major problem in supporting the population with domestic food grain production. Over and above, agricultural crops have suffered from droughts from time to time in both the countries. For instance, Tajikistan was caught in the grip of a severe drought in 2000, considered by many to be the worst in over 70 years. As reported by the FAO, in its crop and food supply assessment mission to Tajikistan, nearly half or 3 million of its population were facing hunger and malnutrition due to drought, combined with a breakdown of irrigation systems. Tajikistan's total cereal production was estimated at only 236,000 tons in 2000 which was down by nearly 50 per cent from the previous year. This was the third consecutive year that cereal production has declined. On the issue of agricultural sector, it was opined by agricultural experts that water shortages and the poor condition of the country's irrigation systems led to uneven cereal harvests from irrigated fields.

Cotton is the most important commercial crop in both states; its production is closely monitored and in many cases controlled by the government. It is one of the major sources of revenues for the Tajik state. Cotton cultivation is a major agricultural activity and about 70 per cent of Tajik population live in villages. But this sector is facing severe problem which is evident from its debt which amounted to over US$ 400 million in 2007 due to high cost, low productivity, poor management, and declining prices for cotton. Over and above, there are vested interest groups which take advantage and are involved in taking benefit at the cost of the state. For instance, according to reports, the National Bank of Tajikistan admitted that in December 2007 it had improperly lent money to investors in the cotton sector. Hence, the IMF cancelled its assistance program to Tajikistan. Subsequently, some corrective measures were undertaken by the Tajik government as a result of which over half a billion dollars in farmer debt was being forgiven, and IMF assistance was reinstated. In fact, in order to give a boost to the development of cotton cultivation, there is need for introducing market reforms and also adopting modern techniques of production, high yielding seeds, etc. Tajikistan is the fourth largest cotton exporter in the world. However, it does not have many value-added aspects of the industry, including ginning and baling facilities and warehouses to support those parts of cotton enterprise. The industries set up during Soviet era for initial processing such as ginning are outdated and even during that time major portion of cotton yield was shipped out of the state to industrial units in Russia and other republics. Hence, textile industry was not well-developed and whatever units were set up have become obsolete.

A positive development concerning this sector is to increase agricultural production. USAID initiated projects to train farmers in modern technologies and management of water and irrigation networks. USAID also supported companies working on food processing, packaging, and marketing. Agricultural production assistance has already benefited 2,81,000 people or 5 per cent of the country's farmers. It is reported that members of 41 USAID-supported water users associations earned more than US$ 5 million as a result of improved water management.

Policy Measures I

After gaining independence, both Tajikistan and Kyrgyz republic undertook policy measures for initiating the process of economic transition from the previous socialist system to market economy which was difficult and painful. Tajikistan's efforts to implement policy measures were halted due to the unprecedented situation of civil war prevailing in the 1990s. In fact, the civil war (1992–7) severely damaged the already weak economic infrastructure and caused a sharp decline in industrial and agricultural production. In comparison to that, Kyrgyz republic was fortunate and it was in the forefront among the Center for Internet Security (CIS) in implementing economic reforms as recommended by the World Bank with regard to privatization, economic liberalization, etc. There was high appreciation of these policy measures by international financial institutions which was evident from the Kyrgyz membership of World Trade Organization (WTO) which was offered to this country in 1998, the first among the CIS.

Mention may also be made of the Kyrgyz government in setting up Free Economic Zones in Bishkek, Naryn, Karakol, and Maimak. The state also provided wide range of incentives such as simplified customs and regulation procedures to attract foreign direct investment (FDI) and joint ventures, waiving of duties on imports of capital goods. As a result of these policy initiatives, according to UN Economic Commission reports, the Kyrgyz republic was able to attract FDI to the extent of US$ 445 million during the period 1992–2001. During this period, Tajikistan received FDI of about US$ 198 million, which was less than half of Kyrgyz republic.

External Economic Assistance

Both the countries have received financial support for various projects which have helped economic development and reduced backwardness to some extent. For instance, in the case of Tajikistan electricity output expanded with the completion of the Sangtuda-I hydropower dam which was finished in 2009 with Russian investment. The World Bank's support to the Tajik energy sector includes improvement in the financial management of Barki Tojik and Tajiktransgas, and investments to reduce energy losses and increase energy supply. Similarly, the smaller Sangtuda-2, built with Iranian investment, is scheduled for completion in 2012. The government of Tajikistan is pinning major hopes on the massive Roghun dam which, when finished according to Tajik plans, will be the tallest dam in the world. The World Bank agreed to fund technical, economic, social, and environmental feasibility studies for Roghun. Favourable reports from these studies could create increased investment in the country. The active portfolio of the World Bank in Tajikistan in 2010 consisted of sixteen projects with net commitment of US$ 223 million. The largest share of on-going portfolio is in agriculture and rural development (31 per cent), followed by energy (23 per cent), water (17 per cent), education (15 per cent), health (8 per cent), economic policy, and public sector (6 per cent). In May 2011, during the visit of World Bank Regional Director for Central Asia, Motoo Konishi, to Tajikistan, expressed satisfaction on the completion of certain projects including second Dushanbe Water Supply project, social safety net, etc. It was opined that the country had potential for sustainable growth by drawing human, hydropower, and agricultural resources. Moreover, it needs to be mentioned that to increase agricultural production, USAID has trained farmers in modern technologies and management of water and irrigation networks. The USAID supports companies working on food processing, packaging, and marketing. Agricultural production assistance has already benefited 281,000 people, 5 per cent of the country's farmers. Members of forty-one USAID-supported water users associations earned more than US$ 5 million as a result of improved water management. It is now the responsibility of the leadership of the country to take initiatives to involve a larger section of the society to develop the economy.

As opined by western analyst, Erica Marat, the Tajik government needed to be credited for its consistency in cooperation with international donors, its ability to learn fast from previous mistakes, and its motivation to acquire new professional knowledge. Moreover, Tajikistan has been cooperating with Russia, Iran, China, and the United States, as well as the World Bank, International Monetary Fund, and Asian Development Bank, to develop its energy sector, transportation system, and agriculture. The Tajik leaders are aware of the fact that to promote its economic development, there is need of foreign investment, particularly for the construction and modernization of hydropower plants.

Challenges of Economic Development

There are several challenges which both the countries face in the task of economic development. The dissolution of the former Soviet Union made a negative impact on the economic development of all the fifteen former Soviet republics, and more so, on these two republics of Central Asia. In fact, as the breakup was sudden, these republics were least prepared for the transition. The Central Asian states was dependent upon the financial support from the Centre, which was no more available after the Soviet breakup. Moreover, what aggravated the situation for Tajikistan was that the country suffered from a rising Islamic fervour and more than five years of civil war after gaining independence, which very adversely affected political stability and socio-economic development. Tajikistan is also concerned about the growing influence of fundamentalist elements during the last two decades. Some social and political activists contend that lack of education and job opportunities in the country is partly responsible for this new phenomenon. While this could be partly true, strong religious hold on the young generation seems to be evident and thousands are sent to Pakistan and Iran for training. The Tajik authorities are concerned about the adverse socio-economic impact of this Islamizing trend, and hence in July 2011, President Emomali Rahmonov warned that foreign religious schools are indoctrinating Tajik students with radical Islamic ideology. He was making this statement in the context when more than 1000 young

Tajiks studying at foreign madrassas and Islamic universities returned home in few recent months.

Apart from this objective factor, there are several challenges and problems which are responsible for lack of economic development during the last two decades. A major challenge facing economic development of both the countries has been the on-going conflicts over the issue of sharing of water resources with downstream countries of Kazakhstan and Uzbekistan. During the Soviet era, Central Asia was considered as a Single Unified National Economic Complex and all economic decisions were taken at the Centre to promote economic development of all Central Asian states. The policy of water management, as stated by S. Alamanov, the former ambassador of Kyrgyz Republic in India, was to maximize area under irrigation in the Central Asian region. In the process, downstream republics of Uzbekistan and Kazakhstan were benefited at the cost of upstream states of Tajikistan and Kyrgyzstan, but they were compensated with resources and financial support from the Centre. Hence, conflicts with regard to water sharing did not arise. With the Soviet breakup, each Central Asian states has given priority to its own national interest being sovereign and independent. Regional consideration and interest have become secondary leading often to differences and conflicts between upstream countries of Tajikistan and Kyrgyz Republic and downstream states of Uzbekistan and Kazakhstan. Tajikistan and Kyrgyz Republic are trying to safeguard their interest for water sharing under the commonly accepted international legal norms such as the Helsinki Convention of March 1992 and the UN Convention of May 1997. Final mutually acceptable solution is yet to be arrived at.

Considering the fact that water and energy resources are unevenly distributed among the Central Asian states, they have become destabilizing factors in the region and very adversely affecting economic development. Experts of international institutions including the World Bank and the Asian Development Bank have highlighted the need for effective implementation of regional programmes which are supported financially for infrastructure projects from time to time. Even as there are efforts made by the Central Asian states leaders for regional cooperation and agreements are signed during summit meetings, overall outcome is far from satisfactory. As pointed out by Martin C. Spechler, there are shortcomings with regard to regional cooperation since each state adopts ad hoc protectionist measures and there is lack of complementarity among the Central Asian states. In the ultimate analysis, being upstream countries both have disadvantage since scope for utilizing river water for generating hydropower and for irrigation has been restricted due to conflict of interest with downstream countries.

Second, there has been lack of implementation of economic policies. For instance, several ministries have been involved in issuing permits to many businessmen for setting up small enterprises. But it has been observed that often there is no follow up action to ensure that units are set up. It is rightly pointed out by the chairman of the Tajikistan Small and Medium Size Business Association, Matlyuba Uldzhabayeva, that business activity must be assertive in nature and responsive to needs for the industrial development for creating job opportunities in the country.

Third, funds received from international agencies are occasionally not utilized properly. For instance, in 2007, the IMF had to temporarily cancel the program of assistance since IMF conditions were violated when the Tajikistan National Bank admitted that it had improperly lent money to investors in the cotton sector which indicated possible linkages between the banking sector and business/bureaucratic circles. Due to some of these policy failures, investment climate was affected, which is further evident from the fact according to World Bank report of 'Doing Business in 2009' that Tajikistan ranked 159th out of 181 countries in world rating. This is an indication of poor investment climate which needs to be addressed by the policymakers urgently.

Fourth, corruption has been a major problem for the Central Asian states that includes Tajikistan and Kyrgyz Republic. Corruption at the highest levels has deep-rooted effects on the Kyrgyz economy and society. It was reported by analysts that the former president, Kurmanbek Bakiev, took millions of dollars from both Russia and the USA on the issue of providing Manas airbase. How much of it was utilized for the development of the country and how much was stashed away is unknown. Subsequently, in May 2010, the Kyrgyz authorities stated that they have found almost US$ 9 million in cash belonging to former Kyrgyz Defence Minister Bakyt Kalyev in a safe-deposit box in a bank in Bishkek, as reported by the Kyrgyz Service reports of May 2010. Even more striking was that Maksim Bakiev, the son of Kyrgyzstan's ousted President, had been implicated in a corruption scandal which involved fuel delivery to the US air base in the country involving millions of dollars. Another factor which has been affecting both Tajikistan and Kyrgyz Republic is that corruption is also linked to drug trafficking which is a major problem affecting both the countries. For instance, as opined by analysts, 'billions of dollars' of drugs pass through Tajikistan en route to Russia and China every year.

Fifth, in the case of Kyrgyz republic, persisting disturbances during the mid of 2010 after ethnic conflicts in southern cities including Jalal-Abad, Batken and Osh have very adversely affected not only social relations among different ethnic communities but also economic development in the country. The Kyrgyz government has succeeded to a great extent to control the situation. According to official reports, clashes were caused by loyalists of ousted Kurmanbek Bakiev. For instance, Usen Sydykov, who was a Bakiev adviser from 2006 to 2008, and Communist leader Iskhak Masaliev were arrested on suspicion of organizing uprisings by Bakiev supporters in the south of the country. Hence, as stated by Almazbek Atambaev, deputy head of the interim government, the government was taking measures to assert its control in southern provinces. However, the situation in the country is far from normal even one year after the ethnic conflicts which has very adversely affected the economic development of the country. It might take some time to heal the wounds between Kyrgyz and Uzbek states.

What has added to the problem for Kyrgyz Republic is that even as the Interim government was struggling to control ethnic disturbances and bring socio-political and economic conditions back to normalcy, Roza Otunbaeva's government faced continued problems due to closure of border with Kazakhastan in May 2010. The Kyrgyz government deputy head Omurbek Tekebaev harshly criticized this refusal to open the border and stated that Astana's decision to close the border had created an 'economic blockade' for his country. This is because the closure of the Kyrgyz-Kazakh border which is the main import-export route for Kyrgyzstan, had seriously exacerbated the country's economic problems. The acting Deputy Prime Minister Omurbek Tekebaev had stated that if the 'unintended blockade' by Kazakhstan and Uzbekistan lasted one or two more months, social explosion was sure to occur. On this issue, Michael McFaul, a senior foreign policy adviser to US President Barack Obama, stated that reopening the border would help stabilize the situation in Kyrgyzstan considering the fact that more than 70 per cent of imported goods reach Kyrgyzstan via Kazakhstan.

Sixth, economic problems are further compounded by social issues during the last two decades. For instance, while in principle, there is equality in the Constitution for all citizens regardless of gender and men and women are equal before the law, in reality there is widespread discrimination and there are reports about ill treatment of women in Tajikistan. Tajikistan has a strong patriarchal tradition and men dominate within the family and in society in general. The population is primarily rural and stereotypes in Tajik culture have the effect of limiting women's opportunities. Women are often confined to a maternal role. It appears that because a large percentage of the male population was killed in the Tajik civil war, many households are now headed by women. Moreover, although in principle, polygamy is prohibited by the Tajik Penal Code, it is still practised and convictions are rare. Women continue to accept such unions largely because of the demographic imbalance prevailing in the country and the deterioration in women's material conditions. Apart from this, there is continued high growth rate of population and the state authorities need to address growing demand of social needs of health, education, and employment.

Conclusion

From what is stated above, it is evident that Tajikistan and Kyrgyz Republic have been less developed economically for various objective and subjective factors. Efforts are being made by them after they have become sovereign and independent states to bring about socio-economic transformation. Even as there is some improvement in their economies, situation has remained fragile due to uneven implementation of structural reforms, corruption, weak governance, seasonal power shortages, and the external debt burden. Civil war conditions in Tajikistan and ethnic conflicts in Kyrgyz Republic added to the problems of economic growth process. Soon after gaining independence, the Kyrgyz Republic had made efforts to reform the economy. During the last few years, Tajikistan has also undertaken measures to implement reforms vigorously. There is appreciation and even support from international financial institutions to enable them to overcome some of the problems they are facing to bring about development in their economies. Overcoming certain problems during the last two decades, the

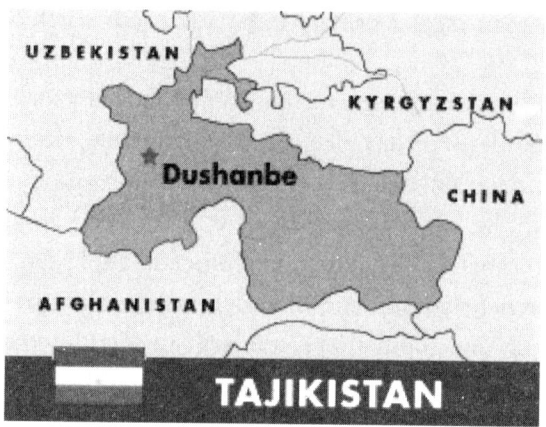

Map: Tajikistan

Growth Rates of Gross Domestic Product of Central Asian States

Country	2000–04	2005	2006	2007	2008	2009	2010 (Est)
Kyrgyz Rep	4.9	–0.2	3.1	8.5	7.6	0.9	0.9
Kazakhstan	10.4	9.7	10.7	8.9	3.2	–2.0	1.5
Tajikistan	9.7	6.7	7.0	7.8	7.9	2.0	3.0
Turkmenistan	17.3	13.0	11.4	11.6	9.8	6.9	7.0
Uzbekistan	4.8	7.0	7.3	9.5	9.0	7.0	7.0

Source: Official data and data from reports on internet on Central Asian states.

leaders of the two countries are looking forward to take their economies forward. They have to overcome several challenges concerning their social, economic, and political development. To deal with problems, there is need for leadership of both the countries to adopt strategy of 'Soft Power' so that the respective governments could facilitate relations with civil society in respective country that would help wider sections of the population.

At the same time, there are certain issues on which the leaders of the two countries have to take policy decisions to sustain economic development and solve problems facing their respective countries. In the case of Kyrgyz Republic, there is a dilemma for the country during the last few months in 2011. Some Kyrgyz political leaders argue about the advantages of joining the Customs Union which is formed by Russia, Kazakhstan, and Belarus. As opined by Prime Minister Alambek Atambaev, joining the CU would have two-fold benefits for the country. First, it would strengthen the borders with both Kazakhstan and Russia. Second, it would facilitate and expand trade and economic relations with them and also improve the living conditions of millions of Kyrgyz citizens who are working in these countries. But those who are not in favour of this proposal make counter argument that this might affect conditions of WTO of which the country became a member in 1998. What is also creditable of the Kyrgyz Republic is that this is the first country in the region which is headed by a woman president, Roza Otunbaeva. Moreover, in November 2010, with due process of referendum the country approved parliamentary system of government and thus made history in establishing a true democratic state and thus becoming the first parliamentary democracy in Central Asia. This is a positive development to facilitate social and economic development of the country in the decades to come. While both the states have received strong support for economic development from Russia, China, and USA apart from the international financial institutions such as the World Bank, the IMF, and the Asian Development Bank, there is an urgent need for effective and strong regional cooperation among the Central Asian states to enable these two small and less economically developed republics to bring about faster socio-economic development in the years to come.

Notes and References

1. R.G. Gidadhubli (2008), 'Economic Development of Kyrgyz Republic: Performance and Prospects', in K. Santhanam and Ramakant Dwivedi (eds), *India-Kyrgyz Relations Perspectives and Prospects*, New Delhi: India-Central Asia Foundation and Indian Council of World Affairs.
2. Gulshan Sachdeva (2003), 'Understanding Central Asian Economic Models', in Nirmala Joshi (ed.), *Central Asia the Great Game Replayed*, New Delhi: New Century Publications.
3. *The Asian Development Outlook 2010 Update*; CentralAsiaOnline.com 2008; Eurasia Daily Monitor, Vols 3 and 4; *RFE/RL Daily Reports*, Prague, January 2005 to June 2011.
4. S. Alamanov (2008), 'Water Rights and Border Issues in Central Asian Countries', in K. Santhanam and Ramakant Dwivedi (eds), *India-Kyrgyz Relations Perspectives and Prospects*, New Delhi: India-Central Asia Foundation and Indian Council of World Affairs.
5. Imtiyaz Ul Haq (2009), 'Economic Transition in Central Asian Republics: Problems and Prospects', in Mushtaq A. Kaw (ed.), *Central Asia Continuity and Change*, Centre of Central Asian Studies, University of Kashmir.

6. H. Umarov (1987), 'Development and Socio-Cultural Transformation: The Role of Education in Tajikistan', in R.G. Gidadhubli (ed.), *Socio-Economic Transformation of Soviet Central Asia*, New Delhi: Patriot Publishers.
7. R.G. Gidadhubli (2011), 'Kyrgyzstan-Violence and Multiple Challenges', in *Journal Central Eurasian News Letter*, April.
8. F. Abazov (2004), 'Kyrgyzstan's Struggle for Democracy and Stability', in K. Warikoo and Mahavir Singh (eds), *Central Asia Since Independence*, Maulana Abul Kalam Azad Institute of Central Asia Studies, Kolkata: SHIPRA.

13

Kazakhstan
Façade of Democracy Veils Stable Despotism

Kuldip Singh

Democracy is widely understood and acclaimed as a system that makes provisions for multi-layered people's participation in the process of governance. This is done with a view to ensure the inclusion of diverse categories of people in the working of the political system. Consequently, a system in which a vast majority of the people is excluded from the process of governance is not considered worthy of being labelled as democratic dispensation. Effective governance leading to positive changes resulting in better life for the people is always accepted as the manifestation of a functional democracy. Protection of minorities, justice for all as per the provisions of well-defined legal system, and with an element of fair play and creating parameters within which dissent is to be permitted and respected, are always seen as the essential features of a democratic polity in modern times. The claims of a democratic set-up being in existence cannot be made exclusively on the basis of constitutional structures as their qualitative working is the real yardstick of a democratic dispensation. In fact, political culture evolved over a period of time leaves a visible mark on the working of structures created for actualizing democratic agenda. This article is an attempt to examine the democratic process in newly emerged Kazakhstan, focusing on the nature of the constitutional structures that have come up in the country and the manner in which these structures have been made to operate. It also analyses the mechanism adopted by the ruling elite for managing 'democracy' from above, where constitutional structures have been moulded in an authoritarian and totalitarian mould that leaves many things desirable from the perspective of a democratic polity.

While examining the state of democracy in Kazakhstan, one should take due cognizance of the fact that the country did not win independence through any long struggle as has been the case in many other parts of the globe, where incidentally democracies are by now well established. Kazakhstan became a sovereign independent country in a unique situation where independence was virtually bestowed on this erstwhile republic of the former Soviet Union. With the exceptions of incidents, such as Kazakh protest against the appointment of Gennadi Kolbin, an ethnic Russian, as First Secretary of Communist Party of Kazakhstan in December 1986, Kazakh Supreme Soviet's declaration of September 1989 declaring Kazakh as the official language of the Republic, leaving Russian as the language of inter-ethnic communication and Kazakh Supreme Soviet's sovereign assertions of October 1990, making exclusive claims over the natural resources of the Republic, there was no strong movement and well-drafted plan for the liberation of the Republic away from the Soviet Union. For most of the time during the eventful tenure of Mikhail Gorbachev, Kazakh leadership remained preoccupied with what was happening in the then Soviet Union, leaving little scope for working out democratic agenda for independent Kazakhstan. It should, therefore, surprise no one that on the issue of referendum on the future of Soviet Union, held in March 1991, a vast majority of Kazaks endorsed the proposal for preserving USSR as the union of sovereign states with equal rights. Kazakhstan has the distinction of being the last of the Republics to declare independence form USSR on 16 December 1991.

The constitutional structures created in post-Soviet Kazakhstan, for actualizing its democratic agenda, did not evolve over a long period of time. These institutions had to be created in response to the situation the Republic was facing following the cataclysmic developments resulting in the collapse of the former Soviet Union. In such a situation, long-term vision of democratic dispensations was destined to be overtaken by urgency and episodic response. Under these circumstances, it was unrealistic to think of major gains on the democratic landscape of Kazakhstan because democratic structures, with well-defined democratic ethos, do not emerge overnight.

If evolution of democracy in India is any guide, it should be noted that unlike Kazakhstan, Indian democracy evolved over a long period of time, through the freedom struggle led by stalwarts like Mahatma Gandhi and Jawaharlal Nehru, who had long-term vision for the country much before it got independence. The nature of the political structures to be introduced in independent India and the broad contours of domestic and foreign policies to be followed after independence were debated threadbare for many decades before independence. In India, large scale mobilization of masses around the goal of freedom took place which in Kazakhstan's case was missing. Therefore, it should not be surprising that even after almost two decades of getting of the independence, many channels that are inseparable part of liberal democracies elsewhere and which serve as training grounds for political recruitment, are missing in this country. Political parties being very weak do not exercise any decisive influence on the working of the political system of the country. Kazakh scholars admit that the influence of political parties on the government is very marginal and their presence on the political horizon of the country does not make them proud because these parties do not reflect popular mood in any meaningful manner and do not even serve as an arena for political recruitment of the ruling elite of the country.[1] Even Nur-Otan, the ruling political party of President Nursultan Nazarbayev, who is at helm of affairs since independence, is no exception. The Party lacks well-defined programmes beyond the policy pronouncements of the President. Many of the opposition leaders do not have anything strikingly different to offer to the people except that they would do a better job, would democratize the system more rapidly, and that they would combat corruption, which is still rampant in the country, more forcefully.[2] Political organs of the country, with sole exception of the office of President, are ineffective. Even the legislature, the key organ in any democratic set-up, has been reduced to the status of consultative body. It is well-known that the legislation does not originate within the legislature; rather it is drafted in the government.[3]

Kazakhstan has a presidential form of government with formal provisions of separation of powers between legislature, executive, and judiciary. Constitutionally, the country is committed to Western-type liberal democracy. It proclaims itself as a democratic, secular, legal, and social state having highest values for individual rights and freedoms. However, in practice, the system is authoritarian and totalitarian. Most of the legislative and executive powers rest with the President. The institution of strong President has been sought to be justified invoking urgency of overcoming problems typical of transitional phase through which the country has been passing ever since it got independence from the Soviet Union. Fate of democratic structures, notwithstanding, the Kazakh scholars take pride in claiming that thanks to strong presidential system being in place in the country it did not face any serious political crisis even in the transitional period. Such elements argue that only President being in control of internal and external policies and having the right to take over the legislative functions of the government could ensure smooth transition from Soviet era totalitarian system to 'liberal democracy'. Default in payment of wages and pension, decline in industrial and agricultural production, alarmingly high rate of inflation, and rising unemployment and politically uncertain future were the hallmarks of Kazakh society in the years following independence.[4] It was Nursultan Nazarbayev's rich political experience in the Soviet Politbureau, coupled with his strong style of governance that brought Kazakhstan out of bad economic predicament and political uncertainty. Kazakhstan, under his leadership, took measures for building market structures and institutions. The regime followed the view firmly held by IMF that the global economy had grown through the system of free trade and capital flows and that the globalization, entailing greater freedom of trade and investment, would expand markets. The leadership took credit for increased economic gains from enhanced capital flows, accelerated investment, and thus creating more jobs, reducing poverty, and attaining human development goals.[5] It was argued that only strong Presidency ensured successful journey on road to economic reforms, for opening up the economy and actively engaging in the world trade system which resulted in Kazakh economy to be ahead of others in Central Asia that was evident from increased per capita GDP of the country to the tune of more than US$ 5100.[6] In the wake of global economic slowdown setting in towards the end of 2008, the rationale for strong Presidency and centralization of powers became even more pronounced and prevalent. The country responded by earmarking US$ 10 billion for extending financial support for safeguarding the bank accounts and deposits.[7] President Nursultan Nazarbayev committed funds for overcoming the ill-effects of the world financial crisis which included the merging of project financing fund and state run national companies, for creating mega holding to foster their national and international competitiveness. The country also undertook to place purchase orders domestically for saving business in the country and in the process making jobs secure. This way the leadership has sought to justify centralization of powers in the hands of President invoking the urgency to take quick measures for tackling pressing economic problems and overcoming the challenges emanating from the transitional phase of Kazakh society and polity.

The justification for the centralization of powers in the hands of the President and putting more and more checks on the legislative body have been more pronounced in the present phase of global slowdown wherein the measures taken by Kazakh government for giving more powers to the President are not seen warranted by the Kazakhs. The office of Vice-President has been abolished. President has got the right to dissolve the parliament. The constitutional court has been replaced by a constitutional council, with President having the power to override.[8] Recently, President Nursultan Nazarbayev, through legislature, indulged in political manoeuvring that virtually earned for him life-time tenure as President of the country. He got constitutional arrangements approved by the legislature, whereby beginning from 2012, the year presidential election was originally due; the tenure of the office was reduced from the present seven years term to five years, with the rider that no one could be elected for more than two consecutive terms. However, this amendment was not to be applicable to Nursultan Nazarbayev as first President of the country, who has been at helm of affairs ever since the country got independence from the Soviet Union. Though the President was to turn seventy two by 2012, the time Presidential election was due, he got necessary arrangement in place, making amply clear that he would contest the next Presidential election as and when held.[9] His political manoeuvring has been demonstrated again in the early presidential election held on 3 April 2011 following his rejection of the constitutional amendment that proposed extending of President's term through referendum until 2020. The idea of referendum was introduced in December 2010 and there were reports of 5 million people having signed in favour of such a move. As the referendum was in progress, it was criticized by political elements within the country as well as the political analysts in the

West. There was also the argument that the President got nervous because of political developments in West Asia, where regimes could not withstand the shocks of popular uprisings despite referendum verdicts being on their side. Therefore, President Nazarbayev rejected the idea of referendum and instead announced early presidential election. The presidential election was scheduled to be held towards the end of 2012 which was preponed by nearly two years. The political opponents of the President did not find time to prepare for the election. And when the election was held, they did not get funds to match Nazarbayev's election campaign run by full state machinery. Also, additional pre-condition such as Kazakh language proficiency test for the candidates eliminated many potential rivals of the President. This reflects the way political system is being run which speaks volumes of totalitarian and authoritarian tendencies of the ruling elite that can go to any extent for safeguarding its political interests. Tall claims, notwithstanding, such a working cannot earn democratic credentials for the country.

The civil society institutions, which are an essential feature of modern day liberal democracies, have not come of age in Central Asia in general and Kazakhstan in particular. There are many factors which do not allow them to function in a fashion in which they work in the other parts of the democratic world. In fact, it would be unrealistic to think of civil society institutions playing any effective role in this part of the world because the democratic structures in these countries are still in a stage of infancy. Kazakhstan may be on a democratic path but by global standards, it is not a mature democracy, with attributes of all democratic institutions in place. Those who argue that Kazakhstan is on the democratic path point out to private-citizens' social movements, independent non-governmental organizations, and government approved organizations which include broad range of public opinion, where citizens can debate and express their views.[10] However, Kazakhstan still does not have a truly transparent and fully independent election commission that guarantees full participation of political parties, NGOs, and social movements. Generally, civil society institutions appear in the diverse spheres of the society when public services rendered by the state come under pressure. Such institutions came into being in Central Asia at phenomenal pace in post-Soviet times, because reduced capacity and role of the state led to huge gap in the performance of the state and people's expectations from it which created wide space for civil society dispensations.[11] This was also the time when the outside powers, due to diverse kind of considerations, wanted new states of Central Asia to shape their polities in accordance with Western values and ethos. This motivated the Western countries to give them political and financial support. A large number of NGOs were funded by the Western countries which took up issues such as human rights, democracy, private farming, and industry. In Kazakhstan, hundreds of civil society institutions were established in various spheres such as environment, human rights protection, health, gender equality, and social support. However, civil society could not register much of the progress because governments in Central Asia remained suspicious of the activities of these institutions and therefore many bureaucratic hurdles were created in their way. This was more so, following colour revolutions in Georgia, Ukraine, and Kyrgyzstan when the role of NGOs came under stricter scrutiny and the governments were less inclined to trust them. Some sections of the civil society even came to be viewed as political opponents.[12] In Kazakhstan, a general disbelief about NGOs has become widely pervasive. The country, like other Central Asian states, has witnessed a sharp conflict between government and civil society.

Well-established mature democracies always produce consensus among major players on vital political issues. Changes are conceived and implemented within the broad structures introduced through the constitutional laws. This is actualized through effective party system where parties gain/lose power in an institutionalized electoral system that should rise above party politics. This kind of structure helps the system get legitimacy and acceptance as democratic dispensation. Most of these features, which are vital for making legitimate claims of democracy, are not visible in Kazakhstan in any effective manner. As noted earlier, Kazakhstan does not have institutionalized party system with mass support base which could produce consensus on vital issues related to the country. Even the electoral system does not carry the kind of credibility that could lend legitimacy to the political system. The independence of judiciary for imparting justice in a fair manner and in the process protecting supreme law of the land is always taken as the key feature of modern day democracies. This is not the case with Kazakhstan where the critics of the President Nursultan Nazarbayev are persecuted on trivial and invented grounds.[13]

The freedom of speech and freedom of press are much cherished values of democracy. Such freedom is not enjoyed by people in Kazakhstan. Most of the newspapers, magazines, radio, and TV channels which have come up in Kazakhstan in post-Soviet era, lack financial viability. The publications and channels which do not face any such financial difficulties and are doing very well are the ones which belong to the members of the ruling family. Doriga Nazarbayeva, daughter of President Nursultan Nazarbayev, holds a strong control over mass media, which ensures positive coverage of the working of the government, especially the office of the President.[14] Any direct or indirect criticism of the top leadership of the country, that includes President, his family members, and persons close to him, is not permitted in the mass media. The publications and channels which do not toe the governmental line are not likely to be spared. The standard practice is that the government officials would unearth cases of tax violations against the elements that dare to criticize the ruling elite of the country. Such highhandedness deters people from criticizing the top layers of the government as unpleasant remarks about them by private newspapers, magazines, and the electronic media would invite reprisal by the government. All this is in sharp contrast to democracy in other parts of the globe where people have the freedom of expression whereby even the top leadership of the country can be subjected to harsh criticism in the press and electronic media. People cannot be made to suffer because their liberties are well protected by the judiciary.

Soviet-type totalitarian mentality, tribalism, and clan system, continue to accentuate the Kazakh political system. Some of the Kazakh scholars attribute the delay in the reconstruction of the society on democratic lines to politically passive population that still has a tendency to bear totalitarian and authoritarian structures. Kazakhs, who for decades during Soviet period, had reverence for supreme authority, are still alien to democracy as it is understood in the Western world. This explains virtual absence of people's movement in Kazakhstan for actualizing democratic agenda in the country. Elsewhere, such agencies have been playing a major role in shaping the agenda of democratic reforms. In Kazakhstan, citizens' initiatives for reshaping polity on democratic lines do not stand any chance of being materialized as people do not figure in any meaningful manner in the political process of the country. There are reports of people's alienation from the ruling elite. However, no channel is available for the manifestation of such alienation. In the absence of people's movements, the ruling elite has a tendency to take credit for initiating 'democratic reforms'. The ruling elite, being in the forefront of political changes, ensures that agenda of 'reforms' remains within the predetermined boundaries set out by the state.

Notes and References

1. Kuralay Baizakova (2006), 'Democratization and Political Stability in Kazakhstan', *Himalayan and Central Asian Studies*, 10(4), October–December, p. 70.
2. Martha Brill Olcott, 'When and How will Kazakhstan Become a Democracy', Testimony before US Helsinki Commission, 22 July 2008. Available at http://www.carnegieendowment.org/publications/index.cfm?fa=view&id=20316. Accessed on 19.9.2009
3. Ibid.
4. Saifolla Sapanov (2006), 'Elections in Kazakhstan', *Himalayan and Central Asian Studies*, 10(4), October–December, p. 78.
5. Michael Camdessus, 'Challenges facing Transition Economies of Central Asia', Address at the conference on challenges to Economies in Transition, Bishkek, 27 May 1998, pp. 2–3. http//www..imf.org/external/np/speeches/1998.
6. Kairat Umarov (2008), 'Kazakhstan is an Idea for Regional Cooperation', in P.L. Dash (ed.), *Emerging Asia in Focus: Issues and Problems*, Delhi: Academic Excellence, pp. 175–6.
7. Embassy of the Republic of the Kazakhstan in India, *Kazakhstan Weekly News*, 169, 28 October 2008.
8. K.N. Baizakova (2009), 'Evolution of Presidentship in the Republic of Kazakhstan', in K. Santhanam et al. (eds), *Democratic Process in Central Asia: India-Kazakh Perspectives*, New Delhi: Aryan Books International, p. 15.
9. 'Central Asia: Country Risk Reports', *Institute for Economic Strategies: Central Asia*, Almaty: Kazakhstan, January 2009, p. 2.
10. Statement of Richard E. Hoagland, US Ambassador to Kazakhstan, in Kazakh Humanitarian and Law University, Astana, 16 March 2009. Available at http://kazakhstan.usembassy.gov/tr-03-16-09.html. Accessed on 19 September 2009.
11. Ajay Patnaik (2007), 'Civil Society in Central Asia', *Contemporary Central Asia*, XI (1–3), (April–August, December), p. 1.
12. Ibid., p. 8.
13. Khojamakhamad Umarov, 'Democracy in Central Asia', in K. Sanathanam (ed.), n. 5, p. 20.
14. Ibid., pp. 22–3.

14

The US Interest in Central Asia

ALI AHMAD ABU ROMMAN

The US involvement in Central Asian republics is not only an opportunity but also a challenge. From acquiring military bases to using Central Asian countries as a transit corridor to Afghanistan to dethrone the Taliban, the US involvement in the region was all pervasive. The speed of US engagement in the region was unprecedented too. To quote Abdul Shakoor, 'Never in the history so much has happened in such a short period of time and in such a peaceful manner as it has been in Eurasia in the past two decades. The disintegration of the Soviet Union and consequent emergence of the Central Asian states has even caught the US policy-makers unawares. Perhaps one of the biggest foreign policy problems for the United States today is to deal with the newly liberated Central Asian states. The problem is biggest in the sense because neither the US academicians and policy-makers knew much about the region, nor the United States has any past experience of interaction to deal with the region.'[1] As Leslie Gelb in *The New York Times* has commented, 'Washington's Soviet experts were mainly experts on Moscow, and with the break-up of the Soviet Union, they have been adrift'.[2] It was also pointed out by an anthropologist, William Beeman that 'Years of neglect have left the United States starved of knowledgeable regional specialists. Only one institution, Indiana University—currently offers courses on the region as part of a regular masters' curriculum.'[3]

It becomes apparent that lack of in-depth knowledge and having no experience at all to deal with the region has created complications for the

United States. One such example is related to the much exaggerated furore over the issue of fundamentalism. The US academicians and policy-makers were making a strategic blunder by taking 'Sufism' as another form of Islamic fundamentalism or extremism. This has clearly become a source of alienation and confrontation among the Central Asian nations on the one hand and the United States on the other. Hence, the main problem for the United States is to define its interests and formulate policies vis-à-vis the Central Asian states in such a way that masses, steeped in age old traditions, are not alienated.

The present geo-political scenario is in sharp contrast with that of the post-1945 era, when the United States readily filled the power vacuum created by the withdrawal of Britain from its colonial world. One fundamental difference is that unlike Britain, Russia does not want to be replaced completely by the United States even though there is a much wider range of cooperation between the two. Russia, despite its severe and pressing domestic political problems, remains keen to retain its hold and influence over the whole region known as near abroad of which Central Asia is an inalienable strategic component. Moreover, the situation also varies from that of a post-World War II era in terms of the number of actors involved in the 'revisited great game'. Along with Russia, the United States has not only to face China as a strong regional power, highly conscious of the Western and the US designs and moves towards the region, but also has to face a number of other assertive actors like Iran, Turkey, and Pakistan. Within this framework of the US policy-making, this paper seeks to address the two following perspectives:

1. Where does the United States stand in the region?
2. How does the US elite tend to visualize or define their interests?

US Standings in the Region

With the Soviet disintegration, for the first time, the United States is now able to inject its political presence in the new post-Soviet republics of Eurasia all the way to the frontiers of China as well as to dominate the Persian Gulf region on the southern fringes of Eurasia.[4] Given the existing regional geo-political vacuum, the case in point is to fill a geo-strategic void and to infuse US political presence in the newly liberated Eurasian States.

On the Asian side, America has to face three states on the southern rim of the Central Asian states—Turkey, Iran, and Pakistan. To have inroads into the Central Asian states, America has to operate either through them or in combination with these three states. Iran, obviously, is a nonentity for the United States. Turkey and Pakistan are the two states which proved instrumental for the United States. Again, the extraordinary rise or the possible establishment of even a secular Pan-Turkic region, which has such potential because of ethnic, religious, and linguistic proximity, is not acceptable either to the European Community or to the United States and Russia. This leaves out Pakistan, once the most allied of allies, to play a crucial and instrumental role for the United States this time, again, because of its geo-political centrality.

Yet there is another option for the United States, that is, Russia with whom America can do business. Already, she has signed a partnership agreement with her. However, any such United States' linkage or commitment with the region is, primarily, contingent upon its intensity of interests-perception. The question arises how the United States visualizes its interests in Central Asia. This leads us to the study of the phenomenon of interest-perception, particularly focusing on four cardinal variables in some details such as containment of fundamentalism, military-strategic interests, peeping off Iran, and economic and commercial interests.

Containment of Fundamentalism

The spread of Islamic fundamentalism in Central Asia is not only a popular bogey, but a conceived real threat in the Western media, especially after the Tajik civil war of 1992–7. The then US Secretary of State, James Baker, publicly warned Central Asian leaders, to stay clear of radical Islam and the influence of Iran.[5] In the words of a leading American strategic analyst, Zbigniew Brzezinski, the horizon of this threat-perception emerging from the phenomenon of so-called fundamentalism is 'for Russia and America the geo-political vacuum which may become a dangerous whirlpool. The political awakening of Islam is generating not only a collision with residual Russian imperialism in the north, but, in time, is also likely to contest American domination in the South.' He further adds that 'the geographical perimeter of this whirlpool may extend from Adriatic sea next to the Balkans all the way to the border of the Chinese Xinjiang. From south to north, this border loops around the Persian Gulf, embracing parts of the Middle East, then Iran, Pakistan and Afghanistan in the South, all of Central Asia along Russian-Kazakh frontier to the north, and all the way along the Russian-Ukrainian border.'[6] Of course, it is a distant threat-perception. Yet, it is essential to stymie such potential Islamic resurgence, when Islamic parties threatened to tear asunder the political fabric of newly independent states, aspiring to build democracy on the debris of socialism.

Strategic Interests

The proliferation of nuclear weapons and weapons of mass destruction is a reality for the Americans, as they are dogged determined to check any such possible proliferation. CIA chief, James Woolsey, told a senate committee that 'nonproliferation poses one of the most complex challenges the intelligence community will face for the remainder of the century'.[7]

The problems raised by Kazakhstan's acquisition of nuclear weapons dominated American and Western strategists. Kazakhstan inherited 104 SS-18 Intercontinental Ballistic Missiles (ICBMs) with a total of 1400 warheads. Each ICBM could travel up to 11.200 km and carry 10 independently targeted warheads, each of which is equivalent to half a million tons of TNT. The point to focus is that Kazakhstan has become the first ever Muslim state which could strike directly at the heartlands of the West. That is why Kazakhstan has become a source of grave concern for the United States whose diplomats have been visiting frequently Alma Ata after the failed coup of August 1991.[8] However, the continuing concerns were set at rest only after Kazakhstan signed the NPT and agreed to dismantle its nuclear arsenal—the first CIS and Muslim country to voluntarily do so.

Sometime back, rumours were rife in the western press that Kazakhstan had sold an SS-18 to Iran and that it was about to provide Tehran with enriched uranium. Speculative media reports in 1992 also spoke of Tajikistan selling enriched uranium to potential Third World customers at the rate of US$ 100 per kg. The nuclear card became a political leverage for Ukraine and Kazakhstan, as both had tried to extract more concessions from Russia and greater financial aid from the USA[9] by using their nuclear lever at that point of time.

However, the hectic diplomacy of the United States had resulted in the signing of a treaty in May 1992, when the President of Kazakhstan agreed to sign the first Strategic Arms Reduction Treaty (START-I) which would eventually allow the elimination of one third of Soviet and the US nuclear weapons.[10] The importance attached to Kazakhstan's possession of weapon could well be judged from the treaty provision that the very first of these missiles to be eliminated would be the SS-18s, the lethal missile on Kazakh soil.[11] This may be the convergence of the American and Russian interests and hence of their security policies.

Containment of Iran

Ever since the fall of the Shah, Iran has become the chief opponent of the United States in this region. In the words of former advisor of American National Security Council, Zbigniew Brzezinski, Iran is clearly an aspirant to regional hegemony and it is prepared to outwit the United States. It has an imperial tradition and possesses both the religious and the nationalist motivation to contest both the American and the Russian presence in the area. With both religion and motivation, conspiring an alien regional hegemony, the current American supremacy in the Middle East is built quite literally on sand. A good illustration of the US limitation of regional control is provided by the fact that even the extraordinary lopsided military outcome of the Gulf War of 1991 did not yield equally commensurate political results: Saddam Hussein's regime remained in power until 2003, and both the Shiite and Kurd revolts, despite American encouragement, were suppressed.'[12] Moreover, a total destruction of Iraq in a Gulf War would have led to the emergence of Iran as a decisive regional leader, which for obvious reasons America did not want. Iraq is half decimated and Iran is yet unbridled. However, the saga of its overtures in Central Asia was checkmated due to overt Islamic fervour and the apprehensions and fears surrounding its spreading influence.

Economic and Commercial Interests

Although US officials regard economic interests in Central Asia as private sector interests,[13] given the huge energy potential, this may turn into an official one or as an alternate to the Middle Eastern oil resources in future. Besides, 55 million people constitute a sizeable market for American and European goods. The past two decades have evidences of American investors and businessmen becoming overtly active in evaluating the region's market potential, particularly in the energy sector. Shafiqul Islam, an economist, in one of his articles says, 'The natural resources that have attracted the attentions of Americans, Japanese and other foreign investors to Central Asia is energy—oil and natural gas.'[14] He also identified that the United States, major European countries, Japan, China, and South Korea are on their way to becoming the region's major trading partners and investors.[15]

In an overall analysis, the nature of American interests may be concluded in the words of a study group's report on Central Asia, published by the US Institute of Peace, which says, 'The only threat in former Soviet Central Asia to have evoked US interests since dissolving the USSR seems to come from some combination of Iran, Islamic fundamentalism, instability and the presence of a nuclear capability. Turkey, Pakistan, and Saudi Arabia are contending for the position of primary American or Western surrogate in containing this threat, with Egypt, India, and Israel coming for similar but lesser roles.'[16]

Given the nature of the US strategic interests, there are several questions asked as to how would these interests be better served? What are the US policies to preserve these very interests? What would be the means to achieve these ends? To answer these interrelated questions, one has to analyse the past and the present trends of the US security policies vis-à-vis Central Asia in the background shadow of continuing crisis in Afghanistan and Pakistan and its impact on the region.

Political Targets

It is being observed that the USA's political targets in Central Asia are primarily to increase stability, to speed up democratization, to settle free market economy and make sure that it smoothly operates, to increase commercial activity, to control nuclear weapons, and to settle human rights standards. Washington promotes all these targets in such a manner of political priority which could be formulated as preventing the development or the activities of radical regimes in the region. In a more general sense, the US purpose is to help the Central Asian countries with their integration into the mainstream world thus making them aware of their own international rights and responsibilities. Therefore, the Republics under discussion will take responsibility in security problems and the ilk by not allowing the rise of anti-Western radical regimes, which may threaten international peace and security.

Although there is a consensus among the American policy makers about the targets listed above, there are divergent views on dimensions of American interference in Central Asia. The group supporting an active policy towards Central Asia is mainly concerned with the negative effects of a probable instability on the neighbouring states which have good relations with the United States, including Turkey.[17] On the other hand, because of the existence of the equipment and resources suitable for producing nuclear weapons in this region, this school of thought draws attention to the danger of a possible arms race and the spread of these weapons to the radical third world countries or to the terrorist organizations. Within this perspective, the United States should increase its support for the region; it should even make efforts in improving bilateral relations. Furthermore, it should not be forgotten that the interests of the allies and the United States are not always overlapping as far as this region is concerned and that a limited amount of fund for aids are apportioned for these friendly states.

Another crucial factor is the belief that the chance of a transformation through direct American involvement is higher, as far as America's prestige is concerned. The advocates of direct American intervention point out that through increasing American aid and investment, the region's dependence on Washington would be enhanced and Russia could be balanced.[18] The last argument is that to lag behind will have a negative effect on America's position in the global competition, particularly when the competition against China, North Korea, and some European states, penetrating the Central Asian market, is becoming intense.[19] The group criticizing America's current policy and demanding less involvement in Central Asia argues that the region does not mean much for American interests, and that the developments in the region remain marginal, as far as America is concerned. Ignoring the claims that there is a threat of Islamic radicalism in the region, and that such a thing would damage American interests in the Middle East or in any other region, the members of this group point out that the regional interests of Washington could be pursued and forwarded by Turkey and other friendly states. While some are stressing that interference in different cultures, for the sake of democratization lead to authoritarianism within the historical process, another group claims that since giving of continuing aid will mean ensuring permanent American interference, which will become the sole means of checking Islamic radicalism. Another approach is that oil and natural resources of these new states are not of vital importance to America, and that it will take years for these states to open up to the Western markets. Yet one more factor which is considered having as much importance as all other factors is the anxiety that any conflict or instability would be dangerous for the American personnel located in the region or in its periphery.[20]

Of these two approaches, which have been touched upon with its main points, the first one is dominant as far as the current conjuncture is concerned. The most obvious proof of this situation is America's swiftness in recognizing the newly independent Republics in early 1992 following the collapse of the Soviet Union in December 1991. The Deputy Secretary of the US State Department, Strobe Talbott, aptly pointed out that Washington took into consideration these countries' characteristics and thus established relations on different dimensions with each country.[21] In this context, the bilateral relations and the characteristics which determined these relations need detailed examination.

Kazakhstan was the first Central Asian country recognized by the United States on 25 December 1991. The cornerstone of the present relations with Kazakhstan is the law of endorsement of Russia's and Eurasia's newly established democracies and their freedom to free markets. A law to this effect was passed in 1992. This law has implications directed at military, political, and economic transformation. Washington sent aid to this country for a smooth transition to market economy. The President of Kazakhstan, Nursultan Nazabayev had paid his first official visit to the United States on 18–20 May 1992. Vice-President Albert Gore's visit in September 1993 was followed by Foreign Secretary Warren Christopher's visit to Almaty in October 1994.[22] During Nazarbayev's second visit to the United States, he and Clinton signed the 'Democratic Cooperation Agreement' which emphasized democratic values, human rights, and the rule of law.[23] After Nazarbayev's visit, another high level contact was realized in April 1995 with Defence Secretary William Perry's visit to Kazakhstan.[24]

In addition to high level visits, the American administration had taken the lead in establishing educational programmes on various subjects in order to help Kazakhstan with its transition to democracy. These programmes consist of different topics such as political party and voter education, election arrangements, public administration, human rights, law and legal reforms, foreign policy, diplomacy, university administration, and English training. Services like translation of articles and books, on the other hand, have also not been neglected.[25]

As could be understood from the US-Kazakhstan relations, there emerged the opportunity of establishing bilateral relations between the newly independent states and the United States after the end of the Cold War. Washington recognized Kyrgyzstan on 25 December 1991 and opened an Embassy in Bishkek in February 1992. The relations with Kyrgyzstan were conducted within the framework of the Freedom law, as with other newly independent states. Then Kyrgyz President Askar Akayev visited the United States on 15–22 May 1993. Akayev made contacts with President Clinton, Vice-President Al Gore, and Foreign Secretary Warren Christopher. During this visit, Kyrgyz Foreign Minister Karabayev and his American counterpart signed a framework agreement on the aid the American administration would provide Kyrgyzstan. Vice-President Gore reciprocated this visit in December 1993. In addition to an agreement that would facilitate bilateral investment relations, Gore also put his signature on a joint agricultural project.

Within the general logic of its relations with the Central Asian states, Washington had taken a series of initiatives for securing and consolidating transition to democracy. Although there were ups and downs, Kazakhstan and Kyrgyzstan were ahead of others in the democratization process, according to reports prepared by the American think-tanks.[26] American authorities are engaged in various services in Kyrgyzstan such as administrative reorganization, and exchange program for local and central government officials, diplomatic training, pluralism, electoral law, political party training, free media activities of cultural groups, university administration, and students exchange. Furthermore, volunteer 'Peace Corps' are working to spread English teaching across the country.

The American administration established diplomatic relations with Turkmenistan in mid-March 1992 and opened an Embassy in Ashgabat.

The relations of Washington with Turkmenistan were on a lower course compared to relations with Kazakhstan and Kyrgyzstan. This is because Turkmenistan had traversed less distance in transition to democracy and free market economy than others. Despite this situation, the American administration did not fail to engage in various projects to build democracy and civic culture in that country.

The United States had recognized Uzbekistan on 25 December 1991, and opened an Embassy in Tashkent in March 1992. Despite early recognition, the relations had not improved to the desired level. The reason why relations were static was Uzbekistan's problems regarding human rights, civil liberties, and transition to democracy.[27] Washington, as in its relations with Turkmenistan, had continued its dialogue in and its call for democratization in Uzbekistan.[28] Defence Secretary William Perry had emphasized on the strategic importance of the country during his visit in April 1995 and had reiterated the American support for democratization and maintenance of stability. The American authorities on the other hand, carried on with training activities in Uzbekistan as well as 'Peace Corps' volunteers who were working for spreading English language training.

The country with which the American administration had the lowest level of relations was Tajikistan. The reason for that was the civil war and instability coming up until 1997 right after independence. Washington recognized Tajikistan on 25 December 1991, and opened an embassy in Dushanbe in March 1992. After this date, the relations developed in the shape of sending in humanitarian aid to Tajikistan to heal the wounds of war. The officials of the American Department of Foreign Affairs had participated in the peace talks between the warring parties in Tajikistan, as observers within the UN Organization. The political reforms in Central Asia thus continued albeit with upswings and downswings in its course.

Conclusion

The US interests in Central Asian republics, together with that of several other European and Asian economic giants are of recent origin, consequent upon the dismantling of the Iron Curtain in 1991. Though freed from the hegemonic control of the Soviet Union, these republics were in the throes of development and desperately needed foreign capital investment for sustained economic growth. This inter-alia required not only support for the independence and sovereignty of these nascent states, but also their integration into the world community in terms of enhanced security and commercial expansion, their increased democratization to be followed by denuclearization.

Combating Islamic fundamentalism, which is being exported by neighbouring countries such as Iran, Afghanistan, and Pakistan, requires a careful and gingerly handling of ground reality in such a way that without appearing to be an enemy of Islam, one may encourage increased democratization of traditional and attendant political structures. Since changes took place with amazing rapidity and speed in this region, from the disintegration of the Soviet Union to the formation of the Commonwealth of Independent States, from the liberation of nationalities to their integration in global institutions, the need of the hour for the US government is not to club these countries arbitrarily into one homogenous mould, but to differentiate between them and recognize their in-built heterogeneity in terms of political awareness, economic development, impact of the ideology of Islam, and multi-national character.

The denuclearization of Kazakhstan, the fourth largest nuclear power and the first Islamic state to possess these weapons, became a matter of utmost priority for the United States, where she found a great convergence of interests with Russia. The states of Kazakhstan, Ukraine, and Belarus were none too keen to use their nuclear card to extract more concessions—political as well as economic, from the United States and Russia. Therefore, Kazakhstan has signed nuclear non-proliferation treaty, volunteered to subject its nuclear arsenal to international inspection and pledged to renounce its nuclear status to be on the forefront of denuclearization process. The nuclear issue of former Soviet republics is also linked with problems of health. A series of surface and underground explosions contaminated the environment of Central Asian states. Areas contiguous to test site of Semipalatinsk have shown an alarming rise in cancerous diseases, infant mortality, and genetic disorders. The major US objective is to ensure that within the framework of START treaties, all nuclear weapons of Kazakhstan, Ukraine, and Belarus are transferred to Russia for liquidation, which has largely been achieved.

The containment of Iran without a total destruction of Iraq is yet another US policy goal in the region. This can be done by developing friendly relations with Pakistan and Turkey but not at the cost of Russia. In fact, the USA accepts that Russia has a predominant role to perform in the region and thereby reducing the role of Pakistan and Turkey on the periphery. Massive humanitarian aid has been pumped into this region by America, Japan, and the UN agencies as part of economic regeneration and cooperation. To offset growing Iranian influence in the region, USA, Turkey, Israel, and Europe have come under a common umbrella to prevent Islamization of Central Asia.

Russia still regards its former republics to be in its interest zone and hence it will not brook any outside interference in this region. At the same time, it is keen to impress upon these republics that their security is inalienably and inextricably linked with Russia which alone is capable of defending them against outside aggression. Because of geographical and ethnic factors, Russia is apprehensive of the designs of China which may use its nuclear and economic clout to gain a foothold in these republics. In any case, all actors in the ongoing 'Great Game' in Central Asia are agog to watch the move of the other in a queer pitch of political quagmire of which the United States is an inalienable part.

Notes and References

1. Saleem Kidwai (1999), 'US Strategy in Central Asia', *Journal of Peace Studies*, 6 (March–April), pp. 33–4.
2. Saleem Kidwai, op. cit., pp. 33–4.
3. Saleem Kidwai, op. cit., p. 35.
4. Abdul Shakoor (1995), 'Central Asia: The US Interest-Perception and its Security Policies', *European Studies*, 2(2), p. 14.
5. Mowahid Hussain (1993), 'Central Asia: Impact on and Implications for Pak-US ties, in Central Asia and the Region', in S.M. Haider (ed.), Lahore: Progressive Publishers, p. 406.
6. Ibid.
7. Zbigniew Brzezinski (1994), 'World Order of the Future', *Dawn*, Karachi, 3 March.
8. Ahmad Rashid (1994), *The Resurgence of Central Asia: Islam or Nationalism?*, Karachi: Oxford University Press, p. 245.
9. Zbigniew Brzezinski, op. cit.
10. Ahmad Rashid, op. cit., p. 236.
11. Ibid., p. 234.
12. Ibid., p. 236.
13. Ahmad Rashid, op. cit., p. 235.
14. Ibid.

15. Zbigniew Brzezinski, op. cit.

16. M.A. Bhatty (1994), 'Pakistan's Perspectives on Central Asia, Strategic Studies' (Islamabad), XVI(3, Spring), p. 36.

17. Shafiqul Islam (1994), 'Capitalism on the Silk Route, Current History', 93(582), April, p. 156.

18. Ibid., p. 159.

19. Robert B. Oakley, 'Afghanistan and Post-Soviet Central Asia Prospects for Political Evolution and the Role of Islam', US Institute of Peace, Washington DC, p. 36.

20. Warren Christopher (1994), 'Towards a Secure, Free and Fully Integrated Europe', *Dispatch*, p. 403.

21. Jim Nichol (1996), 'Central Asia's New States: Political Developments and Implications for US Interests', Washington, p. 2.

22. Strobe Talbott (1994), 'Presidents and Prime Ministers, 1994, an address in Washington DC', 3 May, p. 3.

23. Jim Nichol, op. cit., p. 2.

24. Strobe Talbott, op. cit.

25. *Turkish Daily News*, 11 December 1993.

26. *Turkish Daily News*, 16 February 1994.

27. *Turkish Daily News*, 6 April 1995.

28. *Despatch*, op. cit., 1994, p. 282.

29. Martha Brill Olcott (1993), 'Central Asian on its Own', *Journal of Democracy*, pp. 92–103.

30. Roger Kangas (1992), 'Recent Developments in Uzbek Political Parties', *Central Asian Monitor*, No. 4, pp. 22–7.

31. Jim Nichol, op. cit., p. 3.

Some Important Web Links on Central Asia

http://www.eurasianet.org/
http://www.worldbank.org/eca/
http://www.cagateway.org/
http://www.uzbekistan.org/
http://www.turkmenistanembassy.org/
http://www.armeniaemb.org/
http://www.undp.org/europe/
http://www.cacianalyst.org/
http://www.preventconflict.org/portal/centralasia/
http://www.fpa.org/topics4707/topics_show.htm?doc_id=415867
http://www.centralasianvoices.org/
http://www.crisisgroup.org/home/index.cfm?l=1&id=1251
http://www.adb.org/CAREC/default.asp
http://www.adb.org/Carec/links.asp
http://www.cfr.org/region/264/central_asia.html
http://www.carnegieendowment.org/programs/russia/
http://www.osce.org/regions/13003.html
http://www.state.gov/p/sca/
http://www.state.gov/p/sca/ci/
http://usinfo.state.gov/sa/
http://usinfo.state.gov/usinfo/US_Embassies.html#SA
http://centralasia.usaid.gov/

http://www.eia.doe.gov/emeu/cabs/Centasia/Background.html

http://www.eia.doe.gov/emeu/cabs/Centasia/Links.html

http://www.osac.gov/Regions/index.cfm?region=1

http://fpc.state.gov/fpc/82090.htm

http://fpc.state.gov/documents/organization/67150.pdf - 19 pages available in pdf format.

http://ncseonline.org/NLE/CRSreports/07Jun/RL33458.pdf - 34 pages available in pdf format.

http://italy.usembassy.gov/policy/topics/Russia/default.asp

http://digital.library.unt.edu/govdocs/crs/search/?q=%22Foreign+relations+-+Central+Asian+States+-+U.S.%22&t=dc.subject&PHPSESSID=62af9847884ce4efad7490c80dd25a87 – full-text of several reports

http://www.rand.org/pubs/monographs/MG440/index.html - full document available online

http://www.rand.org/pubs/monographs/MG417/ - full document available online

http://www.efcentralasia.org/ns/main.aspx

http://rfe.rferl.org/reports/FullReport.aspx?report=568

http://www.heritage.org/research/russiaandeurasia/

http://www.csis.org/researchfocus/RussiaEurasia/

http://www.cdi.org/program/index.cfm?ProgramID=26

http://www.fpri.org/bysubject.html#europerussia

Compiled by RAJLAXMI DASH

Contributors

P.L. DASH is Professor of International Relations and ICCR India Chair, University of World Economy and Diplomacy, Tashkent, Uzbekistan.

R.G. GIDADHUBLI is Adjunct Professor at the Centre for Central Eurasian Studies, University of Mumbai, India. He was formerly Director of that Centre.

NIRMALA JOSHI is Director, India-Central Asia Foundation, New Delhi. She is a retired Professor, School of International Studies, Jawaharlal Nehru University, New Delhi.

MUSHTAQ A. KAW is Professor of Central Asian Studies and Dean, Students' Affairs, University of Kashmir, Srinagar, India.

MARLÈNE LARUELLE is Research Professor of International Affairs, The Institute for European, Russian, and Eurasian Studies, George Washington University, Washington DC, USA.

RANJANA MISHRA is Associate Professor and Head, Department of History, M.D. Shah Mahila College, SNDT University, Mumbai, India.

SANJAY KUMAR PANDEY is Associate Professor, Centre for Russian and Central Asian Studies, School of International Studies, Jawaharlal Nehru University, New Delhi, India.

AJAY PATNAIK is Professor, Centre for Russian and Central Asian Studies, School of International Studies (SIS), Jawaharlal Nehru University, New Delhi.

SÉBASTIEN PEYROUSE is Senior Research Fellow with the Central Asia-Caucasus Institute and Silk Road Studies Program, a Joint Centre affiliated with Johns Hopkins University's School of Advanced International Studies, Washington DC, USA.

ALI AHMAD ABU ROMMAN is Assistant Professor, Department of Political Science, University of Jordan, Amman, Jordan.

ANITA SENGUPTA is Senior Fellow, Maulana Abul Kalam Azad Institute of Asian Studies, Kolkata, India.

KULDIP SINGH is Professor of Political Science and Director, Centre for South Asian Studies, Guru Nanak Dev University, Amritsar, India.

SWARAN SINGH is Professor and Chairperson, Centre for International Politics, Organization, and Disarmament, School of International Studies, Jawaharlal Nehru University, New Delhi, India.

K. WARIKOO is Professor of Central Asian Studies, Central Asian Studies Programme, School of International Studies, Jawaharlal Nehru University, New Delhi, India.

LAURA YEREKESHEVA is Associate Professor and UNESCO Chair, Institute of Oriental Studies, Almaty, Kazakhstan.